ISLE OF
CLOVES

COASTLINE
NORTH & SOUTH OF
ZANZIBAR

Miles
0   20   40   60   80 100

KENYA

TO NAIROBI

Kilimanjaro

Galana R.

Malindi

MOMBASA

Msuka Bay

ZANZIBAR

Tanga

Wete   PEMBA
       ISLAND

Pangani

Chake Chake

PROTECTORATE

Mkokotoni

Sadani

Chwaka Bay
ZANZIBAR ISLAND

Wami R.

ZANZIBAR

Bagamoyo

Makunduchi

DAR-ES-SALAAM

Kingani R.

Mafia
I.

Rufiji R.

Kilwa Kivinje

Matandu R.

Kiswere

Mbemkuru R.

Cape Delgado

Ruvuma R.

INDIAN OCEAN

AREA COVERED
BY MAIN MAP

Equator

TANGANYIKA

ISLE OF CLOVES

A View of Zanzibar

F. D. OMMANNEY

THE TRAVEL BOOK CLUB
121 CHARING CROSS ROAD
LONDON W.C.2

This edition by arrangement with
Longmans Green & Co., Ltd.
1957

PRINTED IN GREAT BRITAIN
BY WESTERN PRINTING SERVICES LTD. BRISTOL

To

KEITH AND MARIE YOUNG

ACKNOWLEDGMENTS

The author gratefully acknowledges his indebtedness to the following sources of information:

Zanzibar: The Island Metropolis of Eastern Africa, Major F. B. Pearce, c.m.g. Fisher Unwin, London, 1920.

Zanzibar: Its History and its People, W. H. Ingram. Witherby, London, 1931.

General Rigby, Zanzibar and the Slave Trade, Mrs. Charles E. B. Russell. Allen & Unwin, London, 1935.

The Navy and the Slave Trade, Christopher Lloyd. Longmans, Green, London, 1949.

A Short History of the Coast of East Africa, L. W. Hollingsworth. Macmillan, London, 1951.

Zanzibar Under the Foreign Office, 1890–1913, L. W. Hollingsworth. Macmillan, London, 1953.

Dictionary of Islam, Thomas Patrick Hughes. W. H. Allen, London, 1935.

Encyclopaedia of Islam. E. J. Brill & Co., Leiden, 1927.

Encyclopaedia of Religion and Ethics, Edited by James Hastings. T. and T. Clarke, Edinburgh.

Report on the Civil Disturbances in Zanzibar, July 30th, 1951, Sir James Milner Gray. Zanzibar Government Printing Office, 1951.

ACKNOWLEDGMENTS

The author gratefully acknowledges his indebtedness to the following sources of information:

CONTENTS

Chapter   *page*

1. FROM SEAWARD   1

2. SULTANATE   13

3. THE EMPIRE OF ZINJ   47

4. A HOUSE AT MAZZIZINI   84

5. STRIFE   116

6. FAST AND FESTIVAL   145

7. PEMBA   182

8. ON THE REEFS   201

9. AWAKENING   221

PHOTOGRAPHS

facing page 64
Old Arab
Young Arab

facing page 65
Street scene

facing page 96
European quarter
Arab quarter

facing page 97
African quarter—a wedding celebration
On the outskirts

facing page 160
The coast near Unguja Kuu
"Older than the Faith"

facing page 161
My house near Mazzizini
Dar-es-Salaam

facing page 192
Homali cart
Fisherman

facing page 193
Sokomahogo Street
Watoto wawili wazuri (Two good boys)

Chapter One

FROM SEAWARD

WHAT mystery and surprise invest a coastline viewed for the first time from the sea! Mountains appear astonishingly and unexpectedly high up, like more solid clouds in whose reality and substance it is difficult at first to believe. But presently, in an hour or so, beyond doubt the dim majestic outlines of new land take shape. The blue shadow solidifies among the changing clouds, although for a long while yet it seems to hang remotely in space and one wonders, like an interplanetary traveller approaching a new world, what sort of beings can live on those unearthly uplands. The lower fringe that skirts the sea at length appears, first as a row of dots and dashes, a message in morse upon the horizon—dash, dot, dot, dash—miraged up above the hard skyline. At length these merge into one another, fuse with the skyline and, taking on an intenser blue, become tufted with the shapes of trees. As distance lessens and the land becomes more distinct, the shapes of buildings slowly resolve themselves and houses stare across the miles of water with tiny, pin-point eyes, hostile and aloof. It is a long time before any sign of human activity appears, except for that haze of smoke upon the middle distance where the hinterland fades upwards, line upon line, to the mysterious mountains. What activity, one asks, can that smoke signify? What goes on where that slender chimney bears a black plume aloft above the tree-tops? Where is that train bound for whose trail appears, disappears and diminishes far off among the hills? Who lives, who is born, and who dies among those blank-faced houses by the water's edge? What domes and towers are those that overtop them? Along roads near the sea front motor-cars glide up and down, and crowds of people weave in and out with an air of unreality lent by distance. Familiar sounds come faintly across the water. Can these be human beings like ourselves, living all their lives in this strange land to which we come, nosing our way carefully into the harbour, as though from another world?

Travellers down the east coast of Africa can see the harsh coastline soften towards the south. First they round the cruel, hot spear of Cape Gardafui, like a finger pointing to the east. It is parched and baking in the unchanging sun and the monsoon blows upon it like a breath from an oven. For mile after mile the Somaliland coast is bare, bleak sand with stark promontories, like Ras Hafun, jutting out into the sea. Then, as we get south towards Lamu, the coast begins reluctantly to take on a softer look. Tough vegetation clings bravely to the low cliffs of sand. There are baobab trees and some poor coconut palms. On the long hot beaches hundreds of baboons scamper up and down, chasing the burrowing sand crabs, and you feel you are looking at a human race, dispossessed and driven out of Eden, upon whom a curse has descended, lost denizens of waste places. Small fringing islands stand off the coast, made of black undercut coral rock, often topped with scrub, the home of great flights of terns. The town of Lamu itself is invisible from the sea, hidden behind high sandbanks. South of it the coastline becomes less and less forbidding. A coral reef, defending the coast from the onslaught of the north-east monsoon, leaves between itself and the land a shallow green lagoon where a rainbow population inhabits the warm clear water. Malindi, with its villas and hotels, faces a wide semi-circle of surf. Southward the mangroves gather at the river mouths and the thick plumes of coconut palms line the shore. The land begins to rise behind them, the nearer slopes geometrically ruled with the straight lines of sisal plantations, greenish-grey on brown. Smoke rises into the air from scattered farmsteads and, looking at it from the sea, you think how contented and at peace it all looks.

Yet this is Kenya, land of strife and opportunity. Its thriving, ever-growing seaport of Mombasa stands on what was once a lovely park-like island, recessed into the coast, with coconut palms and huge mango trees and baobabs beautifully disposed about smooth green spaces. But the island is fast disappearing beneath a hideous modern sprawl of Indian construction. The Indians, now fabulously wealthy and

increasingly powerful, own practically the whole of Mombasa.
In fact they own a very great deal of this lovely coastline. As in
Nairobi most, if not all, the big hotels, strictly for Europeans
only, are Indian-owned. They are always full of families waiting
for ships, agitated mothers coping with fractious children, and
red-faced men with moustaches leaning against bars. On the
south side of the island is the port of Kilindini, which means
'at the deep place'. Here the big Union Castle and British
India liners come alongside. Little engines shriek and trucks
clatter in the damp heat. Droves and troops of negro labourers,
clad in exiguous rags, chant and shout above the rattle of the
cranes. On the other, the northern, side of the island is the old
Arab town and the great fort of Jesus, which the Portuguese
built to keep the Arabs down. Here is the dhow harbour where
the last and oldest sailing ships in the world, with lateen sails
and high carved poops like caravels, come to anchor. They
come down on the North-East Monsoon from Arabia, the Persian Gulf and India, spreading their wings and vanishing when
the monsoon changes. The railway and the road cross over the
narrowest part of the harbour on the landward side of the island
and wind up through lush tropical vegetation, coconut palms,
mangoes and bananas. Women with pendulous breasts, and
babies on their backs, stare at the train as it passes. After about
ten miles the tropical greenery begins to thin out and gives
place slowly to the encompassing upland scrub, the bare bald
hills, the mile after mile of umbrella thorn, the dust, the herds
of buck springing, almost flying, from the wayside. Then you
are truly in Africa.

South of Mombasa the coast becomes still greener and still
more lush. It is carved into many islands and protecting reefs
so that small ships can travel a long way, almost through an
inland waterway, without going out to sea, which is useful when
the monsoons blow strongly. Distant mountains rise higher and
higher behind the coast, dim and far off, challenging and
beckoning. These are the mountains which the explorers first
saw who brought the gold from Ophir in King Solomon's time.
They beckoned with promises of untold wealth to Arab slave
traders for hundreds of years, until the missionary explorers in
the nineteenth century saw them and sensed their challenge.
David Livingstone saw them and so did Burton and Speke and

many other famous explorers who opened up Africa for the white man. To the missionaries the hills said 'Come over into Macedonia, and help us.' But to the white men who followed, the message was 'Here it is. Come and get it!'

This is what used to be German East Africa and is now Tanganyika. After the defeat of Germany in the First World War it was handed to Britain who administered it under mandate from the League of Nations. When that essay in international co-operation dissolved in the Second World War, the mandate was continued by the United Nations, which took the League's place. Dar-es-Salaam, the Haven of Peace, is the seaport of Tanganyika about two hundred miles south of Mombasa. Unlike Mombasa, which is very ancient, Dar-es-Salaam is comparatively new and was founded in the sixties of the last century by Sultan Majid of Zanzibar as a possible place of refuge from his enemies. It must be one of the loveliest harbours in the world, a wide, circular, almost completely landlocked pool with a narrow entrance to the sea and a river flowing into it on the landward side. The way in through the entrance is narrow and tortuous. The great liners seem to ride up on to the grounds of Government House and from the European bathing place you can shout to the passengers high up on the ship's decks as you bob in the wash she makes. Behind a shady pleasant waterfront the town lines a semicircle of the harbour shore. It is a thriving, growing place, mostly Indian-owned like Mombasa, but to a visitor it is disappointing and somehow does not seem to fulfil the promise implied by its fine harbour and green waterfront. It lacks the busy, bustling, metropolitan air of Mombasa and the flavour of history and romance that lingers in Zanzibar.

South of Dar-es-Salaam the coast is rich in lovely islands and coral reefs with breakers curling upon them. Here are the ancient Persian and Arab cities of Kilwa and Mafia, and here the great Rufiji Delta opens out through mile upon mile of mangrove swamp. For centuries Arab cities, on the shores of the Arabian Sea and Persian Gulf, have been built with mangrove poles from this vast reservoir of timber, and to-day the dhows still come down on the North-East Monsoon to cut the mangrove poles and take them back on the South-East Monsoon to their own lands where no trees grow.

This is a beautiful and historic coastline, studded with the ruins of dead Arab and Persian cities in which a rich civilization once flourished. The coastal strip is very different from the thorny uplands behind it and from the majestic ramparts of Africa that loom distantly in the west. The inhabitants themselves are different from those of the interior for they have much Arab and Persian blood in their veins and a language, Kiswahili, with many Arabic words, which is a more flexible and cultured tongue than any pure Bantu language. The pure Kiswahili, spoken on the coast, is not understood in the interior though a kind of kitchen-Kiswahili is the 'lingua franca' of all East Africa. The coast people call it contemptuously 'ki-settler'. The coast people have a grace and charm of manner which they derive from their civilized ancestors and none of the bitterness and strife that now prevails up country has yet reached them. On the coast there is no need for Europeans to go around armed to the teeth or to take their children with them when they go out to dine with friends.

Although this is an ancient land, known to and visited by civilized peoples since many centuries before Christ, yet for Europeans it is still a young one. They are still pioneering in it and it is still a land of opportunity, largely undeveloped, waiting to reward the adventurous, the hardy and the astute. For this reason, as one travels up and down the coast, one is constantly meeting with people who display some or all of these characteristics. Adventurers are thick upon the ground in the streets of Mombasa and Dar-es-Salaam. All of them are hardy, some of them are astute. All have wonderful ideas which are going to make their fortunes. The air is vibrant with exciting schemes for making quick money. It is always only just a question of the capital, or the know-how, or the equipment, or anything except the spirit, which is always there in abundance and willing enough. This lends to human contacts on the coast a certain excitement and expectancy which you do not find in older and more established communities. The talk is all of someone's latest venture, So-and-so's latest failure, someone else's prospects.

Most of these schemes and ventures have behind them, as a background, some theory or other. Often the theory is quite wrong and based on wishful thinking, for one can make things seem true if one wants them to be true intensely enough. And while most of these theories are landsmen's dreams, yet some concern the sea, the sea beyond the coral reefs and the shallow warm lagoons. Inevitably there have been schemes for making fortunes out of fishing along the coast, and the theory which they have all been based upon is a simple and, one would have thought, reasonably sound one. It is that there is the wide ocean and it must, as a matter of course, contain a wealth of fish. Unfortunately this theory is not as sound as one might suppose.

There was, for instance, a tough Yorkshireman who came to the coast with an old steam trawler. There must surely be rich hauls, he thought, to be gathered from the wide sandy shelves along the coast. His ship was a strange-looking craft for he built a penthouse on the after deck and lived in it with his wife, the cabins below not having been constructed for the sweaty heat of Mombasa. The homely Yorkshire lady placed blue curtains in the windows, made tea and hung out her husband's washing, just as though she were back at home in Barnsley, and sat outside her penthouse knitting in the evening, while her husband explained about the catches he was going to bring in. But he never did, for the sandy bottoms, which looked so alluring, marked 's' (for 'sand') on the Admiralty charts, were found to be sewn with isolated coral heads which tore the bottoms out of the trawls. What catches he did get were meagre, for sandy bottoms in the tropics, unlike those in northern waters, do not support much fish. He had to find that out.

Another enterprising Englishman had a scheme for making fish-ponds out of tidal mangrove swamp. This is done a great deal in the Far East, in Malaya and Indonesia, where large areas of mangrove swamp are enclosed with banks of earth with sluice gates to let the water in or out or hold it in the ponds. Large edible prawns can be grown in these ponds, African lake fish which can live in salt or fresh water, or grey mullet. In the Far East the Chinese make a fine profit out of culturing fish in this way but in Kenya, unfortunately, the enterprise failed, for the owner spent too much money on building his banks with elaborate machinery instead of using gangs of natives with baskets on their heads.

All over Kenya everybody eats the lake fish, from the Central

African lakes, and gets very tired of it, for it is rather a dull and tasteless little creature. Sea fish is hardly ever seen up country. Accordingly another man of enterprise and imagination had an idea for a refrigerated van to tour the coastal fishing villages. The fish were to be removed from the van, packed in insulated containers and flown from Malindi to fish merchants in Nairobi. I never heard what happened to this scheme but I should have heard if it had succeeded. I suspect that there were too many overheads, which made the price per pound of fish work out at more than it would fetch when it reached Nairobi.

One day we drove some forty miles in a hired car, over rough roads thick with red dust, through sisal plantations and uncleared bush, to a place called Shimoni, on the coast south of Mombasa. The name means 'at the hole'. We thought it was aptly named. The road gradually petered out into a rough cart track, twisting for a long distance through a parched silent scrub, and for over an hour we crawled along in low gear, sweating, with mouths and hair full of red dust. At the end of this unpromising approach there was a mud beach, full of clicking crabs and smelling of decaying vegetation, in a creek among mangroves and scrub-covered islands. There was a native fishing village on the other side of the creek. There were one or two small European bungalows but, apart from that, nothing for miles. In an old Arab house built like a fortress beside the creek lived an Englishman and his wife and a young engineer mechanic. They had a scheme too. They had two or three small motor fishing vessels, which we saw drawn up on the mud, and a small refrigerating plant. The fish they caught they froze and transported to Mombasa on ice. They were keen as mustard and sure they were going to make a lot of money. There must be huge quantities of fish, they said, waiting to be caught out on the reefs and in the deeper parts of the lagoon. For an hour or two we looked at charts and at drawings of fish, made by our host between fishing trips. His wife seemed as keen on fish as he. They both kept referring to fish as 'chaps'.

'Now here's a drawing of a funny chap I got in about ten fathoms just inside the reef the other day. D'you know that chap?'

The others bent forward over the drawing, while I drew back slightly to prevent a bead of sweat from falling on it. Our hostess joined in the discussion with every sign of interest and enthusiasm and we became eloquent over such exciting topics as the number of scales on the cheeks of a parrot fish, the number of scutes on the armoured tail of a jackfish and whether the first three dorsal fin rays are elongated or not. I had another gin and thought about brave women in outposts, and got my thoughts about the scales on the cheeks of parrot fishes confused with our hostess's brave show of interest in them.

We went round the freezing plant and saw fish being gutted and cleaned by dozens of little negro boys, who grinned and danced with pleasure at seeing us. They were like puppies penned in a cage, who leap and wriggle in an ecstasy of pleasure when you approach, not knowing why but for some unexplained reason feeling pleased, sure that you are a good omen and that some good or other must surely come from your attentions. In Africa and the East one is always struck by the capacity of people, especially the young, to be happy and gay and always smiling while leading lives that one would have thought were nothing but unrelieved gloom and drudgery. Nor do they seem to want the artificial amusements of the West until propaganda, and a smattering of what passes for education, teach them that they do.

All these were only a few of the many ideas for mining gold from the sea which were launched like bubbles upon the hot, exciting air of this coast. Most of them spun for a while and then burst with a little pop that hardly anyone noticed. As each one died it was replaced by another, each filled with a lungful of ideas and hope and imagination, reflecting the bright colours of dreams.

One of the reasons why so many fishing schemes and ideas failed on the coast of East Africa was lack of knowledge about the quantity and quality of fish that could be caught. No one starts farming in total ignorance of the soil and general conditions of the land, or if he does no one is very surprised at his failure. Agricultural research has been going on for centuries and is now highly advanced and specialized. But fishery research, which might be looked upon as agricultural research transferred to the sea, concerned as it is no less with soils and crops and seasons, is comparatively in its infancy in Europe and America. It was non-existent on the coast of East Africa.

Yet optimistic people were prepared to sink money in fishing in the sea in complete ignorance of what they might expect to find there.

This ignorance, however, is not at all surprising. The mysterious but diversified world beneath the sea is hidden from mankind. We can only grope in it with our nets and hooks and measure its changes by means of instruments. We do not see its inhabitants when they are alive but only when they are lying dead at our feet, torn from their natural habitat. Or in momentary flashes when they hurtle out of their world into ours for a brief fraction of a second, or swarm before our eyes at the surface of the sea in an ecstasy or under a compulsion the nature of which we can only guess at.

The lagoons along the coast of East Africa are a paradise for the new sport of underwater fishing, with mask and breathing tube and light spring harpoon gun. The water is clear and warm, and the popularity of this pastime is largely due to the fact that you can, for a brief flash and in a ghostly ambience, see the inhabitants of this forbidden world going to and fro upon their normal occupations. Brightly coloured fishes weave in and out of the antlers and cups and convolutions of the coral. Huge shoals appear and disappear and rush past with single purpose, their tiny eyes like jewels. One gets the impression that this is a teeming world, rich in a harvest only waiting to be gathered.

At certain seasons shoals of small sardines come into the shallow water all down this coast, and the surface of the bays and coves froths with them for a while. Then they vanish. Big jackfish and small bonito may be seen hopping in bright arcs through the water while the terns flutter overhead, screaming and diving to kiss it with their beaks. At certain times of the year, it is said, large shoals of Spanish mackerel, long striped fish with pointed heads, come down the coast, bound whither no one knows. Farther out to sea big-game fishermen have taken marline, swordfish and the fierce solitary wahoo. There are barracuda and dorado and many large sharks, which sometimes claim a victim or two in the harbours and lagoons to mark their presence. Yet nobody knows anything about these fishes, where they come from or where they go to, what controls their sudden appearances and their still more baffling absences;

but their occasional capture in large numbers, and the still more occasional capture of splendid specimens, have led, like the coloured idlers round the coral reefs, to a belief that the coast of East Africa is a gold mine, or perhaps a silver mine, only waiting for someone clever or enterprising or industrious enough to come and work it.

It was decided, therefore, that, before any more money was lost, or hearts broken, over fruitless fishing schemes in these waters, some research must be undertaken by the Government. It seemed evident, from what John Wheeler and I had heard about the fishing on the east coast of Africa, that we should be dealing with a type of fish very different from those which we had met with on the banks between Mauritius and the Seychelles. There we had found that the majority of the fishes were of the bottom-living type, taken with hand lines around the coral reefs and on the sandy flats. But along the coast of the mainland we should meet mainly the big, predatory, surface-living fishes, the Spanish mackerel, the jackfish, the yellow-fin tunny, the bonito, the wahoo and others. These are the swift, roving hunters of the sea, moving solitary or in packs, feeding on other smaller fishes.

These are the fishes which are caught by means of lines towing 'lures' at the surface, a method of fishing known as 'surface trolling'. Although only practised by sportsmen on the coast of East Africa this kind of fishing has for many years been an important industry in other parts of the world where large wandering shoals of big surface-living fishes abound. In the Pacific Ocean the Japanese and the Americans fish for the yellow-fin tunny, and other big fish of the mackerel family, with boats towing as many as eight parallel lines a side from booms like fishing rods projecting, one on each side, over the water from the boat's structure. This is known as 'multiple trolling'. The booms act as fishing rods and the lines, progressively longer from the ship's side outwards, are so arranged that they can be hauled in without fouling one another. At the end of each line is a 'lure' which travels on the surface and attracts the fish. It may be made of white bone or feathers or bright metal, concealing a hook. Anything may be used to deceive the fish, which rushes at what looks like a sardine or an anchovy, travelling through the water on, one would have thought, a suspiciously straight and undeviating course. But the fish does not find that out until it is too late. In the Bay of Biscay the Breton tunny fishermen troll with multiple lines for the long-finned tunny or 'germon'. The Spaniards, sailing out of St. Jean-de-Luz, use live bait for the true tunny or bluefin.

We believed that multiple trolling was a method which it might be possible to apply off the coast of East Africa, though neither Wheeler nor I had ever seen it done. Accordingly in the autumn of 1950 I made a trip in a Biscay tunnyman in order to learn something of this method of fishing so that we might, in due course, try it out and perhaps adopt it off the east coast of Africa. I was at sea for three weeks in the Bay of Biscay in a 60-foot motor fishing vessel which towed eight lines aside from long booms or 'tangons', like immense fishing rods stepped into the foremast. We caught the long-finned tunny or germon, and very little else, using lures like large salmon flies made of artificial silk. These were carried on lengths of fine steel trace wire attached to cotton fishing lines dyed with Reckitt's blue to make them less visible. I observed that these fish, unlike the coloured beauties of the tropics, fight very little and that the Breton crews were trained and disciplined to a high degree. They had brought to a fine art the drill of bringing in the fish over the side, one after the other, without getting the lines all tangled up. I returned to England wondering what sort of success we should have with our big tropical fishes which struggle and thrash about in the water, and with a crew of undisciplined and untrained Africans.

Zanzibar was chosen as the centre upon which our researches along the east coast of Africa would be based. Its chief advantage was its central position for, of the other two alter-tives, Mombasa was too far from the southern end of our beat, the mouth of the Ruvuma River at the southern border of Tanganyika, and Dar-es-Salaam was too far from the northern end, which was about Lamu, the northern border of Kenya. For me the old city had many other advantages, but they had nothing to do with fish. It had a romantic flavour and a dreaming air of the past not to be found at either of the two great seaports on the coast.

We were to use our 67-foot trawler-drifter *Cumulus* with which we had worked between Mauritius and the Seychelles. At the beginning of 1950 she was taken to Dar-es-Salaam for a refit. Her accommodation was improved and she was provided with 'tangons' for multiple trolling. When, a year later, the big mail boat on which John Wheeler and I sailed from England to East Africa entered the harbour at Dar-es-Salaam, I saw again our tiny ship lying at her moorings near the repairing yards. I had forgotten how small she was.

Chapter Two

SULTANATE

I

O N the southward route down the east coast of Africa most
of the passengers leave the mail boat either at Mombasa or Dar-es-Salaam. The Administrative Officers,
Agricultural Officers, the Forestry Officers, the school teachers
and the entomologists, their wives and their children, who have
been your agreeable companions for the past three weeks, come
to say good-bye. 'Any time you're in Nakuru, old boy, come
and look us up.' You say you will be delighted, but you know
you are not very likely to be in Nakuru in the near future.
Vaguely military-looking men and determined ladies go down
the gangway to the Nairobi train, preceded by chains of porters
carrying their baggage, as on safari. Only the 'all rounders',
people doing the whole circular tour round Africa from Great
Britain and back again, now remain—elderly ladies, studiously
seeing everything there is to see, and younger ones determined
to have a perfectly marvellous time, even if it kills them. Personally I never can understand why anyone should travel all
the way round Africa in a great liner for pleasure. A gregarious
nature and a high noise tolerance are the qualifications required
for such a test of endurance.

The ship seems empty after one's friends of these weeks have
left and there follows a pause, an intermission, before she reaches
Durban where she undergoes a sea change. For there she
ceases to be outward bound round the Suez Canal and becomes
instead homeward bound round the Cape. New faces appear
and new voices are heard, new and yet how much the same!
The purser, having relaxed after Dar-es-Salaam, braces himself for further prodigies of organizing ability. He takes down
from its hook in his cabin the mask of geniality which has been

13

hanging there since Mombasa. Junior officers watch the passengers coming aboard from aloof positions on the boat deck and speculate as to which they would like to mingle with if mingling were allowed. The stewards, entering the brandy belt between Durban and the Cape, prepare themselves for orgiastic expeditions ashore.

It is during this pause between the outward-bound hilarities, which end at Dar-es-Salaam, and the even more uproarious homeward-bound ones, which begin at Durban, when the first-class lounge has the hushed and restful air of a Lyons' Corner House or the Cumberland Hotel during a slack hour, that the ship calls at Zanzibar to take water.

This small, flat, green coral island between Mombasa and Dar-es-Salaam has the sweetest and purest water on the coast. On the mainland, water famines are a recurring feature of life and water is a luxury at all times, but on Zanzibar Island it bubbles up cool and clear from many springs in the coral rock of which the island is composed. According to the laws of Islam no charge may be made for supplying water anywhere at any time, an adaptation, as many of the laws of Islam are, to a nomadic life in a hot and desert country. But the harbour authority is allowed to make a charge for transporting the water in its lighters. And it does so. The mail boats lie in the open road-stead, towering above the flat coral islets, the dhows in the anchorage, the low palm-fringed shore and the waterfront of white, blue and saffron houses. They do not stay for long, usually only a few hours, but long enough to fill the narrow streets of the little town with strange, even grotesque, unfamiliar figures, red-faced, perspiring and somehow too large, which is always what I feel myself when I go ashore in oriental ports.

2

The dominions of the Sultan of Zanzibar consist of the two islands of Zanzibar and Pemba, which lie off the coast of Africa approximately opposite the boundary between Kenya and Tanganyika where the continent has a kind of tropical waistline north of Madagascar. Zanzibar is about 25 miles from the mainland and Pemba about 40 miles. But in addition to these two islands His Highness has also, nominally, dominion over a strip of territory about 170 miles long and 10 miles wide extending along the coast of Kenya from the town of Kipini, on the mouth of the Tana River in the north, to the Umba River, the border of Tanganyika, in the south. This strip of land, originally part of the mainland dominions of the Sultan, was conceded to the Imperial British East Africa Company in 1887. A strip to the south of it was conceded to the German East Africa Company. The Germans lost theirs when they lost East Africa in 1918, but the British coastal strip has been administered by the Kenya Government since its formation. For this reason, among others, Kenya is officially styled 'the colony and protectorate of Kenya'. The rent paid for this narrow and once virgin strip of coastline is £11,000 a year, but since the beginning of the lease the great port and prosperous township of Mombasa, the holiday resort of Malindi, together with numerous industries and undertakings, have grown up on the coast so that nowadays voices are sometimes heard in Zanzibar declaring that the rent is not high enough and that this is another case of imperialist exploitation. The Sultan's flag, plain red and undefaced, flies above Fort Jesus in the old town of Mombasa during Mohammedan festivals, and the Sultan, as titular head, sometimes pays a state visit to the city.

Zanzibar, with all the Sultan's dominions, is a British Protectorate, ruled over by the Sultan who is the head of the State, but the Government is carried on by a British Administration under a Resident. The Sultan's subjects are known as 'British protected persons' and carry Zanzibar passports stamped to that effect. The Residency, where the British Resident lives— a pleasant but undistinguished house with castellations and old Portuguese cannons—is one of the only two places in Zanzibar where the Union Jack is officially flown. The other is the Neomoorish entrance of Her Britannic Majesty's Court of Justice. Everywhere else, outside the Palace of the Sultan, on the Municipal Building, outside all police stations and on the sterns of Government ships, the plain red flag of His Highness the Sultan is flown. On all ceremonial occasions the Sultan's anthem is played before 'God Save the Queen'. Visiting strangers are prodded in the ribs at the opening bars.

The island of Zanzibar is about 54 miles long and 24 miles across at its widest point. It is, in fact, about the size of Hertfordshire and very much the same shape. The city stands on the western side of the island, and looks across the strait to a blue coastline and high, dim mountains above which towering cumulus clouds build up by day, and by night the lightning glimmers like the flames of distant war. The island is built of coral rock with sand and humus deposited upon it, and forms part of the long coral reef, part fringing and part barrier, which runs down the East African coast from Gardafui to somewhere off the coast of Mozambique. The bays and inlets on the western coast of this flat island, which is nowhere more than 200 feet above sea-level, are bounded by low, undercut, flat-topped cliffs of black coral rock. They are intricately sculptured by the tropical rains of millions of years, and the dead, branching corals, which once built up the reefs of which these cliffs are the remains, can be seen still standing in the position of growth within the rock. They show that the island is part of a reef which was once beneath the sea but has now been lifted up. Many of these bays and long arms of shallow sea on the western side of the island merge into the land, the coral body of the island itself, in a cloud of green mangroves so that it is hard to know the dividing line between land and sea, which fade into one another in a clicking of mud crabs and the hot noise of crickets, until the coconut palms lead the eye away into a forest of tall slender stems and waving plumes. Long low headlands, pencil thin and shimmering in the heat, reach out to embrace flat, insubstantial islets, floating upon air. The native, paddling his dug-out canoe across the glassy water, seems airborne, a ghost borne upon the tremulous heat. But on its eastern side the island fronts the Indian Ocean and the South-East Trades with a long straight stretch of white coral sand, plumed with coconut palms and guarded by a fringing reef for nearly fifty miles. For mile upon mile the coconut palms bend to the hot damp monsoons and the breakers pound and wink upon the coral reefs. There are a few fishing villages of thatched huts with outrigger canoes drawn up on the sand and nets hung out to dry, but on the long lonely beaches between them myriads of sand crabs scuttling to their burrows at low tide are the only living things to be seen.

The island of Pemba, or El Huthera, the Green One, is the second of the Sultan's two islands. It lies about 25 miles to the north of Zanzibar and some 40 miles off the coast of the mainland. It is the smaller island of the two, about 42 miles long and 24 across at its widest part, and is slightly larger than Huntingdonshire. Its western side is even more strangely indented and sculptured than that of its sister island for, inside a guardian barrier of flat islets made of the same uplifted black coral rock, undercut and topped with scrub, lies a lovely shallow lagoon with long arms running into the body of the island itself. They too merge into the land in mangrove thickets, keeping the ranks of coconuts at bay. But on the eastern side again there is a long straight coast protected by a fringing reef.

Pemba is primarily a coral island, like Zanzibar, and is built of old coral rock, broken down into chalky deposits, sand and red earth. It, too, forms part of the barrier system of the East African coast, but while Zanzibar was evidently recently joined to the mainland, Pemba is divided from it by deep water and must have been separated from it for a very long time.

Pemba is little known and seldom visited, for mail boats never call there, so that European faces are rare in the little towns of Wete and Chake-Chake. A dear old steamship, with a high yellow funnel and curious whining noises in her vitals, sails once a week from Zanzibar with her decks packed with Indians, Arabs and Africans. When she arrives at her destination she noses her way with caution to an anchorage far out in the lagoon. But very few tourists make the journey and the only Europeans permanently resident in the island are Government officials and doctors. Yet, neglected though Pemba is by the world outside, it supplies by far the greater part of the cloves which are exported all over the world from Zanzibar and for which the city is famous. It is in aspect more striking than its sister island for it is hilly and carved into quite deep valleys with ridges between them along which run the roads and from which can be seen prospects of wooded distances and glittering arms of the sea. In both islands the luxuriance of the vegetation is astonishing. The coconut palms in orderly ranks, the dark towering mango trees, the bananas with their tattered

wings, together with a mass of glaucous foliage, seem to enfold
the landscape in deep shadow and plume the middle distance.
Pemba is slightly cooler than Zanzibar but also somewhat
damper, so that all the wonderful, heavy-scented and brilliant-
flowering shrubs that grow in Zanzibar bloom in Pemba with
an even more generous beauty and abandon.

The climate of these two islands is one of the most enervating
in the world and very hard for Europeans to bear. It is hot
and very damp from about November to May. During
these months the North-East Monsoon blows from the Equator.
Yet the temperature seldom reaches 90°F., though in March
1951 there was exceptional heat when it reached 96°F. The
humidity, however, is very high so that one lives in a state of
unbecoming dampness and nothing seems to dry. The shirt
you discarded at lunch time is still damp the following morning.
The suit dry-cleaned in London before you left shows, after
hanging up for a month, the marks of the soup you spilt on it
three years ago outlined precisely in mould. A white hoar frost
forms on all your shoes and on anything made of leather.
Metal rusts and bright surfaces soon grow dim. Tender complexions fade and even the loveliest English rose soon looks
wilted, wan and shiny. A feeling of extraordinary lethargy
overcomes even the most energetic. After a few months
nobody is, in fact, very active and after a few years most people
have succumbed altogether. It is an insidious process that one
scarcely notices. On first arrival one thinks everybody terribly
lazy and wonders why it is so difficult to get anything done in the
place. Does nobody ever get a move on? You'll soon show
them. But after a few months one no longer particularly wants
to get anything done and finds it hard to move oneself. To-
morrow will do. You develop an extraordinary inventiveness
in thinking of reasons for doing things not to-day but to-morrow.
A capacity for sleep is also a noticeable symptom of the general
torpor which Zanzibar induces. It is possible to sleep without
waking from nine in the evening until eight the following
morning and, as the disease advances, one finds oneself sleeping
innocently and soundly, as though after a heavy day's work, in
the afternoon as well. Offices open at seven o'clock in the
morning, though I think it unlikely that you would find anyone,
certainly no European, there at that hour. They close at 1.30

and after that the day is finished. In actual fact most Europeans arrive at work about eight o'clock and then absent themselves about half past nine for breakfast. There are not many people at their desks at half past twelve.

Yet one is never ill. I endured much clammy discomfort, and often felt and looked as though I had been rung out under a shower bath and put through a mangle. Yet I was hardly ever unwell and never suffered from those horrible chills and colds which always seem to be waiting for me when I step ashore in England. It is, in fact, during the months of the North-East Monsoon at least, a rather unpleasant but healthy climate, especially now that medical science has overcome the fevers and miasmas, malaria, yellow fever, blackwater fever and cholera, that not so long ago made of Zanzibar a white man's grave. Nowadays one just becomes, as I did, indecently fat and lazy.

In about May a welcome change takes place. It begins to rain. Heavy black clouds build up over the island and spill their contents in crashing downpours which advance through the coconut plantations with the noise of an express train. At first these refreshing cloudbursts are sporadic and everyone is thankful for them, but they become more and more frequent until they coalesce into a nearly continuous cataract which lasts throughout the month of May. Long before it has ceased everyone, including myself, having greeted the arrival of the rain and the merciful drop in temperature with joy, is praying for it to stop. Roads become impassable. The narrow streets of the city are racing rivers of murky water. Water spouts solidly with a ceaseless clatter from every pipe and gutter. Broad lakes, pocked by the pitilessly falling pencils of rain, cover every square yard of flat ground. The natives paddle about under umbrellas, holding up their white robes about their knees. Rich Indians, driving along in their new motorcars, spatter everybody with fine abandon. The mosquitoes, and every other insect imaginable, rejoice and arise in clouds singing. Then, quite suddenly, the rain stops and the sun shines again.

These are the 'Long Rains', the 'Masika', and they usually last for about a month. Occasionally they do not occur and in 1952 there was only about a week of rain, heavy but sporadic. The big rains failed, with disastrous effects upon the crops on the mainland. Zanzibar, however, never lacks water. On the other hand in 1951 the rains were heavy and prolonged. A stranger in those parts, I went to stay in Dar-es-Salaam during May, taking with me in my ignorance no provision against wet weather at all. I became virtually a prisoner in the Dar-es-Salaam Club for about a fortnight.

The 'Masika' brings a miraculous change in the climate. For as the rain belt moves away up north the South-East Monsoon, or South-East Trade Wind, comes in behind it. It blows hard at first and the Sultan's little steamship, which makes the forty-mile passage to Dar-es-Salaam once a week, takes quite a tossing for about half an hour when she gets clear of the southern end of Zanzibar island. But after about three weeks the wind loses its ardour and relents. Then for five months the green islands and their crowded capital enjoy a paradisal climate, cool and bright and rainless, though still somewhat relaxing for Europeans. During this cool season it is possible to grow English vegetables, crisp lettuce and enormous tomatoes, if you dig in enough manure. But everything comes up with a rush, all together, as though there were not time to get the business of growing, flowering, fruiting and dying down safely over and done with before the cool season ends. So those who have gardens, such as myself, can make friends and influence people by giving them lettuces, tomatoes, beans and radishes with al-most feverish generosity, for otherwise they soon find themselves with a wilderness of rotting stalks, since the soil is poor and sandy and the lack of rain soon dries everything up. The landscape, which had burst into a riot of heavy green during the 'Masika', soon takes on a thirsty look and it is with relief that the earth, at any rate, greets the 'Vuli' or 'Short Rains' in November.

These only last a week or two and they mark the change back from the South-East to the North-East Monsoon. The monsoon comes in like a fierce, hot, damp breath, covering the surface of the straits between the island and the mainland with white horses and dark squalls. The little ships and boats dance in the roadstead. Every day the wind blows hard but falls away about sunset to give place to those serene and silver nights that are one of the glories of that part of the world. In January the wind dies away altogether, and during February and March the heat increases in the narrow streets of the town to an almost unbearable crescendo of sweatiness in April.

Zanzibar owes its existence to these regular and predictable monsoon winds and is the most southerly Arab city in the world to-day because of them. As long ago as the seventh century before Christ dhows, very little different in appearance from those that throng the roadstead to this day, sailed down the African coast from Arabia on the North-East Monsoon and, on the South-East, took back gold from Ophir, tortoise-shell, ivory and slaves. Hippalus, the Egyptian, revealed the existence of these monsoons to the western world in 45 B.C. and, in so doing, gave the West the key to the East. The Arabs, the Phoenicians and the Hindus, however, had known about them for centuries before that but kept their knowledge secret. In the seventeenth and eighteenth centuries a great trade in slaves grew up on the East African seaboard, based upon rich and prosperous Arab towns, Kilwa, Mombasa, Lamu, Zanzibar and several others. In the nineteenth century Zanzibar became the metropolis of the western Indian Ocean and the chief centre of the African slave trade until the trade was abolished in 1845. The same dhows, scarcely changed by the passage of over two thousand years, and manned by crews whose respect for law and order and human life had changed as little as their ships, carried on this pitiless commerce, sailing southwards on the North-East Monsoon with knives and spears, and metalwork and beads, and finally with firearms with which to tempt the African chiefs to barter their people into slavery. To-day they still come, with their sails like the crescent moon and their wild fierce crews, chanting and beating drums. They come in November and December, when the North-East Monsoon sets in, but they bring dried fish and roofing tiles and general cargoes, and also carpets and brass-bound camphor-wood chests, which were once very cheap and are now very expensive. They take back cloves and mangrove poles when the monsoon changes. Exactly as they might have been seen centuries before Christ you may see them to-day, poised on the northern horizon like a flock of birds, their wings bright in the sunshine. They come to roost in the anchorage and ride there, as strong as and older than the Faith, with their high carved poops and forward-raked masts. The narrow, odorous streets of Zanzibar, especially the particularly narrow and especially odorous ones of the Arab quarter, are thronged with fierce-looking

visitors, bearded Arabs from Oman and the Hadhramut with
curved silver knives stuck in their waistbands, slender Somalis
black as midnight with delicate hands and wrists, hook-nosed
Persians and Pakistanis, chattering Hindus from Bombay.
Rhythmic chants and drum beats sound far into the night.
By the end of the 'Masika' rains they are all gone and the
anchorage of Zanzibar, which in April is a forest of raked
masts, is quite empty by the end of May.

The dhows are the last sailing ships making regular runs on
the world's seas. But they are fighting a losing battle and every
year fewer of them come to Zanzibar. The number of quick,
regular motor-driven coasters is increasing and making it more
and more difficult for the dhows, dependent for sailing on wind
and weather, to get cargoes. The oil fields and refineries of
the Persian Gulf and Arabia are drawing away young Arabs
from the sea and making the recruiting of crews more difficult.
And the little city of Zanzibar, with its air of history and past
grandeur, is sinking into the background, easily outstripped
nowadays by Mombasa and Dar-es-Salaam. One day, perhaps, it will become just a curiosity, a museum piece, and the
red-faced, loud-voiced people from the mail boats, clicking
their cameras around its alleyways, will be its major industry.
However, that melancholy time is not yet, for Zanzibar has
another shot in the locker. The two islands, Zanzibar and
Pemba, are together the principal centre in the world for the
cultivation and export of cloves.

One usually associates cloves with apple tarts or with tooth-
ache, for which in my schooldays they were a temporary and
inefficient antidote. Seeing the great black perfumed pyramids
of them drying in the godowns of Zanzibar harbour, the sacks
of them borne on the backs of chains of labourers and descend-
ing into the holds of lighters for loading into great ships, one is
amazed at the hitherto unsuspected popularity of apple tart.
Or the high incidence of tooth-ache in the islands of the east for
which those ships are bound. Nevertheless, cloves have other
uses. In the Far East, particularly in Indonesia, they are mixed
with tobacco in the manufacture of cigars. One of the greatest
buyers is Singapore which re-exports them all over the east,
but especially to Java and Sumatra.

Zanzibar cloves are supposed to be the finest in the world,

though some are grown in Brazil and some in Madagascar. I believe, however, that a kind of snobbism has grown up in the select circles where cloves are bought and sold, so that those which are not grown in Zanzibar are taken there to be re-packed in order that they may go out into the world's markets stamped with that ancient and romantic name.

The clove tree was introduced into Zanzibar in 1828 by the first Arab Sultan to make his home in the island, Seyyid Said-bin-Sultan. He obtained the seedlings from Mauritius whither they had been brought from the East Indies by M. Pierre Poivre, with many other spices, to stock his famous botanical gardens at Les Pamplemousses. Said planted his seedlings in the garden of a palace he had built outside the city of Zanzibar and found that in that hot, damp climate they did very well. Accordingly he ordered every Arab estate owner, growing coconuts, bananas or mealies, to plant three clove seedlings for each coconut palm in his plantation, or forfeit his estate. And that meant every plantation owner. This was an astonishingly far-sighted action and laid the foundations of the Sultanate's prosperity for many years to come. Naturally it angered the estate owners at the time, but they had no choice but to obey or lose their estates and, perhaps, their heads, for there was no possibility of that quick and easy return that Arabs love—and who does not?—and nowadays have grown to expect as of right. Clove seedlings planted in very favourable positions may perhaps flower after the first five years but, as a rule, they do not do so for seven years. Rich Arabs in Zanzibar to-day, scented and luxurious in their new cars, bought with the profits from cloves planted by their forefathers, should bless the name of Seyyid Said who forced this effortless prosperity upon them. But I do not suppose they do. I rather suspect they think it is all due to their own skill, prowess, innate intelligence, charm and personal attractions—especially the last.

The clove is a compact and handsome tree with small, dark, shiny leaves. It looks not unlike a large bay tree and has a cultivated appearance. It gives to the landscape, particularly in Pemba where it is seen at its best, the aspect of a garden, formal and arranged, almost of a graveyard because of its close-growing habit and dark foliage. Usually it is irregularly planted, but sometimes it stands in avenues and aisles that make one think of graves and worms and epitaphs. The clove itself, which eventually finds its way into the apple tart, is the yet unopened bud of the little star-like cream-coloured flower which hangs in heavy clusters. The buds are picked before they open and then spread out on mats to dry in the sun. Those which are not harvested, but remain on the tree and come to flower, are known, after the flower has died, as 'mother of cloves' and from them the seeds are taken for future planting.

The dried cloves are brought to Zanzibar in sacks and stored in godowns near the docks, where their spicy fragrance mingles with other odours less fragrant but equally pungent. From the godowns they are carried to the docks through the streets on four-wheeled, wooden 'homali' carts, man-hauled by a central shaft, which are the familiar and characteristic vehicles of Zanzibar. For the little town, with its narrow streets and awkward corners, must be one of the last remaining places in the world where man is still a beast of burden. The motor-car and the ox cannot tackle the difficult corners and the many twists and turns so easily or efficiently as the teams of four or five grunting, straining blacks who man the shafts of the 'homali' carts. With a curious rhythmic chanting and backs gleaming like polished stone, they push and pull their creaking waggons through alleys that are deep channels of heat. Their rank *'odeur d'Afrique'*, so evocative and compelling, is one of the other fragrances of Zanzibar which mingle with the smell of cloves.

Since the 'homali' teams are paid piece-work rates, at so much a load, the more journeys they make in a working day the more they earn by their humble labour. For this reason, when their carts are empty, they race back to load up again, charging at a rattling full tilt through the streets, shouting as they run, streaming with sweat and naked except for a wet breach clout. When their loads are heavy they bend their muscled backs in time to a rhythmic and scarcely human grunting, a zoo noise which, it would seem, helps to make their burden lighter. It sounds like the grunt of a sub-species of ape trained in the service of a higher one. The 'homali' men are said to be a wild, uncouth lot among whom trouble flares up quickly and murder is soon done. And, under the circumstances, this is not surprising.

I remember, on one occasion when I tried to take photographs of them, they became very angry and threatening and made it plain that they looked upon my presence, and that of my camera, as an insult. Some only turned their heads away as they passed with their carts. Others shouted their disapproval, while others bore down upon me with their carts and made as though to run me down. I had to jump for it.

Dislike and fear of the camera is common among the simpler people in Africa. They fear its evil eye which brings bad luck. All people who do menial work especially object to being photographed while doing it and consider it an affront to their dignity. I have heard it said that this is a kind of psychological hang-over from the days of slavery. The lowest and least skilled menial work, performed under the public eye, carries with it a loss of face, especially now when it has become the ambition of every coloured man, once he has achieved even a smattering of education, to wear a tie and shoes and part his woolly hair and to order others about, preferably from a sitting position behind a desk. The 'homali' men are not alone in this consciousness of the indignity of their calling. The men who go round with the sanitary cart at dead of night disguise themselves with palm leaves and daub their faces so as to be unrecognizable by any of their friends who might be out and about at three o'clock in the morning. They also have to be very highly paid to compensate for the degradation of their profession.

The harvesting of Zanzibar's clove crop begins in November and goes on until April throughout the months of the North-East Monsoon. It is carried out with the maximum of ruthlessness and the minimum of skill. The trees are just torn asunder without care or thought in order to strip off the buds. If a branch is too high to be reached by hand or by ladder, it is broken off and stripped on the ground. For this exceedingly unskilled labour, which for some reason does not carry with it any loss of prestige at all, the harvesters get very good money so that a great migration of hopefuls, whose only qualification is a pair of destructive hands and strong arms, takes place every year from the city into the countryside, from Zanzibar to Pemba and from the mainland to the islands. Gangs of casual labourers come over from Tanganyika to work in the clove plantations during the harvesting. During the rest of the year they live more or less off the country like an invading army. No thought whatever is given to the clove trees, or to what may be left of them to survive the harvesting for next year, and the result is that every good crop is succeeded by a number of years during which the trees bear very little because they are slowly recovering from the damage done to them in the good year.

Nowadays the clove plantations of Zanzibar and Pemba have a blighted and stricken appearance because of a mysterious disease which has overtaken them. Hundreds of trees, and individual branches of hundreds more, stand as dead white skeletons against the green of those which still survive. The plantations look in places as though fire had swept through them leaving the trees white instead of black. The death of the whole tree is caused by the 'sudden death' disease of cloves and that of individual branches by the 'die-back' disease. These have been the two chief headaches of the Zanzibar clove-growers for some years, and at one time looked as though they might ruin the clove-growing industry in the islands. Whole trees just died where they stood and there seemed to be no evident reason for it. In the 'die-back' disease individual branches withered and whitened and the whole tree slowly succumbed limb by limb.

In 1948 a team of British scientists under a brilliant botanist, Dr. John Nutman, was sent from East Africa to carry out research into these mysterious diseases. They were baffled at first, believing the cause to be a virus, that is, some agent so small that it cannot be isolated or cultured or stopped by the finest filters made, but whose presence can only be inferred from the way it appears to behave. Accordingly, it seemed, after two or three years of fruitless work, that the only possible remedy was the drastic one of cutting out of the clove plantations all the dead trees, and also all the living ones that showed any sign of the disease. Only thus could the rest of the trees in the islands be saved. This, of course, faced the Government with a serious political problem, for the Arab plantation owners knew nothing and cared less about non-filterable viruses and Koch's postulates. All they knew was that the infidel Government was out to destroy their clove trees, many of which were only partly dead and could still bear crops for some years. Bitter resentment was aroused even though compensation was offered for every tree uprooted. Here was fertile ground for the seeds of discontent and, though elaborate plans were made for it, the cutting out of the clove trees was never in fact undertaken. Perhaps it was just as well that this bonfire was never lit for later the scientists were able to trace the diseases to a fungal origin, the fungi, carried by ants, possibly entering the wood through the wounds made during harvesting. It seems now that more careful harvesting must be the remedy.

In addition to the cloves there are always, of course, the coconuts. Those palms, marching across the two islands in companies and battalions, have become for me symbols of breathless heat, of hot damp winds, of still, metallic moonlight. They form the backdrop of every tropical scene, of the fierce colours, the woodsmoke and the fires winking in the twilight. They advance and retreat like a chorus, now crowding in thickly, with aisles and lattices of grey and green, now suddenly retreating as though in fright to leave wide plains covered only with scrub under cumulus skies. They stand far off on the sky-line and bend their heads together, take courage and come trooping back again, some taller than the others, nodding and beckoning them on. The rattle of their fronds in the monsoon, and the hiss and roar of torrential rain upon them, are the sounds with which one lives.

The copra is prepared in the usual way by splitting open the nuts and drying the pith in the sun, or over fires made of the husks. But, whereas in the Seychelles it was the custom to wait for the nuts to fall to the ground before gathering them, in Zanzibar the natives climb the trees and cut the nuts down. This is done four times a year, but the trees bear all the year round so that the gangs of labourers work over the island continually and almost every morning, somewhere or other among the coconut palms, you may hear their fine strong voices singing. Five or six negroes, accompanied by a very superior Indian and a very disinterested donkey, work through the plantations. The negroes climb every tree and throw down the nuts to the Indian who keeps a tally and loads them into sacks on the donkey's back. The men bind their ankles together with cords and climb up the smooth grey trunks of the palms with the

motion of a looping caterpillar, feet up together, then arms up
gripping the slender trunk. Their agility and strength are
astonishing and climbing a hundred-foot-long, smooth, swaying
stem seems the easiest feat in the world. Each man has a heavy
knife stuck in his loin cloth, which is all he wears. He slashes the
nuts off one by one and tosses them down. The coconut cutters
sing all the time as they work in a high, monotonous and yet
agreeable ululation in order to keep in touch with one another
and with the Indian tally man and his donkey. Often you wake
at dawn in Zanzibar to hear their voices warbling among the
trees, their laughter and the heavy thump of falling nuts, and
to see the donkey nonchalantly breakfasting among your
vegetables.

3

The town of Zanzibar, like all the Arab cities of that coast,
was built on an islet, cut off from the main body of the island
by a narrow lagoon. This was for safety against the maraud-
ing hordes of savages who lived on the other side of the lagoon.
Mombasa, Lamu, Kilwa and other East African Arab cities
are similarly built on islands for safety against the natives
on the mainland. Zanzibar, however, nowadays stands
on a peninsula and most of the lagoon has been filled in to make
a fine green open space. On this the British play golf and the
natives football. On Empire Day the police force parades on
it with martial ardour, chests and bottoms stuck out and bare
feet twinkling, while the Resident salutes, sweating in his tight
white uniform and plumes. On the feast of Id-el-Fitr, at the
end of the fast of Ramadhan, the Arabs do sword dances and the
Indians make money and still more money out of stalls, draining
the African of his cents. Originally the reclaimed land on which
the golf course was laid out was given by the Sultan for the use
and enjoyment of the people of Zanzibar. That was long before
the craze for fresh air had filtered down to Indians, Arabs and
Africans. In those days nobody but the British ever thought of
playing games or of taking great gulps of air for its own sake.
But since the war the coloured people have taken to all sorts of

things they never thought about before. They pursue footballs with passion and skill and with loud cries of enjoyment. They even hit golf balls with force and accuracy and giggle when they observe their betters foozle. Their women, in their lovely flowing robes, walk abroad in the cool of the evening, chattering like birds and surrounded by droves of children. All this has become most embarrassing. 'Good Heavens!' said a British resident of many years' standing. 'When I first came here one never saw Indian women walking about. They stayed indoors!' So the golfers find they no longer have so much room to swing in, especially when the ladies in their saris seat themselves in busily chattering circles on the greens and do not seem to understand when 'Fore!' is shouted at them. And now that the Indians and Arabs are getting so rich they drive over the fairways, and even over the greens, at night in sleek motor-cars to their necking parties, American style, among the casuarinas by the shore. After dark the cars are dotted all over the golf course with their lights out, and furtive squeaks can be heard coming from inside them. One corner of the golf links has become what might be called a 'cyclodrome' where African and Arab boys teach themselves to ride bicycles, wobbling round and round upon the turf with their skirts tucked up round their thighs, shrieking with laughter.

Laughter, I think, is always somewhere around in this hot crowded little city. It is part of the orchestration of the dusty, narrow streets, with the blare of radios, the half-articulate noises of people who sell things, the clink of coffee sellers' cups, the cries of sweetmeat sellers. Perhaps the strangest cry of all is that of the old man who walks round the town selling palm tips. This is the crown of the coconut palm, the growing point, and is a great delicacy, known as 'Chui'. The call of the bent old man who sells it can be heard far ahead of him down the street—'Cho-oo-oo-oowee! Chooi-chooi—cho-oo-oo-oo-wee!' And children of all colours dance with joy as presently the old man appears and cuts off nutty-flavoured lumps from the concentric cylinders, cylinder within cylinder like an onion, which he carries under his grubby armpit. But chiefly the radios blaring from every shop front, balcony and window—the triumph of the twentieth century—at certain times of the day drown every other sound. In the evening the people of Zanzibar relax and let their minds empty themselves. They take a noise bath and let great throbbing waves of screeching, rhythmic sound sweep over them, driving out thought and care and, in fact, all mental processes whatever. The mixture is astonishing and must be most beneficial for those who care for that kind of treatment. As you walk down the street you pass from bizarre Arab music, with no beginning nor end nor perceptible melody, to Indian music, always apparently on the verge of a nervous breakdown, a tropical hysteria; thence to the American crooner mooing like a cow, and 'swing', the voice of the west, melancholy and sex-frustrated, full of vague longings for something to be got without effort, 'blew skies and yew'. But above and through all the cacophony, comes the laughter like the repeated statement of a theme in the narrow smelly streets, in the thronged markets, among the thatched mud houses, under the huge mango trees—laughter and the incessant beating of drums, remote, intangible and somehow disturbing.

The old stone-built town of Zanzibar, known as the Stone Town, is almost but not quite cut off from the main body of the island, on which stands the African town of mud and palm thatch, by a creek which is a horrid, slimy tentacle of the sea. At low tide this becomes an expanse of black mud which stinks and, everyone says, is quite disgraceful. I suppose it is, and yet I must confess I found great charm and beauty in it. It is there and refuses to be denied, like the human soul in the atomic age. I am sorry to say that, as part of the campaign to make Zanzibar as much like Surbiton as possible, the creek is being rapidly obliterated by filling in with banks of compacted refuse, a little more every day. When it is all gone some valuable building land will have been added to the town and visual horrors will no doubt replace the olfactory ones, but something characteristic, oriental and picturesque will have been lost to it. For, black and smelly as it is, exhaling a breath like all the rotten eggs in the world, it is really quite harmless. No one dies of a nasty smell, but hideous commercial modern buildings are death to the spirit. Anyhow the creek is nothing now to what it used to be. In the middle of the last century the rotting corpses of slaves, camels, dogs, donkeys and all the refuse of the town were consigned to it. In return, in generous measure, it gave back cholera, malaria, blackwater fever and dysentery. It

contributed largely to the climatic terrors of this sweltering
Arab city, terrors now quite overcome. To-day the creek is
innocuous. You merely put your handkerchief to your nose,
say 'Phew!' and drive on. Yet I suppose in this sterilized age
it ought not really to exist.

It would be hard to catalogue the smells of Zanzibar, almost
as hard as cataloguing the sounds. In this part of the town,
where the ramshackle buildings seem to step down into black
mud, like pilgrims into a holy river, the dominant note is
certainly rotten eggs. In the alleyways of the old town itself,
where the houses are so close together you can almost touch
the two opposite sides of the street at the same time, there is
the garlic breath of many Indians, a spicy, curry odour from
open doorways, mixed with something stale and unwashed
from within the dirty, crowded dwellings. From almost perpetually open shop fronts, with all the goods piled towards the
entrance, come the smells of hardware, of stuffs, of cosmetics.
Everywhere is the hot negro smell of sweat and urine. But in
the European part of the town, among the great Arab houses
converted, rather badly and often most inconveniently, into
flats, there is the soft, swooning perfume of frangipani, the
resinous tang of the casuarina, and the heavy fragrance of the
Millingtonia, the Indian cork tree, which weeps its tiny white
trumpets all over the road.

As for the sounds, the drums are always there, vaguely and
often intangibly. Sometimes they are low and scarcely heard, a
pulse in the ear, at other times insistent, throbbing like a headache. You have to pause, incline your ear, and say 'Hark! the
drums!' They beat in the African quarter for the trance-like,
shuffling dances or the wild, frenzied gyrations, when rhythm
seems to possess both mind and body. They throb monotonously
on the dhows in the harbour, far into the night, accompanied
by the wild chants of the Arab crews. These sounds, so old, so
moving and mysterious, used to keep me sometimes spellbound
at my window. In the still, silver night it was the voice of
Africa. Occasionally when in bed at night I have woken to
hear the distant drums and got up, put on shorts and a shirt,
got out my car and driven round the town at dead of night,
trying to follow the throbbing beat. But it was like a will-o'-
the-wisp. You could never track it down. Nor can you really

understand what that strange, monotonous, insistent voice is saying through the soft darkness. A few, perhaps, can get the message, for it speaks, I think, only to the initiated, those who have lived in Africa for a lifetime, sweated and been lonely and hated it, eaten and drunk and slept with it and, at last and against their will, become part of it. But they are a dying race. A few lingered in Zanzibar, but soon there will be no one left who understands the drums.

4

The part of the town which the visitor sees, when he comes ashore from the mail boat, is the Stone Town, built on the peninsula which was once an island. Its narrow streets, which twist and turn as though built for the concealment of the worst crimes, give an impression of extreme age, a monumental city brooding over its dark and bloody past. The great Arab houses, three, four and sometimes five storeys high, white, saffron and blue, jostle one another for space, frowning down upon the narrow ways between them. And yet this impression is quite false, for Zanzibar, as we know it, is not, in fact, very old. It dates only from the thirties of the last century when the Sultan of Oman, the same Seyyid Said who imported the cloves, made it the great centre of the Arab slave trade and finally, enchanted by the lush green of the island after his own arid land, decided to settle in Zanzibar and make it his home. None of these great houses, at which the visitors gaze with veneration, with their heavy, carved doors, fine courtyards and archways, and the 'poor man's rose' sprouting from the masonry, is really more than about 120 years old. Originally they were flat-roofed, like all Arab houses, but nowadays they are covered with corrugated iron sheets and with various erections added comparatively recently, so that from the air the city has the look of a shanty town with spires. The spires are Christian, the Anglican and the Roman Catholic cathedrals. The Mohammedan mosques, though very numerous, are so inconspicuous and unpretentious that it is hard to know where they are. One of them, near the docks, has a pointed phallic tower, but it is hidden and no one coming out of the dock gates would guess that it was there.

Some of the Arab mansions still remain as private houses. The house of the famous Arab slave trader, Tippoo Tib, remains very much the same to-day as it was when he lived in it. The old house where Sir John Kirk, the great British Consul, lived stands forlorn and derelict, four miles out of town, surrounded by the fine trees which Kirk collected during his lifetime. The house of David Livingstone has been turned into laboratories for the clove research team. But most of the big houses have been converted into flats for European civil servants. The German legation, to which the Pretender escaped after the bombardment of his palace in 1896, now houses three families. From the narrow windows of these palaces, from which the veiled ladies once timorously peeped, bathing costumes and baby linen are now hung out as signs of the changed times. The spacious halls in the basements, where the household slaves once slept and where the weary could rest and refresh themselves, are store places now for prams and bicycles. But the external features of the houses remain. Chief among these are the magnificent brass-studded doors with elaborately carved lintels and architraves. But even these are fewer than they were some years ago, for when the tourist trade began the Arab owners of the houses took to tearing out whole doors with their lintels and architraves for sale to America. This practice, one may record with gratitude, has been stopped by the Government. In the African quarter there is a little house with a carpenter's bench outside it where an old gentleman, with a gang of young men, makes doors and carves them. He and his boys make a lot of money at this craft, it is said, though if that is so, Heaven knows what they do with it.

When the doors are polished and oiled they are a splendid and unique sight. The lintels and architraves are carved with intricate patterns in which the same ancient devices are always to be seen. The fish at the bottom of the door-post is the ancient fish-god of the Egyptians, the waves of the sea climbing up it represent the livelihood of the Arab merchant to whom the house belonged, the lotus flowers entwined are the Egyptian emblems of fertility. The faces of the doors themselves are studded with big conical brass nail-heads, the purpose of which,

C

it is said, is to make it difficult for elephants to butt the doors open with their heads, or any other part of their anatomy. This seems improbable, though an Arab traveller, writing in A.D. 915, recorded that the island abounded in elephants. They must have been extinct long before the Arabs built their houses in the Stone Town so that the brass nail-heads may be derived from some other part of the world, possibly from the Arab cities on the coast.

The greater the wealth and social position of the owner of the house, the larger and more elaborately carved his front door. You were, and still are, known by the size of your front door. In the African quarter to-day quite humble houses of mud and palm thatch have heavy, carved double doors, even though the back of the house may be an affair of kerosene tins and bed ends. This is one of those matters where one has to keep up with the Joneses.

These big old houses do not lend themselves very willingly to European needs. Steps are now being taken by the Government and by commercial firms to move their European staff into new quarters outside the town. But for years past married couples with young children have been living in flats, mostly badly converted and far from desirable or convenient. The lower part of the building is useless for a start. Here, in an earlier day, the household slaves slept on stone shelves around the walls. Here, too, came the poor, the weary and the hungry to take shelter, to rest and to receive a portion of free rice or mahogo (cassava root), part of the tribute which Islam decrees the wealthy shall set aside for the poor. To this day any subject of the Sultan may take shelter in the basement of the palace and receive his portion of mahogo. From the empty ground floor of the Arab mansion a stairway ascends, often round three sides of a courtyard, to the first floor, which is the habitable part of the building. The rooms are long and narrow, with tiny windows and high beamed ceilings. As a rule the rooms have been thrown into one another by knocking gaps in the walls, but the windows remain as they originally were because the walls are so thick that to knock larger holes in them would cost too much. So Government servants stifle, even if they have ceiling fans, which few do. Extra rooms are often built, penthouse fashion, on what was once the flat roof of the house and are reached by wooden stairs. The suites of apartments that result from these surgical operations on such old bodies seem to cover an immense area without providing very much accommodation and, because of makeshift party walls, not much privacy. One makes long journeys up and down steps, along airy balconies with roof-top views, through graceful arches deprived of their meaning and purpose, in order to find conveniences most inconveniently located. 'I'd better show you,' says your hostess. 'I'm afraid it's a little difficult.' And, having escorted you, leaves you wondering if you will ever find your way back again.

The Stone Town presents quite a handsome front to the sea. There is a broad road on a sea wall and several considerable buildings. The most important of these is the Beit-el-Ajeib, the House of Wonders, built by the famous Sultan, Seyyid Barghash-bin-Said, in the eighties of the last century. It was originally part of his palace but in 1896 there was a slight dispute about the succession, and the palace was bombarded by the British fleet and partly destroyed. To-day the House of Wonders is the Secretariat, a tall square building of four storeys with verandahs all along each storey supported on continuous columns that reach right up to the roof. It has a square central courtyard, roofed over now with steel and glass like a railway station, but the magnificent carved doors, the finest in Zanzibar, the wide staircase with silver knobs on the banisters, and the general air of spaciousness and grandeur are still preserved. Yet these are the least wonderful things in the House of Wonders. There is, for instance, the clock in the central tower which astonishes visitors by being always, apparently, six hours slow. At three in the afternoon it points to nine. At seven o'clock it shows one. This is, in fact, because it is keeping Mohammedan time which, very sensibly, measures the day from sunrise to sunset all the year round, an excellent arrangement in these latitudes where the sun always rises and sets at the same time to within half an hour. The day, therefore, starts at twelve o'clock, which to the infidel is 6 a.m., and noon is the sixth hour. It ends again at twelve o'clock, which to us is 6 p.m., and our midnight is six o'clock in Islam. This is good mind training for European visitors, who have to do a mental exercise whenever they ask a native the time. The other wonder in the House of Wonders, which enormously excites the natives and moves them to expressions of awe and admiration, is an exceedingly ancient electric lift, the only one in the two islands. It is operated by an affair of wheels which emits blue flashes and angry clicking sounds in a cage under the stairs. Inside the lift a notice reads 'Five Persons Only', and gives to the uniformed lift attendant a measure of power and authority of which he is proud and which he uses with condescension. Often I have seen fierce-looking bearded Arabs, with coloured head-cloths and silver, curved sheath-daggers at their waists, watching with amazement this marvel of twentieth-century technical achievement, this evidence of western mechanization and advancement. Little groups of boys in white robes and round embroidered caps gaze upwards wide-eyed, in awe-struck silence, as clerks and secretaries ascend and descend, while safely imprisoned fireworks and the clanking of heavy wheels accompany their movements.

There is an open space of worn, exhausted grass in front of the House of Wonders with a fountain and some trees. This is the Maidan, and is something of a wonder in itself, for the grass is like a threadbare carpet worn thin by thousands of bare feet. The trunks of the trees and the barrels of the old cannon, unattractive trophies of the First World War, are polished bright and shiny by years of friction and the fountain is never without its living frieze, seated upon and astride its rim. A walk through this open space in the evening inevitably fills the mind with Malthusian reflections. For black and brown human life seems to pullulate upon this wide triangle of tired ground. A stroll through a colony of birds or a rookery of seals gives the same impression of swarming, urgent, fecund life, full of a blind force and powerful by sheer numbers. The noise, too, heard in the mass, is much the same as that produced by a vast multitude of birds, a continuous high-pitched screaming and chattering without discernible meaning. The little brown and black creatures swarm and tumble over the beaten earth, all but engulf the fountain, climb into the trees, straddle the guns and flow over the sea-wall into the sea. In the midst of the up-roar African 'ayahs', attendant on the better-to-do Indian children, sit around impassively in their black cloaks with the mild, gentle look of contented cows. Each little brown or black entity, I used to reflect as I strolled among them, meant ten more little entities in fifty years' time and a hundred more in a hundred years' time.

'Good Lord!' said the English resident of many years' standing. 'When I first came here one never saw anyone on the Maidan at all!'

The House of Wonders, or Beit-el-Ajeib, is flanked on one side by a castellated fort and on the other by the Sultan's palace. The fort was built by the early garrison of Omani Arabs in the eighteenth century and is the oldest building in the city. Four stout walls of yellowish, gravelly rag, with round towers at each corner, enclose a pleasant garden which for years was used by the purdah ladies as a place of recreation. Unobserved by the lewd eyes of males they could walk there, embroidering and gossiping and twittering together in the evening. But some years ago the top floor of an overlooking building was turned into government offices and the ladies lost even this retreat.

The modern palace of the Sultan is a very modest affair. It was built for him by the British at the beginning of this century and is a two-storeyed white house with castellations and moorish arches, appropriate to its function. Were it not for the sentry in a tarboosh at the gate you might take the palace for a block of municipal offices or a school. It has no garden and only a small yard in front and it always struck me as odd that under the roof of the verandah, which, with a row of moorish arches, forms the base of the façade, myriads of house martens have made their home, as they do everywhere in the city if not disturbed. Their dirty nests of mud and feathers hang down in festoons above the Sultan's threshold, giving to the entrance an air of extreme dinginess. The birds fly endlessly to and fro, keeping up a ceaseless chatter and covering the ground with their droppings. Since no effort seems to be made to clear them away one can only suppose that the benign old monarch likes to have them there.

Altogether there is a homeliness, a total lack of display or pomp, about the residence of the Sultan of Zanzibar. The inside of the palace is as plain and unremarkable as the outside. The main throne room, which was the only apartment I had a chance to see, might well have been a large school class-room.

It has hideous lighting arrangements and equally hideous windows of coloured glass.

A certain puritanism has always characterized the Sultans of Zanzibar, with one or two exceptions. One of the reasons for this is that they are descended from the Sultans of Oman, who were originally men of the people, elected by suffrage to the Sultanate. Another reason is that the sect of the Mohammedan faith to which the Sultan of Zanzibar belongs, and of which he is the head, is a strict and puritan one, almost the equivalent of the Calvinists among the Protestant Christians. All display and ceremony, as well as ostentation of wealth, are frowned upon. The frown was maintained for ten centuries, since the first Imam of Oman was elected. But now, when sleek motor-cars, glittering wrist-watches, luxurious radios and American-pattern ties have appeared, and Allah has provided, out of cloves, the money with which to buy them, the frown has relaxed. To-day it is disappearing, especially among the young, and giving place to the dazzling and charming smile of the Arab.

The Sultan lives to the sound of bugles, which can be heard at frequent intervals throughout the day, sounding extremely British and martial calls within the oriental precincts. At six o'clock, sunrise, his red flag is hauled up to the 'Reveille' and at six o'clock, sunset, it comes down to the 'Last Post'. The Sultan's guard and bugler, in high red tarbooshes and with bare feet, march softly through the town each morning and evening to relieve the duty guard at the palace. They form single file in the narrow main street to avoid being squashed against the wall by newly acquired bulbous motor-cars, and never can a sovereign have had a gentler, more unwarlike bodyguard. They march with a soft, padding, almost inaudible tread and, like the police, salute all Europeans indiscriminately in the belief, not altogether unsound, that every European is certain to be Someone or Other.

At the entrance to the palace, near where the sentry stands, is a small kiosk with a visitors' book. This is the Book, which civil servants must sign several times a year and visitors should sign at least once a visit. There is another Book outside the British Residency, artfully concealed in a shrubbery. This also has to be signed several times a year by civil servants, on arriving, on leaving, on the Queen's birthday, on New Year's Day and after attending an official function. Failure to sign one or other or both of the books on the appropriate occasion leads to embarrassing telephone calls and tart little reminders. Book signing, in fact, in a small British Colony is a fetish which is becoming a menace, for there are other, lesser Books lying open in other, lesser entrance halls, with pen, ink and blotting paper all ready for really conscientious signers. I am afraid I was not a very conscientious book signer and left these lesser volumes, that of the Chief Justice, the Secretary to the Government, the Chief Medical Officer and so on, innocent of my signature. The changing times, however, are tending to relegate the sport of book signing to the limbo where other luxurious and polite conventions have gone, for the expense of providing these heavily engraved, gilded and printed tomes—and nothing shoddy will do, of course—is becoming prohibitive. In some Colonies one is asked to be sparing with one's favours and sign only on important occasions, or on arrival or departure.

In the kiosk outside the palace of the Sultan of Zanzibar a little framed notice hangs above the Book. It reads—'It is not customary for ladies to sign His Highness's Visitors' Book.'

Every evening, somewhere around six o'clock, a large scarlet motor-car, with a crest in Arabic characters on the panels, and the red flag on the bonnet, drives out of the gates of the palace and proceeds slowly in the direction of Kiwani, about six miles northward along the coast. Here there is another palace, a summer residence, modern and unpretentious like the one in the town. Inside the motor-car sits a fatherly old gentleman with a dark skin and full, white beard. He wears a long blue robe and Arab head-cloth. Next to him sits a plump Arab lady, unveiled, showing bright, twinkling dark eyes. His Highness the Sultan of Zanzibar, Seyyid Sir Khalifa-bin-Harub-bin-Thuwaini-bin-Said, K.C.M.G., K.B.E., and his Sultana are taking their daily drive. His loyal subjects bow and touch their foreheads as he passes by or lay their hands upon their breasts in the native greeting which so gracefully combines dignity with humility. British visitors bow stiffly and smile. The red motor-car rolls silently along in the middle of the road at a steady fifteen miles an hour with its off-side traffic indicator out. It does not give way and no vehicle may overtake it.

To hoot loudly behind it would be a breach of good manners that oriental courtesy forbids. It would take no notice in any case. When you meet the red motor-car on the road you first look to see if the flag is flying on the bonnet—if you have time. Its presence means that His Highness is in the car. You pull in to the side and stop until the royal barouche has passed— again, if you have time—and make as good an imitation of a courtly bow as you can from inside a Morris Minor. I some-times managed to pull this off, but not always. Sometimes the royal car, with the flag fluttering on its nose, would be upon me, and I upon it, before I could collect my wits. I would pull up with a jerk and a screech and bow out into the empty road after it had passed. At other times I would pull into the side with dignity as the royal car approached, make a bow over my steering wheel and then realize that the royal car was empty. I had not noticed that there was no flag.

Behind the House of Wonders, the Fort and the Sultan's palace, which are the city's brave face to the world, the Stone Town lies as a maze of narrow and crooked alleyways between high, shabby houses and mean buildings, tiny squalid shops and humble habitations. It is easy to get lost among them. One walks on and on, twisting and turning this way and that, always hoping, but never quite sure, that one is heading in the right direction. One becomes drenched with sweat and in-creasingly apprehensive. Are we here for ever? Shall we walk round and round in perpetual circles and never get out at all? The more lost and bewildered I felt myself during my earlier explorations among these purlieus the more purposeful the air with which I strode along, down this narrow crack and up that tortuous alley, putting up an appearance of conviction and *savoir-faire* that I was far from feeling. Soon my shirt was clinging to me like a bathing suit. At last I could keep up the pretence no longer and looked undoubtedly what I was, hopelessly lost in an oriental city, as impenetrable as, apparently, but kindlier than, the Kasbah. Yet it was never necessary to look lost for long. Some brown or black gnome was sure to materialize out of the ground, grinning broadly and holding out a pale palm. 'Shilling, English Club?' Following his soft, sure footsteps I would suddenly find myself, in a couple of twists to the right and one to the left, at the place where I had come in an hour, or maybe more, ago.

As in most towns in the East, for this part of Zanzibar belongs to the East rather than to Africa, the streets tend to be distinguished by the trades that are carried on in them. This tendency, like other marks of individuality, is slowly diminishing as the years go on and the distinctive characters of the various streets are becoming blurred. A western standardization is creeping upon the town like a slowly rising tide, proclaimed by familiar advertisements on the walls of houses, mercury-strip lighting in some of the little shops and even, here and there, electric signs. Nevertheless it is still possible to find oneself in a street, or in a part of one, which is inhabited mainly by clock makers, or cobblers or tailors, or hardware merchants. One whole, gaily coloured little passage is given up to the sale of those brilliant African garments, the printed cotton 'kanga', which the women wear, the more sober 'kikoi', which the men wear like a skirt round the waist, the long white linen 'kanzu' and the round embroidered caps. It is a street of a thousand sewing machines, clicking merrily all day long outside the little shops. In the hardware street venerable old gentlemen, of cunning and Confucian appearance, sit at the entrances to caves which are full, literally, of everything that opens and shuts. They passively contemplate the Universe or add it all up in enormous books. In the street of the clockmakers hundreds of dials proclaim as many different hours, but there is not a clock among them to tell the time or one which you would care to have in your house. They are all without exception of the kind which it is embarrassing to receive as a present, hideous but obviously very expensive and one just has to take the will for the deed. In the recesses of these caves of the hours, among the many expressionless faces, the proprietor may be seen with lens in hand, poring over the disarticulated innards of your watch by the light of a single electric bulb. Your watch has succumbed to the general lassitude that overtakes all in Zanzibar, and it is most unlikely that the proprietor's ministrations with the forceps will do it any good. In the cobblers' shops they cobble almost in the dark, in caves that smell of leather and dust, sitting on their hams in that extraordinary oriental attitude, their thighs horizontal at right-angles to the body, and the soles of the feet together. Hour after hour, in this posture, they cobble, as, indeed, they work with silver wire, or ivory, or sit tailoring London-style suits for you to wear, with an application and industry almost incredible and, for a European, quite impossible. In the caves of the cobblers they squat upon the floor, while in those of the tailors, among the stuffy smell of fabrics, the clouds of motes like a mist in the thick air, and the wilderness of clippings, Indian and African boys squat upon benches, tirelessly plying their scissors and their sewing machines.

The industry of oriental peoples, particularly of the Indians and Chinese, gives to the cities of the East a formidable, even a slightly alarming, aspect. A nest of ants or a hive of bees is scarcely busier and, it would seem, only slightly more mindless. Work goes on, often, one would think, under the most forbidding conditions, in squalor, with the minimum of light and air, hour after hour all day and sometimes long after sunset. Food is taken at any time and sleep anywhere, on the floor, on a table or under it, on a bench or under it. Where or when love is made, one can scarcely imagine, but it obviously is made, for all the dingy premises swarm with children. Ponderous, slow-moving women-folk screech and chatter in the background, presiding over their fusty kingdoms like queen ants, enormous and for reproduction only, while the busy workers toil incessantly to support them.

To an Indian shopkeeper his shop is his life and the reason for his existence. The making of money for its own sake, and more of it than his neighbour to the right and left and opposite, is his only aim and ambition. It has nothing whatever to do with a wish for a better or fuller life. He worships the golden calf. He provides education for his children in order to equip them to compete even more efficiently in the game, for game it is, of accumulating wealth. Education is not looked upon as a means to broaden the intellect or to improve the mind, nor to acquire the standards inherited from Greece and Rome. Naturally, of course, for what are Greece and Rome to these children of the Malabar coast? An artist who came to visit Zanzibar, and used to set up his easel in the streets, was always bombarded by eager questions from Indian boys. 'Could I learn to paint? How much money could I earn as an artist?

How much do you make from your pictures?' And when the goal of wealth is achieved, as the pile of gold accumulates, there is little change in the way of life. All the increasing family, generation upon generation, continue to live in the same over-crowded, foetid apartments. But the neighbours must be shown how successful the business has become so the proprietor, who has worn the same shirt for many arduous years, hangs his money in trinkets on his stout, comely wife, or buys the largest and shiniest motor-car he can, fills it full of his enormous family, and drives round and round the town in it every evening, honking loudly.

In 1951 some eager official in England, with the zeal for standardization prevalent nowadays, or in the fashionable belief that all the world is just one big, jolly Trade Union, or ought to be even if it isn't, caused the British Administration in Zanzibar to introduce a modified Shop Hours Act. Hindus and Moslems were ordered to close their shops on Sundays like good Christians. No juveniles under a certain age were allowed to be employed for more than a certain number of hours and a register of persons employed had to be displayed prominently in the shop. This would have meant the paralysis of most of the businesses in the town which employed all the juveniles in the whole family all the time. The order was resented and widely ignored and the Administration wisely did not press the matter. On the first Sunday when it was in force there were two mail boats in the anchorage and the town was full of visitors. The shops were open as usual with scouts in the streets coaxing the tourist to come in. There was a record trade in brass Indian cow bells, fretwork inlaid coffee tables and elephants crossing bridges.

Zanzibar has an indefinable quality, an air about it, which is noticeable in certain towns and cities but lacking in others. It has the air of being a capital city in its own right. Perhaps this is the reek of history, the lingering flavour of great and sometimes terrible events now long past. In the places where mankind has suffered, some sort of imprint remains. In newer cities, like Nairobi, this is lacking and there is as yet no sense of haunting in the streets.

In Zanzibar there is an urbanity in the way the people stroll about, talking and enjoying each other's company. A

young Arab, who had been to London, once told me that two
things impressed him about our western metropolis. One was
that we do not spit in the street, the other that we seem to hurry
along 'everybody minding his own business'. This, he thought,
was a most exemplary state of affairs and a sign of the superiority of our culture. Yet, strolling through the streets of his little
capital, while the sunset flamed above the mountains of
Tanganyika, I found it hard to share his enthusiasm for our
haste and concentration. Other people's business is far more
interesting that one's own, and it was a cheerful, apparently
unworried throng that strolled up and down around me, lingered and sat and lay about, passionately interested in each
other's affairs and spitting everywhere with fine abandon. Arab
coffee sellers, with their conical brass pots on charcoal pans,
wove through the crowd clinking their porcelain cups. Elders
sat around at café tables, drinking the strong black coffee,
talking animatedly, regardless of the 'Voice of Zanzibar' bray-
ing over them all from loudspeakers in every direction. Fierce-
looking Arabs, ebony Somalis, Africans, Indians and women of
many races, gaily coloured as flowers, made a constantly
moving pattern that one could watch until the stars came out
low down over the earth and lightning flared over Africa. The
grace and beauty of the people in hot countries is one of the
spectacles of the tropics and part of the magic.

Across the bridge over the black creek you pass from the
Near East into Africa. On the one side of the creek are the
dark, shaded alleys of an Arab city and high, overhanging,
crumbling walls. Here, but modified and made respectable
by sixty years of British rule, are the sudden encounter, the eye
glance, the soft pad of feet, the giggle of invitation, the squeak
of surprise. On the other side are the wide, hot, dusty streets of
an African village, full of movement and colour, deafening noise
and smells. There is a feeling of sky and space and tall palms
waving above thatched roofs. The air vibrates with the heat,
the sky quivers with the noise of radios, the beating of drums
and the wide-mouthed, thick-lipped laughter. The jostling,
chattering African crowd, the white robes of the men and the
black hoods ('bui-bui') of the women, fill the street. Islanded in
it are 'homali' carts with their grunting teams, and impatient
motor-cars adding to the din with loud blasts of the horn. The

feeling of life and vitality soon imparts itself to you and you want to laugh and shout too. You have to shout anyway, to make yourself heard above the din.

The African quarter of Zanzibar is known as Ngambo, which is the Swahili word for 'on the other side', and its main street curves slightly uphill between the little square mud houses with roofs of palm thatch or of flattened kerosene tins. Some of the houses are more pretentious than others and are made of coral rag with heavy carved doors. But all the houses are of much the same height and of much the same size. They are mostly very sparsely furnished inside, with low trestle beds or mattresses on the floor and bright cotton coverings; but it is all very clean, for the African is meticulous in his habits and in his person. His ablutions are prolonged and elaborate. There are washing places in many different parts of the town and they are well attended all day long by Africans washing themselves and their clothes. The main street of Ngambo is festive with colour. Nearly every shop sells the printed cotton squares of brilliant colours, red, black, orange, yellow and blue, known as 'kangas', which the women wear gracefully draped around their figures. The kangas are hung out in the street like banners to attract the passer-by and give to shops that sell them a gala appearance. In each little decorated cavern, like a spider in his web, sits the Indian shopkeeper surrounded by his seductive wares. With siren voice and beckonings he lures you in.

The kanga is the African female costume. The Arab ladies usually wear a plain black silk covering (the 'bui-bui') over the head and the western-style frock underneath. African women often also wear a bui-bui over their kanga. The bui-bui can be drawn across the face with varying degrees of coquetry, and high-heeled sandals or block-heeled shoes twinkle provocatively beneath it. A heavy perfume lingers in the air long after the clicking of the heels has faded. The kanga is usually of agressively bold design. The square has a decorated edge and a device of some sort in the centre. Some of the designs, though bold, are gay and tasteful. Others are simply hideous and others slightly suggestive. It is becoming increasingly smart to wear a crude picture of a battleship, or a bedstead or even a suite of furniture, printed in the middle of

the kanga, so arranged that the centre piece is squarely over
the protuberant behind. Sometimes the words '*Karibu, Bwana*
—Welcome, Mister' or something even more daring are worn
in that conspicuous position.

When I visited the Comoro Islands, which are a French
Protectorate, I noticed that the kanga worn by the women
of those islands was usually of a finer and more delicate design
than that worn by the women of Zanzibar. As you go up
country on the mainland the design seems to get uglier and
coarser. This I took to be an example of the superiority of
French taste, which had been passed on to the natives, as had,
I found, the superiority of French cooking. However, I discovered that this pleasant female garment, whether found on
the mainland or in Zanzibar or in the Comoro Islands, is
manufactured in Manchester, and now, increasingly, in Japan.
Yet I may still be right. In Zanzibar some of the British ladies
amuse themselves and turn an honest artistic penny by drawing
kanga designs, which they sell to an enterprising Indian
importer. Perhaps the French ladies do the same in Grande
Comore—though somehow I rather doubt it.

The African quarter peters out into the hinterland of the
island, into a zone of sports clubs, football grounds, schools and
prisons. It trickles away as a kind of ribbon development of
little square mud houses and erections of kerosene tins along
the main roads leading north, south, and east out of the town.
When finally you have passed the last group of boys strolling
along hand in hand, the last aged crone with a bundle of faggots
on her head, the last perverse chicken scuttling across the road
under the front wheels, then the coconut palms come crowding
round and the mango trees like dark cumulus clouds, the
bananas, cassava plants and tall, coarse grasses. The fugitive
uproar of the cicadas pursues you on your way, overtakes you
as a hissing wave of sound, falls back and then comes on again.

Chapter Three

THE EMPIRE OF ZINJ

I

THE east coast of Africa was almost unknown to the nations of the west until the sixteenth century when the early Portuguese navigators explored it on their way to India and the Far East and planted garrisons upon it. But the nations of the east, the Arabs, the Persians and the Hindus, had known about it and traded along it for centuries before Christ. For at least three thousand years dhows, not very different from those which sail up and down the coast to this day, have come south from Arabia, Persia and India on the North-East and returned on the South-West Monsoon. In ancient days they came for ivory, spices and slaves.

These eastern peoples knew of the wild lands that lay behind this coastline as the mysterious empire of black men, which stretched beyond the end of the world into the territory of the dwarfs and monsters. To the Arabs this great territory was known as Zinj-el-Barr, the land of the 'Zinj' or Black Men. In modern Kiswahili *bara* means a land or country and in Zanzibar and Pemba the term refers to the mainland, as distinct from the islands.

In the records of early travels along the east coast of Africa, and in early maps of it, the Arabic words '*Zinj-el-Barr*' appear in many forms. The word 'Zinj', in fact, is believed to be traceable in several African names, in Zimbabwe, for instance, and in the Swahili name for the city of Zanzibar itself, Unguja. It survives to this day in Europe in the words 'Czingary', 'Tsigane' or 'Zigeuner', a gipsy, an Egyptian or black man. Until the fourteenth or fifteenth century the name was applied only to the mainland, but Vasco da Gama mentioned a place on the coast called Jangiber and in fifteenth-century maps there are ill-defined localities marked Xangibar, Zanguebar and Chancibar. The name Zinj-el-Barr was probably first transferred definitely to the island now called Zanzibar by the anonymous Arab historian who wrote the *Chronicles of Kilwa*. Kilwa was a Shirazian (Persian) city state situated near the Rufiji Delta south of Dar-es-Salaam. It flourished from the tenth to the fifteenth century when it was destroyed by the Portuguese. After the arrival of the Portuguese the island of Zanzibar was always referred to by that name which is thought to be a corruption of Zinj-el-Barr introduced by Indian traders.

The land of Zinj was peopled by the Bantu race, the sons of Ham, who at various times in several separate waves of invasion came from Asia into Africa and mingled with the original negro peoples whom they found there. The present natives of the coast of East Africa are known as Swahili, which means 'coast people' from the Arabic word '*sahil*', meaning 'coast'. They are Bantu people with a strong mixture of Arabic and Persian blood. Their language, Kiswahili, is a Bantu language, strongly diluted with Arabic words. Their way of life and culture they derive from the Arabs and their religion is that of Islam.

Some of the original Bantu people settled down on the coast and became a race of fishermen. Some crossed over to the islands in their canoes, which were dug-outs with outriggers practically the same as those which may still be seen on the islands. These first-comers to the islands were larger than the people who now inhabit them and they worshipped trees and the sun. The *Periplus of the Erythraean Sea* mentions an island called Menouthias, which is probably Pemba. 'Along this coast,' the author says, 'live men of piratical habits, very great of stature and under separate chiefs for each place.' The descendants of this ancient race, the first African inhabitants of Zanzibar and Pemba, are still to be found in remote corners of the islands. On the east coast of Zanzibar lives a race of fishermen, the Wahadimu, who speak their own language, are larger in stature than the Swahilis and are thought to be descended from the Zinj who came over from the coast centuries ago before the Arabs arrived.

In the centuries immediately before Christ and in the first century of the Christian era the land of Zinj was under the dominion of the Kingdom of Saba or Sheba, whose queen visited Solomon and marvelled at his wealth. The Sabaeans were a great maritime people, the descendants of Joktan (Genesis 10: 26–9), and they inhabited a large and prosperous kingdom in southern Arabia. In the seventh century B.C. they were supreme in Arabia and dominated the carrying trade of the east, controlling all the spice trade and supplying the eastern world with gold, slaves, tortoise-shell, ebony and ivory, which they brought in dhows from the coast of Zinj. The Sabaean kingdom lasted until the first century B.C. when the Indian trade ceased to be carried by sea and went by land. The decline which then began was speeded by a terrible disaster to the great dam which irrigated the country. The whole land dried up and the capital city, Marib, became a ruin.

The rise of Islam in the seventh century united the Arab states, which after the decline of Sabaea had been in a state of hopelessness and disintegration, into a great host of the Faithful who set out on a war of conquest, sweeping northwards eventually as far as Constantinople and westwards across Africa along the shores of the Mediterranean to the western gate of Christendom. It was a Holy War to convert the infidel world to Islam by the sword. A vast Mohammedan empire was formed, with the Caliph as its head, stretching from India to Morocco. But at the end of the seventh century A.D. a split developed in Islam when the Shiites broke away and founded their own Caliphate with Baghdad as its capital. The Caliphate of Baghdad lasted until the thirteenth century in a state of more or less continual war and ferment. There was continual war also among the Arab states themselves over the succession to the Caliphate.

The conquests of the Saracens after the rise of Islam and the constant war and unrest in Arabia and Persia stimulated a series of waves of emigration from these lands to the coast of Zinj, the lush green shores of which became for the inhabitants of those war-torn and barren countries a sort of Eldorado, a land flowing with milk and honey. There was peace there and freedom to trade. During this period, therefore, Arab and Persian (Shirazian or Shiite) cities arose all along the coast, fortified and built on islands to protect them from the savage Zinj. Some of these colonies were founded as early as the sixth century, but most were founded later than that, after the rise of Islam which drove people from their homelands. Zanzibar was probably first settled by the Persians in A.D. 701, though the oldest Persian building in Zanzibar island is a mosque which dates from 1107. On a small islet called Tumbatu, cut off from the northern tip of Zanzibar except at low water, are the remains of an ancient Shirazian city. The people who live on the islet, the Watumbatu, are an aloof, timid race who are said to be of Persian descent. The natives of Pemba are also believed to have a large mixture of Persian blood. Pemba, according to an Arab traveller, was colonized by Omani Arabs and Persians in A.D. 703. In the tenth century the Shirazian city of Kilwa was founded and attained great wealth and prosperity, and a high state of civilization in succeeding centuries, until it was destroyed by the Portuguese. Its domain extended to Sofala from which the gold of Zimbabwe was shipped. About this time, too, arose all the other Arab cities of the coast and grew to prosperity each on its island under its own Sultan— Mombasa, Lamu, Malindi, Mafia, Warsheik, Patta, Brava and several others. Their houses were built of stone and the people were dressed in fine silk and cotton clothes, while their women went 'bravely decked'.

Thus, when the Portuguese arrived on their way to India at the beginning of the sixteenth century, they found separate flourishing and civilized communities in fortified island cities dotted along the coast from Mozambique to Gardafui. On Zanzibar and Pemba islands, however, the Arab and Shirazi settlements must have been very small ones. It seems that in the main the native Zinj in these two islands were left alone under their own rulers, and, in fact, remained so until well into the nineteenth century. The last native ruler, the Mwenye Mkuu (the Great Lord), died in 1830. The Zinj continued to trade peacefully across the strait in the fruit, rice and millet which they grew, using boats sewn together with coconut fibre and having palm-leaf sails.

The Portuguese did not arrive in East Africa on any colonizing mission. They were looking for a route to India and they left garrisons in the Arab cities, which became victualling and repair bases for ships bound to and from their Far Eastern possessions. During the two and a half centuries of their domination of the coast they did not concern themselves with the cities they garrisoned, except to keep them in subjection, and took no interest in the welfare of the people. In the larger cities, such as Mombasa, the garrisons lived in forts and held the population down with the utmost brutality. Mombasa was the scene of intermittent bloody war throughout the whole period of Portuguese occupation, and to this day the native name for the city is Mvita, the warrior. Legend and tradition on the coast have nothing to say about the Portuguese, who were feared and hated. The modern Swahili word for Portuguese is '*Afriti*', a devil. When at length they were driven out it was as though they had never been, and the only remnants of their occupation are now the old fort at Chake-Chake on Pemba island and the curious custom which has survived there of bull-fighting, which is still carried on in a tame and rather jolly manner. There are also in Zanzibar a few bronze cannon captured by the Persians when they took Ormuz from the Portuguese in 1622.

Bartholomew Diaz was the first Portuguese navigator to round the Cape of Good Hope and he gave it that name in 1486. In 1497 Vasco da Gama sailed up the coast with four ships. He was received with hostility in Mombasa and went on to Malindi where a friendship arose between the Arabs and the Portuguese which was never broken. Da Gama built a pillar on the shore there which may still be seen, one of many which he raised to mark his progress up the coast. From Malindi he sailed for India in May and reached Calicut in twenty-two days. He was again on the East African coast homeward bound in January 1499. His expedition led to the opening up of the Cape route to India and the Far East by the Portuguese, and many expeditions followed placing garrisons in the Arab cities and exacting tribute from them, often with bloodshed.

One of the ships of an expedition in 1503, under the command of Admiral Antonio da Saldanha, discoverer of Table Bay, became separated from the main squadron and, after waiting in vain at Mozambique and at Kilwa, cruised off the island of 'Zemzibar'. It captured twenty dhows laden with ambergris, ivory, tortoise-shell and other produce. The king of the island protested and manned all his canoes with 4,000 men, but the captain of the Portuguese vessel, Ruy Lourenço Ravasio Marques, lowered two boats armed with cannon and, at the first shot, killed thirty-four men, putting the rest to flight. After this the Portuguese landed and soon overcame the slight resistance they met with. The king sued for peace, which was granted, and a tribute was imposed of £57 a year.

Thus in 1503 Zanzibar came under Portuguese dominion. However, the Portuguese did not apparently regard the island as of much importance for they built no fort there and the garrison probably lived in a stockaded encampment. The tribute levied was a small one compared with that which other cities had to pay, Kilwa £1,100 a year and Mombasa about £715 a year.

At first the Portuguese easily kept the mastery over their garrisoned Arab outposts. Nevertheless from the beginning there were constant local wars all along the coast and, with the motherland so far away and her manpower drained to the limit, it became extremely difficult to keep in subjection a people themselves bloodthirsty, cruel and treacherous.

In 1580 Portugal became subject to the Spain of Philip II and remained in subjection until 1640. This event marked the beginning of a slow decline of Portuguese power over the coast. The Portuguese empire had become too far extended, for distances were immense and sailing ships were slow. It took over a year for a sailing ship from Portugal to reach her possessions in India. Further, the motherland, a small agricultural country, could not supply the manpower for her many garrisons scattered all over the East and along the route to India, nor could her economy support the constant minor wars and many major ones in which it was necessary to engage in order to maintain so large an empire. The morale of the people at home was undermined by the Inquisition and by subjection to Spain. In the garrisons overseas it was undermined by the implacable hatred of the subject Arab and African peoples.

General rebellion in the Arab cities of the coast was touched off by a Turkish pirate, Ali Bey, who made a raiding cruise down the coast in 1586. He claimed that he had the authority of the Sultan of Turkey and was the vanguard of a great liberating Turkish fleet. The fleet never turned up, but Ali won the submission of several Arab cities and fanned the flames of rebellion all down the coast, except in Zanzibar and Malindi which remained quiet.

In the following year a horde of savages of Zulu origin, called the Wazimba, swept up from the south, took Kilwa and killed and ate 3,000 of the inhabitants. They appeared before Mombasa where the Arabs, oppressed by the Portuguese, let them into the town. For their pains the Wazimba fell upon them and ate almost the entire population. In the middle of this Ali Bey reappeared with five ships, as did also a Portuguese expedition of twenty sail which had been sent from India to deal with him. The Portuguese took Ali prisoner and transported him to Lisbon where, with a little persuasion from the Inquisition no doubt, he became a Christian. The Wazimba were driven out of Mombasa and settled down in the surrounding country.

In order to keep the unruly city of Mombasa in subjection the great bastion of Fort Jesus was built in 1594, and another at Chake-Chake in Pemba to overawe that troublesome island. The Viceroy of India wrote to the Commandant of Mombasa Fort in 1598—'I order you to put down the insurrection in Pemba, as it is from this island that all movements are made against the fortress.'

After this there were uprisings against the Portuguese all along the coast. They began with the massacre of all the garrison in Pemba and of the few settlers who owned estates in the island. In 1627 the Sultan of Mombasa murdered the Portuguese Governor, and there was a bloody rebellion. All the Portuguese locked themselves in the Convent, but, after a siege of some days, agreed to submit on condition that they were allowed to leave the town unmolested. No sooner had they left the building than the Arabs slaughtered every one of them.

In 1652 the Portuguese lost Muscat, capital of the Arab state of Oman in southern Arabia, having already, twenty years previously, been driven from the important island fortress of Ormuz by the Persians, assisted by British ships. The Arabs of Oman, future rulers of the coast, now appeared off East Africa for the first time in force, attacked Zanzibar and killed all the Portuguese there. This gave rise to another rebellion which the Portuguese quelled in 1653, with the help of men from Malindi, razing the native capital of Unguja Kuu to the ground.

The Portuguese power on the coast continued to decline in the face of increasingly successful rebellion and of attack by the Omani Arabs, but the Portuguese were not finally driven out of Mombasa until 1698, when they also lost Pemba. In 1710 Zanzibar was garrisoned by Omani Arabs and the Portuguese lost for ever all their African possessions, except Mozambique, which they hold to this day.

2

Neither the British nor the French seriously contested the Portuguese dominion on the coast of Africa. Neither played an important part in the history of Zanzibar until the slave-trading days of the mid-nineteenth century. Nevertheless, they, with the Dutch, were rivals of the Portuguese on the Cape route to India, although they appeared late in the field.

The first English ship to round the Cape was Sir Francis Drake's *Pelican*, homeward bound westward in 1580 after her circumnavigation of the globe. She found it to be 'the most stately thing and the fairest Cape we saw in the whole circumference of the earth', and so, indeed, it is.

On 28 July 1591, an expedition of three English ships under Captain (later Sir James) Lancaster dropped anchor in Table Bay. This was the expedition which led to the establishment of the British trade route to India and to the founding of the British East India Company of which Sir James Lancaster became a director. One of the three ships turned back at the Cape, carrying home the sick, and another foundered in a storm off Cape Corrientes. But the third, the *Edward Bonaventure*, went on alone and, after losing her mainmast and four of the crew in a thunderstorm, reached the Comoro Islands where 'the King came aboard in a gown of crimson satin, pinked after the Moorish fashion down to the knee, whom we entertained in the best manner'. This did not prevent the islanders from murdering a party of thirty men of the ship's company who went ashore in a boat to fetch water.

On 17 November 1591, the *Edward Bonaventure* arrived off Zanzibar Island and dropped anchor opposite Unguja Kuu, presumably a long way out since the bay is shallow at low tide. Her crew drew water from the ancient well which may still be seen there. 'This place,' they wrote, 'for the goodness of the harborough and watering and plentiful refreshing with fish, whereof we took a great store with our nets, and for sundry sorts of fruits of the country, as cocos and others, which were brought to us by the Moores, as also for oxen and hennes, is carefully to be sought for by such of our ships as shall hereafter pass that way. . . .'

They captured a priest or 'sherife' and held him to ransom for two months' victuals, but treated him with kindness and delivered him safely at the end of that time, 'which the King took in very good part, having his priests in great estimation'.

'These Moores informed us of the false and spiteful dealings of the Portugals towards us, which made them believe that we were cruel people and man eaters, and willed them if they loved their safety in no case to come near us, which they did only to cut us off from all knowledge of the state and traffic of the country.'

The *Edward Bonaventure* left Zanzibar on 15 February 1592, and shaped a course for Socotra, thence across to India. Her crew suffered terribly and she arrived at Sumatra with only thirty-three men and a boy. Here the crew became discontented and she turned homeward, but in the Atlantic was driven off her course to the West Indies and lost.

When the British, with the French and Dutch, entered the Indian Ocean it was for India and the Indies that their ships were bound, steering east of Madagascar for the Chagos Islands. The Dutch often made course due east from the Cape and turned north in the longitude of Sunda Strait.

Thus the East African coast was left alone and the Portuguese empire was not disturbed by European rivals. Up to 1823, when Captain Owen arrived on the coast on his surveying mission, only three British ships had visited the coast north of Zanzibar. When Admiral Blankett touched there in 1799 on his way north to the Red Sea and Suez he was told that no British ship had called at Zanzibar within living memory. His voyage, occasioned by the fear of Napoleon breaking through into Arabia and India, marked the beginning of European, and especially British, interest in the east coast of Africa.

3

The Arabs of Oman, whose capital was Muscat, had been a seafaring nation since several centuries before Christ. They were descendants of the same Joktan who was also the ancestor of the Sabaeans, and they traded between the Red Sea and India and the east coast of Africa. It was largely from Oman that the Arab, as opposed to the Shirazian, cities of the coast were peopled before the coming of the Portuguese. It was natural that the Arabs of East Africa should turn to Oman for help in their struggle against their oppressors.

In the early eighteenth century the fortified Arab cities of the East African coast, after the Portuguese had been driven out, came under the suzerainty of the Imam or Sultan of Oman, who appointed governors, each with a garrison. In 1728 civil war broke out in Oman about the succession to the Sultanate and the losing side appealed for help to the Omanis' traditional enemies, the Persians. This led to a Persian invasion and occupation of the whole country with much destruction and bloodshed. The Omani governors in Africa took advantage of these disorders at home to set themselves up as independent princes, Mombasa declaring itself independent in 1730. Zanzibar, however, remained faithful to Oman.

The Persians were driven out of Oman and utterly defeated in 1741 by the great Imam Ahmed-bin-Said, who was thought by many to be divinely appointed for this purpose and directly descended from Joktan, founder of the Omani state. He was the first of the Albusaid dynasty to which the present Sultan of Zanzibar belongs. Although there is some doubt about the true descent of Imam Ahmed, it seems that the Sultan of Zanzibar is at least in the running for the longest traceable genealogical tree in the world, going back in a direct line to Genesis.

Ahmed died in 1775, leaving seven sons and three daughters. The fifth son, Seyyid Sultan-bin-Ahmed, succeeded to the Imamate after much family quarrelling, acting at first as regent for his weakling elder brother. He was killed in a sea fight with pirates in 1804 and succeeded by his son, Seyyid Said-bin-

Sultan, who became a great ruler, destined to lift a small green island off the coast of East Africa into a position of great, though shortlived, prosperity and prestige with undefined dominions extending to the Great Lakes.

The word '*Seyyid*', which is prefixed to the names of all the members of the ruling house of Oman and Zanzibar, means 'ruler' or 'prince', member of the royal house. It is a title used by the present Sultan of Zanzibar and his five sons, whom one addresses as '*Seyyid*' in the same way as in English one would say 'Sir'.

Seyyid Said was only thirteen when he succeeded to the Imamate of Oman. At the age of seventeen he murdered his cousin, who was acting as his regent, stabbing him in the stomach at a palace reception. He spent the first twenty years of his reign bringing order to Oman and suppressing the rebellious and fanatical Wahabi tribe. He then built himself a navy of three frigates, four corvettes and several smaller vessels and sailed with it to settle accounts with the unruly governors of the east coast of Africa. He subdued Mombasa, using Baluchi cavalry troops which he garrisoned in the town, and sailed for Zanzibar. He fell so much in love with the green island that he decided to make it his capital and in 1840 took up his permanent residence there. The reign of Seyyid Said brought great days to Zanzibar which were to last until the scramble for Africa by European powers in the 'nineties when Said's great amorphous empire was torn apart. At the end of his reign of fifty years it was said of his capital city—'When one pipes in Zanzibar, they dance on the Lakes.'

4

In the nineteenth century, Zanzibar became the centrepiece of two great events, two chapters in the story of human progress, in which Great Britain took a principal part. One was the suppression of the slave trade, the other is what is nowadays called 'the scramble for Africa'. We may be proud of our country's part in the first of these for it was by her efforts that a great weight of misery and unhappiness was lifted from the shoulders of the black races. The conscience of Great Britain, and the pity and kindliness of her people, were aroused against the slave trade by the reports brought back by the early missionary explorers who penetrated into the interior of what was then in truth the 'Dark Continent'. The chief of these were the Germans, Krapf and Rebmann, who discovered Mount Kilimanjaro and Mount Kenya; Speke, who discovered the southern shore of Victoria Nyanza; David Livingstone, the greatest of them all, who explored the Zambesi, the Shire district of Nyasaland and Lake Bangweolo and died in doing so. These men brought back stories of the horrors they had seen and gave a great impetus to the abolitionist movement which had already, in 1839, resulted in the foundation of the British and Foreign Anti-Slavery Society. But it fell to the Royal Navy and to some men of high courage and faith, who were British Consuls in Zanzibar, to do the spade work and bear the brunt of the battle.

In the competition for space in East Africa, which developed between the European nations towards the close of the nineteenth century, Britain in the end won the largest slice, but we need feel no pricks of conscience on that account. If we had lost that race it would have been won by another European power, almost certainly Germany, whose rule might perhaps have been less enlightened and would certainly have been less liberal. During their short period of dominion on the east coast the Germans made themselves feared and hated by the Arab and the African alike. The rebellions they provoked, by harsh and overbearing conduct, they ruthlessly suppressed, using in the process many high-sounding words like 'Christianity', 'civilization' and 'humanity'. The British Government, on the other hand, won the biggest slice almost, it seemed, by accident, appearing to fall over itself in its efforts to show that it had no aggressive or expansionist intentions, frequently letting down its own side and confounding both those who served it faithfully and those who trusted it for support.

The slave trade was almost as old as the Continent itself. Slaves had been the merchandise which brought the earliest visitors to Africa from Asia. When the European nations began to visit Africa in the sixteenth century they also took part in the traffic in slaves, largely shipping them westward to the

Americas. The traffic was carried on under conditions of the utmost brutality until, towards the end of the eighteenth century, the nations of Europe began to realize the enormity of the crime that was being committed. In 1807 the buying and selling of slaves was forbidden in all British colonies and their carriage was forbidden in all British ships. However, it remained quite legal to own slaves, though not to buy, sell or transport them, in British dominions until the condition of slavery was entirely abolished throughout the British Empire in 1834. It was abolished in French dominions in 1848.

Outside the British dominions, however, slavery and the trade in slaves continued. The Arabs had carried on the traffic for centuries, making forays into the interior of Africa as far as the Great Lakes and bringing back caravans of slaves to the coast for export by dhow to Arabia, Persia and India. Zanzibar, an island twenty-five miles from the coast, was the natural centre for this trade and the average number of slaves imported into Zanzibar annually in the early years of the nine-teenth century was 15–20,000, of whom about 10,000 a year were re-exported. So great was the flow into the state of Oman itself that in 1835 one-third of its population consisted of negroes. No count was taken of the numbers of those who died in thou-sands on the terrible journey from their homes to the coast and the still more dreadful one by sea to Zanzibar. It was believed that the number of those who perished on the journey was twice as great as that of those who survived it.

When Seyyid Said established his capital at Zanzibar he realized the uniqueness of its position as a centre for the slave trade all along the coast and he encouraged his subjects, many of whom followed him from Oman, in their profitable raids into the interior of the mainland. As a result of the activities of the slave caravans Said became the nominal, if not the actual, master of a vast, undefined empire extending from the coast to the Great Lakes and embracing the territories now known as Kenya, Uganda and Tanganyika.

The caravans, penetrating ever farther and farther inland, consisted of scores or hundreds of white-clad Arabs, marching under the red flag of the Sultan of Zanzibar, each man armed with a long musket and sword. Fortified stockades guarded the lines of communciation. If the caravan passed through country inhabited by weak, unwarlike tribes, its work was easy. The Arabs would steal up to a village at dusk and surround it while the villagers were at their evening meal. Any who tried to resist or escape were shot. The rest began the long, terrible journey to the coast. But if the caravan passed through country inhabited by more warlike people, a different plan was adopted. The Arabs would settle in the district and encourage the tribes to make war on one another. They then bought from the victors, for a few beads or a few yards of cloth, the prisoners they took in battle.

The captured slaves were roped or chained together in single file, or secured one behind the other, each slave's neck in a forked stick about six feet long supported on the shoulders of the slave in front. Thus they were driven down to the coast, a distance possibly of five or six hundred miles, flogged along the forest paths with strips of raw hide. Usually they all, even women and children, carried on their heads loads of ivory which was the other merchandise for which the caravans made the journey inland. If the escorting Arabs were mounted on horseback the slaves had to trot the whole way. If any fell sick, or if the women or children stumbled, they were shot without mercy and left to die by the forest path. If a woman became too weak to carry both child and ivory, the child was speared or had its head dashed against a tree. A companion of Livingstone described how he saw 'bands of them—four or five hundred at a time—newly captured, as one could see by their necks all chafed and bleeding, their eyes streaming with tears, principally young men from ten to eighteen years of age, driven along in the most inhuman manner'.

The caravans made for the coastal towns of Lindi, Kilwa or Bagamoyo, the name of which means 'here we leave our souls'. These were the ports at which the slaves were embarked for the even more horrific journey by dhow to Zanzibar. Those who had survived the overland journey were placed in stockaded barracoons and given a meal while waiting for the dhows which were to take them across the strait, a voyage which normally took twenty-four hours. But frequently the dhows were becalmed and took days or even weeks to make the passage, the slaves packed literally like sardines below deck with neither food, nor water, nor air, nor sanitary arrangements of any kind. The human cargo was packed in tiers in the dhows, lying or squatting, adults with children packed in between them. Above each tier a bamboo platform was laid, an inch or two clear of their bodies, supporting another tier and so on up to the level of the gunwales. Those who lay could not move or change their positions, those who squatted could not lift their heads from between their knees because of the platform above them. Out of 200–400 stowed in this way it sometimes happened that, after ten days, scarcely a dozen were left alive when the covers were taken off in Zanzibar.

Those of the cargo who were in a fit state to walk up the beach were taken to the slave dealers' houses where they were kept for a time to put on flesh before being sold at auction in the slave market. Those who were not in a fit state to walk up the beach were left there to die, and Colonel Hamerton, British Consul at Zanzibar in the time of Seyyid Said, complained of the stench of the rotting corpses outside his consulate.

A healthy adult slave cost between £2 and £7 in 1859 and a boy or girl between £1 and £2 10s. A donkey, on the other hand, cost between £4 10s. and £12. In 1871, however, slaves seem to have become much cheaper for the British Consul reported that 'this year slaves have been sold in the interior for half a dollar a head, and five slaves given in exchange for a cow or a bullock'.

Business in the slave market began at four o'clock in the afternoon when the heat of the day was diminishing. Each dealer led his slaves through the market-place and the principal streets of the town. The youngest slaves walked in front of the crocodile and they increased in size and age towards the rear. The dealer walked at the head of the procession 'holding forth in a kind of sing-song the good qualities of his slaves and the high prices that had been offered for them'. On each side of the procession walked two or three of the dealer's domestic slaves armed with swords and spears. If a possible buyer in the crowd took a fancy to one of the slaves in the procession, the crocodile stopped while an inspection took place 'which, for minuteness, was unequalled in any cattle market in Europe'. The intending purchaser, having found out that there was no defect in the faculties and no disease present, and that the slave did not snore in his sleep, which was considered a very grave fault, then paid over the agreed price and marched his goods away.

Those slaves who were re-exported to Arabia, Persia or northern India had yet another hellish journey by dhow to undergo. But of those who found a buyer and a new home in Zanzibar it may be said, as a general rule, that their troubles were over. The Arab plantation owners, though they were hard task-masters, were not often cruel. The Arab was too easy-going by nature and, on the whole, treated his slaves pretty well. They were flogged if they did not work or tried to escape, but they were well fed and looked after as it is written in the Koran. A rough and not unkindly feudalism existed in Arab houses which the slaves understood.

The first shots in the battle against the East African slave trade were fired in the 'twenties of the nineteenth century, during the reign of Seyyid Said, by two distinguished British naval officers.

In 1822 Governor Farquhar of Mauritius sent Captain Fairfax Moresby to Muscat, which was then still Said's capital, to negotiate a treaty with the Sultan, if possible, prohibiting the sale of slaves to any Christian nation. He returned with Said's signature to this undertaking and to a further agreement that any Arab vessel which violated this decree could be seized by the Sultan's own ships or those of the Royal Navy if found south or east of a certain line. The line ran from Cape Delgado, on the mainland opposite the northern tip of Madagascar, to a point sixty miles east of Socotra and thence to Cape Diu, on the coast of India north of Bombay. This still allowed the shipment of slaves from Zanzibar and the east coast of Africa northwards to Oman within the territorial waters of the Sultan's dominions. It forbade it, so far as Christian nations were concerned, outside those limits.

Said, however, was an exceedingly wily ruler. He knew that such a decree as this would bring him the enmity of his Arab governors and slave-owning subjects. On the other hand he knew that the British, fired with this unaccountable zeal on behalf of black slaves, the lowest form of life, were the dominant sea power in the Indian Ocean. He foresaw that he would probably stand in need of their protection both against his own disaffected subjects and against other powers. He also knew that, magnificent as his act of self-abnegation appeared, it would have practically no effect since his dhows still had free passage up the coast from Zanzibar to southern Arabia. It was their custom to hug the coast in any case. In the vast Indian Ocean outside his territorial limits British warships were very few and it was most unlikely that any dhow would ever be challenged. On the other hand he had placed himself under the British umbrella at very little real expense to himself.

Said's policy paid dividends two years later when the next skirmish in the war against the slave trade took place. This was a private battle fought and lost by a Welshman, Captain Fitzwilliam Owen, an upright and God-fearing man and one of the most distinguished surveyors the navy ever produced. The charts which he made of the whole of the east coast of Africa remain almost unaltered as his memorial to this day. In 1824 he voyaged up the coast on his surveying mission and was disgusted with what he saw of the slave trade, especially the Portuguese trade on the Mozambique coast, which had by then degenerated into a string of miserable villages, all that remained of a once proud empire. No attempt whatever was being made to observe the Moresby treaty.

When he visited Mombasa Owen found the Mazrui tribe of Arabs, who ruled there, in open rebellion against Sultan Said. They offered their country, through Captain Owen, to the British Crown for protection. Owen went to Muscat and had an interview with Said, demanding the complete abolition of the slave trade, both Moslem and Christian, within three years. He told the Sultan that he was sailing for Mombasa and intended to take the rebels under the British flag for protection. The Sultan bowed, said he would be only too delighted if that were to happen, presented the captain with a gold-hilted sword and accepted several copies of the Bible. When Owen had gone the Sultan wrote a vigorous protest to the Governor of Bombay.

When Owen arrived at Mombasa again he accepted from the Mazrui Arabs the voluntary and unreserved gift of their country for His Majesty the King of England. He then sailed away, leaving what he considered to be an ample force in charge of his new protectorate, a lieutenant, aged twenty-one, a midshipman, a corporal of marines and three seamen. But when he arrived at Mauritius, after sailing up the coast threatening the Arabs with the dire consequences of carrying on the slave trade now that the British flag flew over Mombasa fort, he found to his dismay that his whole plan was in ruins. A letter from the Secretary of State had arrived. In view of previous engagements with the Imam, it stated, nothing further was to be done at Mombasa. Said had won.

He scored again in 1840 when the French, having annexed some of the Comoro Islands and Nossi Bé, off the coast of Madagascar, began making inquisitive movements up the East African coast as far as Barawa, 400 miles north of Mombasa. Lord Palmerston told them that Great Britain 'was concerned to maintain the integrity of the Sultan's dominions'. But his price was another concession with regard to the slave trade.

The price was extracted by Colonel Hamerton, the British Consul, from the reluctant Said after much argument and stormy interviews. It took the form of an agreement forbidding the export of slaves from Africa to Arabia altogether. The transport of slaves from one part of the Sultan's African dominions to another was still allowed, but His Majesty's ships and those of the East India Company were authorized to seize any of the Sultan's ships which could be proved to be violating this decree. Said, however, knew quite well that this could not be enforced for there were not sufficient British ships in those waters. The agreement did not forbid domestic slavery and how was a British naval officer, unable to speak Kiswahili or Arabic, and conducting his inquiries through corrupt and often hostile interpreters, to know who was who on a dhow at sea? Everyone on board could be said to be a domestic slave, the men working the ship, the women the owner's concubines. This bargain again, then, was not really a very difficult one for Said.

Seyyid Said died in 1856, having made Zanzibar the metropolis of the East African coast. The population rose during his reign from 5,000 to 60,000 and Indians, encouraged by the Sultan, flooded into the town to do business while the Arabs, too feckless and lazy for business, remained the owners of clove and coconut plantations, run by imported slaves. Europeans and Americans competed to make trade treaties with the Sultan.

OLD ARAB

YOUNG ARAB

STREET SCENE

Zanzibar was the capital of a vast empire where no writ ran. It was an empire of death. In 1843 the explorers, Krapf and Rebmann, reported that 'slavery was fast depopulating that side of the Continent, barbarizing the residents on the coast, carrying death and desolation far into the interior, and effectively neutralizing every attempt to introduce Christianity'. The forest paths where the caravans had passed were strewn with stinking corpses and over huge tracts of country, where a few years previously there had been a native village every two miles, there was now no human habitation for hundreds of miles. And, in order to make themselves un-attractive to the dreaded slave raiders, the women of that country took to distorting themselves and making themselves hideous. They wore rings in their lips and ears, and bone skewers through their noses. They tattooed their bodies with hideous designs and made scars upon their flesh. These grue-some decorations are still the vogue among many African tribes, though the necessity for them has long since passed, and may be seen in the streets of Zanzibar to this day.

Said died leaving 112 children by 70 wives. On his death the Asian and African portions of his empire fell apart and have remained separate ever since. A younger son, Majid, suc-ceeded in Zanzibar, while an elder son, Thuwaini, succeeded in Muscat. This arrangement, however, was unacceptable to Thuwaini who, backed up by another brother, Barghash, set sail for Zanzibar with a fleet intending to seize the throne by force while Barghash, aided by the French Consul, collected an enormous armed band of cut-throats in the town. They were to have gone into action when the fleet arrived. However, it never did arrive for Lord Canning, Governor-General of India, had it intercepted by the Royal Navy and Thuwaini was persuaded to turn back. Barghash then entrenched himself in a country house with some of his rabble and breathed defiance until forcibly removed by naval parties from H.M. ships. He was sent to Bombay where, with a house, a carriage and Rs. 1,000 a month, he spent fourteen years until he himself ascended the throne of Zanzibar in 1870.

The war against the slave trade had, on the whole, not made much headway during the reign of Seyyid Said. The British Consul, Colonel Hamerton, did not feel that he could battle

D

with his friend the Sultan over a system deeply entrenched in the way of life and religion of the people. After the death of Said, however, and the retirement of Hamerton, things became very different and war was declared in earnest not only upon the traffic in slaves but on the status of slavery itself.

Sultan Majid was a weak, rather timid young man who, in the early days of his reign, went in terror of armed insurrection among his subjects. Several attempts were made to assassinate him and he came to rely more and more upon the support of Colonel Rigby, the British Consul. Later in his reign he became increasingly dissolute.

Rigby was appointed Consul in Zanzibar in 1858. He was a fierce, fire-eating soldier and a man of very high principles. Before coming to Zanzibar he had served in Persia where he had contracted a loathing for slavery and everything which it entailed. One day, during his service in the Persian Gulf, a slave rushed into his tent and threw himself at Rigby's feet, clasping his knees and begging for protection. His arms were raw to the bone from the bonds from which he had escaped. A few days later the chief of the tribe, to whom the slave belonged, sent one of his officers to demand that the slave be given up. Whereupon Rigby, seizing a rhinoceros whip, gave the officer a thrashing and told him to tell his master he would get the same if he dared come near him. When he arrived in Zanzibar Rigby was even more appalled by what he saw. Outside his house slaves lay dead and dying on the beach. He saw long files of them, emaciated and with bulging eyes, in the last stages of disease and starvation, staggering ashore from the reeking dhows. Those who could not walk fell and lay where they fell or were clubbed by the dhow crews to get them out of the way. In the latter years of Said's reign the trade had enormously increased and no attention was paid to either of the treaties negotiated by Moresby or Hamerton.

Rigby wrote long reports to the Bombay Government and begged for an increase of naval power to suppress the trade. He never got it, and the number and types of ships used against the slave trade on the coast remained pitifully inadequate. The ships were hopelessly old and slow. The hunting for slavers was done mostly from open boats for which the warships acted as base ships. These open-boat parties were often away from their bases for months in pursuit of dhows, their unsuitable craft loaded to the gunwales with stores, arms and ammunition. Casualties among the crews from disease, malaria and dysentery were very heavy and many lie buried on Grave Island in Zanzibar harbour. Nevertheless, the toughness of the officers and men accomplished much and, in the last year of Rigby's consulate, two old ships, H.M.S. *Lyra* and H.M.S. *Gorgon*, captured between them sixty dhows. The *Lyra* became known to the Arabs as '*El Shitan*', the devil.

Meanwhile, in Zanzibar town itself, Rigby made a frontal attack single-handed against slavery in general. He began with the Indians who, having recently immigrated, were British subjects. He posted a notice at the Customs House and at his Consulate ordering all British subjects in Zanzibar owning or trafficking in slaves to bring them to the Consulate to be emancipated, and the penalty for failing to comply with this order was to be a fine of £100. This caused a great commotion and indignation in the town. No one had ever interfered with or questioned the condition of slavery before and the Indians rather naturally considered that they had as much right to their slaves as anyone else. They accordingly prepared to ignore the Consul's order. England was considered to be done for in those days, as so often since, and the Indians believed that the British had lost India as a result of the Indian mutiny, an idea sedulously cultivated by the French consul. Rigby, however, to show that there was life in the old dog yet, seized and imprisoned in the fort a particularly fat and wealthy Hindu, after fining him heavily for appearing in his office with his obese torso uncovered, an act, Rigby declared, of disrespect to Her Majesty the Queen. He marched his rich and influential prisoner through the town in irons and kept him in the fort until he had consented to give up his slaves. There was great astonishment at this, angry protests and threats against the consul's life. But the fierce soldier was undaunted. He used to make personal raids in the town quite regardless of the risk to his life, entering the houses of British Indians and dragging out slaves himself. He showed beyond all doubt that he meant business. By degrees the slaves began to be brought to him to be legally freed and, as the months went on, the owners brought them in increasing numbers, so that before he left

Zanzibar in 1861 he had personally set free 8,000 slaves. Many of them were given portions of their masters' land, others found work on clove or coconut plantations, some went to sea and years afterwards the Consul met them again in ports on the Indian coast, wearing the certificates of emancipation, which he had signed and sealed for them, in amulets around their necks like charms. Other slaves went to the Seychelles where their descendants still are.

The French constituted themselves a terrible thorn in Rigby's side. They were determined to have slave labour for their colonies in Madagascar and the island of Bourbon or Réunion. They pointed out indignantly that they had no reserve of Indian coolie labour to draw upon such as the planters had in Mauritius, where slavery had been improvidently abolished by the British. However, in order to placate public opinion in metropolitan France, and to reassure their own government, they instituted a fraudulent system whereby the slaves they bought from the Arab dhows were said to be *libres engagés*, freely engaged. Each slave was confronted on his transfer from the dhow by a menacing individual who rattled off a rigmarole in rapid French, a language the slaves did not understand anyway. This purported to be a questionnaire asking him if he agreed to be freely engaged to work on the plantations in a French colony. The slave was told to nod his head, which, not understanding a word, he miserably did and passed into a bondage far more oppressive and cruel than anything suffered at the hands of the Arab plantation owners in Zanzibar. The mortality was enormous on the Réunion plantations and the demand for *libres engagés* was insatiable. At one time the French became extremely menacing. One of their warships appeared in Zanzibar harbour and demanded the supply of slaves under threat, while a formidable array of scoundrels, who represented France as consuls, insulted Rigby and the Sultan, obstructed the work of the Royal Navy and gave every possible assistance to illegal slave trading. Rigby wrote thunderous denunciations to the Foreign Office, but it was not until 1871 that the French African slave trade was finally checked by an arrangement which allowed the recruitment of labourers in India for work on the plantations in French colonies.

Rigby left Zanzibar in 1861, taking two little slave boys

with him, one of whom became his devoted servant and retainer. He took leave thankfully of the shifty Sultan, Majid, who became more unreliable and dissolute as the years went on. Rigby wrote in his diary—'I hope never to set eyes on the false vile scoundrel again.'

Five years is a short time, and if Rigby had not succeeded in that time in getting rid of the condition of slavery, which he hated so much, he had at least left the Arabs and their Sultan in no doubt that the fight was on, and that it was the firm intention of the British Government to make an end of the business. It is, of course, easy to take up a self-righteous attitude towards the Arabs. But it must be remembered that slavery was centuries old in the east and part of the structure of the Mohammedan way of life. As for the Sultan, he found himself always caught between the upper millstone of the British conscience, backed by naval power, and the lower one of his subjects' deep-rooted religious and social customs.

Sultan Majid died in 1871 and was succeeded by his brother, Barghash, who had been living in Bombay since the rebellion at the beginning of Majid's reign. Barghash was a magnificent oriental potentate after his subjects' hearts, more sophisticated and more educated than any of his predecessors. Former Sultans knew very little about the world beyond Zanzibar, which they believed to be the greatest city on earth. It was reported that when Barghash went to live in Bombay he was amazed to find that there were other cities as large as Zanzibar which he had always thought of as the capital of the world. He introduced into his court a lavishness and splendour it had not known before. He built the House of Wonders and several other magnificent palaces which are now the haunts of bats and flying foxes. He built an aqueduct to bring water to Zanzibar and once a year placed a ship at the disposal of those of the Faithful who wished to make the pilgrimage. On the other hand, true to the oriental tradition, he was exceedingly autocratic and would, without hesitation, seize any of his subjects' property that took his fancy from a jewel in someone's dagger hilt to his clove plantation.

During Barghash's reign Dr. John Kirk became British Consul and it is perhaps to him more than to any other single individual that the eventual suppression of the Arab slave trade

is due. He came to the British Consulate as surgeon in 1866
and became Acting Consul soon afterwards when the Consul
himself was ill. In 1873 he was appointed Consul and, owing
to the deep respect and friendship which grew up between him
and Sultan Barghash, he ultimately became a sort of unofficial
Grand Vizier, deferred to and consulted upon almost everything.

In spite of Rigby's efforts during Majid's reign, and the exer-
tions of the naval patrol, the slave trade was more flourishing
than ever when Barghash came to the throne. Large numbers
of slaves were smuggled every year to Arabia and Persia, and
Zanzibar itself was constantly subjected to the attacks of slave-
raiding pirates who descended upon the town and carried off
children by night. Dr. Kirk made a somewhat unpromising
start against all this for he was instructed to approach the
Sultan with a view to negotiating a stricter version of the
Hamerton Treaty wrung from Said in 1845. The export of
slaves from the coast to any port except Zanzibar and Pemba
was to be forbidden and the slave market in the town was to be
closed. This met with a blunt refusal by the Sultan and, accordingly, in 1873 a mission headed by Sir Bartle Frere was sent out
from England to negotiate a new treaty. It was largely due to
the tact and influence of Sir John Kirk that Barghash was
eventually induced to sign a new and far more drastic decree.
The Sultan was in a difficult position for Sir Bartle Frere explained the indignation that the continuance of the trade was
causing at home and the fixed resolve of the British Government
to put a stop to it. On the other hand the Arab subjects of the
Sultan remained bitterly hostile to any infringement of their
rights and convinced that the abolition of the slave trade would
mean the ruin of the clove plantations. 'A spear is held at
each of my eyes,' the Sultan exclaimed. 'With which shall I
choose to be pierced?'

The Sultan hesitated for a long time and tried to play off
the British against the French. At last, in June 1873, he agreed
that there should be a total cessation of the export of slaves
from the coast, whether from one part of his dominions to
another or to foreign parts. All slave markets in his dominions
were to be immediately closed.

As a reward for swallowing this pill Barghash was invited to

Britain, stayed with Queen Victoria at Windsor, went to the races at Ascot and Doncaster and was given a firework display at the Crystal Palace. He was also taken proudly to see some of our larger manufacturing towns. Unfortunately the Sultan's comments on all this have not come down to us.

In 1876 there were two more proclamations, for it was found that slave smugglers were evading the provisions of the 1873 decree by marching slaves along the coast and selling them in the towns, so avoiding the British naval patrol. New proclamations, accordingly, forbade the conveyance of slaves by land under any conditions, and forbade the approach of slave caravans to the coast.

In order to enforce these anti-slavery decrees, and to stop smuggling, a young naval officer, Lieutenant Matthews of H.M.S. *London*, was given the task of training a preventive force of about 300 Africans. The *London* was an old wooden two-decker which was moored permanently in Zanzibar harbour to act as a base ship for open-boat parties which cruised up and down the coast enthusiastically harrying the smugglers by sea. Matthews' idea was to harry them equally enthusiastically by land. By 1880 he had 1,300 men under his command. A year later he retired from the navy and entered the service of the Sultan, who bestowed the rank of 'General' upon him. Ten years later he was appointed First Minister to Sultan Seyyid Ali, Barghash's successor, and became thus Grand Vizier in name as well as fact, whereas Sir John Kirk had been Grand Vizier to Barghash in fact but not in name. Matthews was in charge of the general administration of the country which had, in 1890, been declared a British Protectorate. Sir Lloyd Matthews, as he became, lived in Zanzibar for twenty years, a long time in those days of malaria, dysentery and various other diseases, which usually finished off Europeans in a year or two. He was one of the greatest men who ever served his country in Africa and, although not a particularly good or efficient administrator, he was immensely successful because he was loved and respected by the local people, Arab and Swahili alike, who referred to him always as the 'Bwana Mkubwa' and would journey overland for days to come to Zanzibar to lay before him their troubles and their disputes. He died in Zanzibar of fever in 1901 and was buried in the European cemetery outside the town.

The slave trade thus came to an end officially in the reign of Seyyid Barghash. The market, the scene of so much misery for many years, was closed and in due course the Anglican Cathedral arose upon its site. Yet the smuggling of slaves continued, often by means of dhows unofficially flying the French flag, and the legal status of slavery in the Sultan's dominions was not abolished. It was not forbidden to own slaves, but forbidden to import or export them.

Barghash died in 1888, having been ill for some years with consumption and elephantiasis. He died a disappointed and embittered man for during his reign he saw his empire torn asunder by Germany and Britain. The rapacity of the Germans in this was only equalled by the irresolution of the British Government, which managed to let down its friend the Sultan and its loyal servant Sir John Kirk in the best manner which, fifty years later, came to be known as 'appeasement'.

Barghash was succeeded by his brother, Khalifa, who, having been imprisoned in a dungeon under the palace for six years under suspicion of intrigue, was somewhat weak in the head. He only reigned for two years and was, in the words of the British Consul, 'abnormally ignorant of affairs of the world outside Zanzibar'. He was succeeded by another brother of Sultan Barghash, the youngest, named Ali, who was so delighted at suddenly becoming Sultan, for Khalifa had died unexpectedly, that he was easily prevailed upon to sign an anti-slavery decree more drastic than any which his predecessors had agreed to. All exchange, sale or purchase of slaves was forbidden. Houses of slave brokers were closed. Slaves of an owner who had no children were to become free on his death and every slave was entitled to buy his freedom for a reasonable price.

During the reign of Sultan Ali, in the year 1890, Zanzibar was declared a British Protectorate. In the same year, at an international conference held at Brussels, a General Act was signed 'putting an end to the crimes and devastations engendered by the traffic in African slaves . . . and ensuring for all that vast continent the benefits of peace and civilization'. The act provided for the suppression of the slave trade by sea and land, and for the restriction of the import of alcoholic liquor and of firearms, which the slavers had not hesitated to supply to the

Africans in exchange for slaves. Regulations were laid down for
the search of native vessels on the high seas, compelling them to
fly a national flag and to provide lists of crew and passengers.
In Zanzibar an international bureau was set up whose task was
to collect information about the slave trade.

Yet still the legal status of slavery was not abolished and
smuggling continued, especially into the island of Pemba where
innumerable creeks and large areas of mangrove swamp formed
an ideal hide-out for illicit goings-on of all sorts. Pemba, as a
matter of fact, had remained largely outside the anti-slavery
campaign, although all the decrees applied to it equally with
Zanzibar, largely because of its remoteness and because there
were no resident Europeans there and no police to enforce
the Sultan's word.

After Zanzibar came under British protection, and the
Brussels agreement had been signed, the Anti-Slavery Society
in Great Britain turned the blast of its propaganda upon Zanzibar, organizing meetings up and down the country to protest
against the continuance of slavery in these islands now under
the British flag. But the men on the spot, the British Consul,
Sir Arthur Hardinge, and the First Minister to the Sultan, Sir
Lloyd Matthews, who knew and understood the Arabs, were
against any sudden and drastic abolition. They knew how
deeply interwoven into the Arab pattern of life the system was.
All the wealthier Arabs, for instance, kept concubines, chosen
from among the family slaves, in addition to their wives. It was
a practice recognized and regularized by the '*sharia*', the religious and secular laws of Islam. When a concubine bore her
master a child she ranked almost equally with the wives and
there was no distinction between her children and those of the
wives. Sultans Barghash, Khalifa and Ali had all been themselves sons by concubines. Yet the abolitionists clamoured for
the immediate end of this system and the abrupt emancipation
of all concubines, a proceeding which Hardinge knew would
turn them all at once into prostitutes, overturn the entire social
system in a Moslem city and cause intense resentment among
the Arabs. He believed also that abrupt abolition would bring
about an outbreak of lawlessness and vagabondage because all
the most useless slaves would demand their freedom first and
make no effort to find work. He foresaw widespread destitution

among the freed slaves and the ruin of the clove industry, the mainstay of the islands' economy.

Nevertheless the abolitionists thumped and roared for total and complete abolition. The Liberal *Daily News* called for 'an end, once and for all, to the scandal of slavery under the protection of the British flag'.

In 1896 an event occurred which gave the abolitionists the chance to demand that the Sultanate should be brought to an end altogether and the Protectorate made a Crown Colony. This was Zanzibar's Great Rebellion and the bombardment of the Sultan's palace by the British Navy.

Sultan Ali had been the last of the great Said's sons and the last of Barghash's brothers. When he died, after a reign of only three years, the British Consul decided that the most suitable claimant to the throne was one Hamed, son of that Sultan Thuwaini who, on the death of Seyyid Said, had taken over the Sultanate of Muscat. Hamed was rich and influential and more likely, it was thought, to make a satisfactory and amenable ruler than his eighteen-year-old rival, Khaled, son of Barghash, an obstinate, sullen and proud young man, a hater of Europeans and their works. When Ali died, Khaled made an unsuccessful attempt to seize the palace and install himself on the throne, but was dissuaded by a posse of British marines. He retired to brood over his defeat, but he had not long to wait for Hamed, like Ali, only reigned for three years and died in August 1896. The British Consul, Sir Arthur Hardinge, then recommended the Foreign Office to recognize Seyyid Hamoud, a grandson of the great Said and a cousin of Khaled, as Sultan. He was the oldest male member of the royal house and more likely to fall in with the wishes of the protecting power than Khaled. This time, however, Khaled made a bolder attempt. He had about 2,000 armed men at his command, including the Sultan's bodyguard, who had become disaffected. He forced his way into the palace with about sixty men by climbing in through a window, announced that he was the Sultan and raised the Sultan's red flag on the flagstaff. Unfortunately for him, but fortunately for everyone else, there were three naval ships in the harbour at the time and they were reinforced by the timely arrival of two others. It was decided to eject Khaled and his supporters, all of whom were before long encamped in the palace square. Armed parties from the ships were posted around the town and, on 27 August, an ultimatum was sent to Khaled telling him that unless he hauled down his flag and gave himself up before nine o'clock the following morning, the British ships would open fire. But Khaled and his Arabs laughed, for had not the witch doctors prophesied that the ships' guns would only spout water? Even water, they might have reflected, could have done some harm since the ships were anchored only 150 yards from the palace. At nine o'clock, accordingly, they opened fire at this range on the palace and in forty minutes had reduced a large part of it to ruins, killing about 500 of Khaled's supporters. There was only one British casualty. Khaled, aghast at the ruin and destruction, fled to the German Consulate. The Germans, at that time on unfriendly terms with the British in East Africa, escorted him to a waiting gunboat. The story goes that the German Consular staff formed themselves into a ring with Khaled in the centre and marched thus through the town, protecting him with their diplomatic immunity, past the squads of British marines and seamen, back to their Consulate. The gunboat came alongside a jetty at the bottom of the Consulate garden and so took Khaled away without his setting foot outside German property. He lived at Dar-es-Salaam until the defeat of the Germans in East Africa during the First World War. Then he was sent to St. Helena and to Seychelles, those havens for political exiles, until, in 1925, on his promising to be good, he was allowed to return to Mombasa where he remained until he died in 1927.

This was not, perhaps, the most glorious victory ever won by the British Navy, but the abolitionists were delighted. They gloated in a way that sounds very strange to-day. Now was the time, they declared, to force upon the Arabs total and immediate abolition, 'while the memory of the blazing palace is still fresh in their minds'.

Sultan Hamoud signed a decree, on 5 April 1897, declaring that 'his courts would decline to enforce any alleged rights over the body, service or property of any person on the ground that such a person was a slave'. The decree thus abolished the legal status of slavery but, in response to the earnest plea of Sir Arthur Hardinge, who went to the Foreign Office in person to put his point of view, it was agreed to pay compensation to Arab slave owners for any slaves lost to them and concubines were to be regarded as inmates of the harem in the same sense as wives. This decree, which to the Arabs must have seemed rather like the bomb on the House of Commons during the Second World War, was announced by the Sultan at a Baraza or Council in the palace. The Sultan's private secretary was so overcome that he expressed doubts whether his religious scruples would permit him to read such a document in public. Accordingly the Sultan retorted that unless a curb could be speedily placed on such scruples the possessor thereof would receive sixty lashes, and the decree was duly announced and became law.

As is often the case in reforming movements the objects of the reform, the supposed beneficiaries, were not consulted. If they had been, and if they had formed any opinions on the subject, it might have been discovered that most of the slaves regarded freedom merely as freedom to starve. It meant for them the exchange of a possibly, though not by any means always, harsh yet secure existence for a precarious and insecure one. It meant leaving the warmth and intimacy of a feudal relationship for the cold and impersonal one of employee and employer of native labour. In an Arab household the slaves were part of the establishment in the same way as the dog in his kennel, the chickens that scratched in the yard, the donkey and the oxen that took the cloves to market. They were conscious of no disgrace or humiliation whatsoever in this position and status. They were blissfully unaware of the dignity of man or of the sanctity of the human spirit. They did not bother with metaphysics and only knew that as paid labourers they were treated with inhuman coldness. No one was responsible for them or cared whether they lived or died. They were adrift and became wage slaves instead of real slaves, but chattels none the less. The slave market was the site of a cathedral but the labour market, much more inhuman, existed in its place.

To anyone who understood all this and knew the Arab and the African, to Sir Arthur Hardinge for instance, it was not in the least surprising that after the abolition decree there was no rush at all on the part of the slaves to gain their freedom. At the end of the first year only about 2,000 had claimed emancipation, out of perhaps 50,000 or 60,000. Somewhat over 2,000 more made private arrangements with their Arab masters to work as free labourers without claiming emancipation papers. Those who claimed their freedom first were, as Hardinge had foretold, the malcontents and ne'er-do-wells, so that there was, again as Hardinge had prophesied, an outbreak of lawlessness, and bands of unemployed hooligans roamed the countryside committing murders and robberies.

But to the reformers at home this was all most mystifying. Accordingly they vented their astonishment and anger upon the district courts which were responsible for the machinery of emancipation. They accused the Arabs in charge of the courts of obstructing the working of the decree and of corruption, and the British officials of connivance. The Quakers, who were especially active, sent to Pemba an industrial mission whose head, arriving with the faith that moves mountains but finding no mountains to move, raised such a hornets' nest that Sir Arthur Hardinge had to go to Pemba to investigate the charges which were being made and refute them. The refutation was made publicly in the House of Commons in the debate on the Queen's speech, on 10 February 1898, by the Foreign Secretary, Mr. Nathaniel Curzon.

Sultan Hamoud died in 1902 and was succeeded by his son, Ali, who was a schoolboy at Harrow, where he was affectionately known as 'Snowball'. He was very Anglicized and could not speak Kiswahili so that when he came back to Zanzibar from England, it is said, he had to speak to his own mother through an interpreter. During his reign it was decided that after 31 December 1911 no further compensation would be paid to owners on the emancipation of their slaves. After that date, too, every concubine was to be free whether she stayed with her master or left him. If she stayed with him, or left with his consent, she was entitled to the custody of her children by him, and to inherit the property of her sons if they predeceased her.

The legal status of slavery came to an end on the British mainland sector in 1907 and, as in Zanzibar, 31 December 1911 was fixed as the last date upon which claims for compensation would be paid. In the German sector, now known as Tanganyika, the legal status of slavery was not abolished until

1922. Yet it is very doubtful if slavery has completely ceased to exist among the peoples of this part of the world even now. In the Red Sea and the Persian Gulf slave running was still going on in 1927. Even to-day children still sometimes mysteriously disappear from Zanzibar and it would still be very difficult to tell exactly who is who on board an Arab dhow.

In the same year, 1911, when the last vestiges of slavery were removed from Zanzibar, King George V of England was crowned and Sultan Ali, who was in poor health and spent most of his time in Europe, went to England for the Coronation and never returned. He abdicated on 9 December and died in Paris seven years later. He was succeeded by the present Sultan, Khalifa bin Harub, whom Allah preserve, a constitutional monarch beloved of his people.

5

The scramble for East Africa at the end of the nineteenth century was an affair between Britain and Germany. France had agreed in 1862 to scramble in the opposite direction for she was at that time chiefly interested in Madagascar and the Comoro Islands. In a treaty between them Britain and France agreed to respect the independence of the Sultan of Zanzibar. Germany was then, in the eyes of the world at any rate, a land of amiable professors of music and philosophy, who wrote music that no one could play and philosophy that no one could understand. It was not until after the war of 1870 that Germany suddenly appeared in a different guise, trumpeting for a place in the sun and proclaiming that her new-found nationhood demanded colonies in Africa, for raw materials and commerce, but most of all for prestige.

The most likely part of the globe for Bismarck's Germany to look for territory was the vast, undefined, unregulated and unsanctified empire, without law or order or system of government, which the Arab slave raiders had built up for the Sultan of Zanzibar. It was an untamed wilderness with Arab sheiks, ruling in strongholds, scattered among the native tribes, owing only formal allegiance to the Sultan.

In the middle of the nineteenth century missionary explorers, many of whom were Germans, had traversed the interior and penetrated as far as the Great Lakes. David Livingstone was the most famous of these. Others were the Germans, Krapf and Rebmann, who saw Mount Kilimanjaro and Mount Kenya, and Burton and Speke, who discovered the Great Lakes. These travellers and their contemporaries were interested in pure discovery, but their discoveries drew attention to the commercial possibilities of this virgin country.

During the reign of Sultan Barghash the British Consul, Sir John Kirk, foresaw that this vast stretch of territory would not be allowed to stay very long in its unregulated condition but would sooner or later have to be taken in charge by some power more responsible than the Arabs. Accordingly in 1880 he sent Sir Lloyd Matthews to the mainland to set up a fortified post about 120 miles inland from the port of Bagamoyo opposite Zanzibar. His idea was to build a chain of such blockhouses inland along the caravan route to Tabora in order to establish the Sultan's authority. However, the Foreign Office refused its support to the scheme and it came to nothing.

Germany made the first move in 1884 when a Dr. Karl Peters formed an organization known as the *Gesellschaft für Deutsche Kolonisation* and landed at Bagamoyo with the object of furthering his country's colonial ambitions. He persuaded a number of native chiefs to sign treaties surrendering large tracts of mainland territory to his society. In each was a clause stating that the signatory chief was in no way dependent upon the Sultan of Zanzibar and had never even heard of him. In the same year Kaiser Wilhelm I convened an international conference in Berlin in order to draw up rules for what he saw as the coming scramble for other people's territory. It was agreed that no nation would annex any part of Africa without giving due notice to other would-be annexers, and that territory so annexed would be effectively occupied. The day after the delegates dispersed from this agreeable session the Kaiser announced that Germany had taken under her imperial protection all the territories, about 60,000 square miles, newly acquired by Dr. Peters. This territory included and engulfed the military post set up four years earlier by Sir Lloyd Matthews, the one part of the mainland where, if anywhere, it could be said with truth that the rule of the Sultan of Zanzibar was up-held. Barghash protested furiously to the Kaiser and Kirk to the Foreign Office, but neither protest had the least effect. Mr. Gladstone was in power and appeasement was in the air.

In the following year the Germans announced that they had established a protectorate over the Sultanate of Witu, on the coast north of Mombasa at the mouth of the Tana River. They demanded Barghash's recognition of this as well as of Dr. Peters' bag of the year before. When the Sultan demurred they backed up their demand with a squadron of five German war-ships. Barghash, deserted by the British, agreed to the dismem-berment of his empire literally at the pistol point.

At this stage the three scramblers, Britain, France and Ger-many, agreed to appoint a commission to decide what were to be considered the exact limits of the Sultan's territory. As was fashionable in those days the Sultan was not consulted or even invited to attend the deliberations, which took place in Zanzi-bar in December 1885. The British representative was Colonel H. H. Kitchener. Finally Britain and Germany signed a treaty recognizing the Sultan's authority over the islands of Zanzibar and Pemba, and of Mafia in the south and Lamu in the north, and over a coastal strip about 700 miles long and 10 miles wide stretching from the River Ruvuma in the south to the Tana in the north. North of the Tana the Sultan was still to hold the towns of Barawa, Merka, Mogadishu and Warsheik. The vast hinterland behind this strip was to be divided into two spheres of influence. The northern part from the River Umba to the Tana was allotted to the British. The southern part from the Umba to the Rovuma went to Germany.

Thus, by a stroke of the pen, the empire of the Sultan of Zanzibar was disposed of. The Imperial British East Africa Company was formed to develop the British sphere with a con-cession to administer the Sultan's coastal strip adjacent to it, and the German East Africa Company, similarly formed to develop the German sphere, had a similar concession to deve-lop the strip of coast adjacent to it. To-day all that remains of the Sultan's empire are the islands of Zanzibar and Pemba and the coastal strip adjacent to the British sphere, now the coast of Kenya, which is still administered on lease by the Government of Kenya. The island of Mafia has become part of Tanganyika and Lamu part of Kenya. Italy, in 1893, bought the towns of Barawa, Merka, Mogadishu and Warsheik and the adjacent Benadir coast for a cash payment.

The Arabs and natives in these sectors were, of course, not consulted about their future any more than was the Sultan. In the German sector they soon rose in revolt against their new masters and murdered a number of German missionaries and officials. The rebellion, largely brought about by the over-bearing conduct of the Germans, was put down with the utmost ruthlessness with the use of German marines and Sudanese troops, and the leaders of the rebellion were hanged.

Intense rivalry and ill-feeling developed between the British and German companies and when Dr. Karl Peters again became active, this time in Uganda, it appeared to the chief conspirators that the time had arrived for a settlement of their rival claims to other people's territory. Accordingly in 1890 Britain and Germany came to an agreement. Germany agreed to give up her protectorate at Witu, on the north of the British sphere, and all claims to territory in Uganda, and to recognize a British protectorate over Zanzibar and Pemba. In return Britain ceded Heligoland, in the North Sea, to Germany and 'prevailed upon' the Sultan of Zanzibar to cede abso-lutely to Germany the coastal strip of territory which he leased to the German East Africa Company, in return for the sum of £200,000. The Sultan considered this to be a paltry sum but added that he was in the hands of God.

Although the Germans were pleased to get Heligoland, which was of importance to them in view of the fine new canal they were building at Kiel, the agreement was not popular in Ger-many, and certainly not with Dr. Karl Peters, who arrived at Bagamoyo in time to hear the news with his pockets bulging with a new treaty with the King of Uganda. He was so shocked that he had to shut himself up in a room for several hours in order to recover. In England most people were pleased, although there were some notable exceptions. One was Mr. Labouchère, who protested vigorously in the House and propounded the novel idea that Africa belonged to Africans. Another was the great Queen herself, who, in initialling the document, let fall one of those *multum in parvo* remarks that royalty sometimes bring forth. 'Giving up what one has,' she said, 'is always a Bad Thing.'

This story of land grabbing and scrambling for other peoples' territory reads strangely to-day when ideas, in Britain at any rate, seem to have changed so much. But people thought differently in those days and only a few voices were raised on behalf of the natives of the lands in question. Nowadays, sixty years later, no one can have any doubt that what happened was best for the general happiness and welfare of the people.

The Protectorate remained under Foreign Office control until 1913 when it was transferred to the Colonial Office under a British Resident. In general, since the date of the formation of the Protectorate, satisfactory progress can be reported towards the desired goal of ordered respectability and social advancement. Yet such is the perversity of human nature, and Arab human nature at that, that in spite of the advance of the Welfare State, of elected provincial councils, of modern maternity hospitals, of new schools and social centres and welfare clinics, in spite of the fine new harbour and the wide esplanade, the busy coming and going and rattle of typewriters in the House of Wonders, the agricultural stations and the clove research, the Arabs of Zanzibar look back nostalgically to the days of Seyyid Barghash as to a Golden Age. In those good days all the customs revenue and all the export duty on cloves went straight into the Sultan's pocket. No tedious accounts were kept and a host of favourites, dependants, hangers-on and scroungers hung perpetually around the palace and did very well out of it. The only public charity was that which the Sultan dispensed in accordance with the laws of Islam and hundreds daily received their portion of rice and mealies. All justice was in the Sultan's hands and his word was law. He had the power of life and death over his subjects. The town stank and the corpses of slaves, donkeys and dogs rotted together in the creek. The fashionable complaints were malaria, cholera, blackwater fever, yellow fever and plague. Zanzibar was one of the most unhealthy places in the world and Europeans were lucky if they survived five years there. But the magnificent bat-haunted ruins of palaces, crumbling under the mango trees and the frangipanis, testify to a glory that is past and old Arabs sigh and shake their heads when they pass by them.

The First World War only slightly disturbed the sweltering calm which British rule had brought to the little town. That was when the Germans sank the ancient cruiser *Pegasus* in the harbour. The Second World War hardly touched it, except that most British officials found themselves stranded in Zanzibar for the duration. It is now rapidly becoming very much like any other town on the face of this standardized globe, with its cinemas, its radios, its golf course, its Saturday football matches and its shiny motor-cars. I am glad to have seen it before it loses its identity altogether.

Chapter Four

A HOUSE AT MAZZIZINI

I

WHEN I first visited Zanzibar in 1949 the site of my house was a large virgin coconut plantation. The locality was known as Mazzizini, literally 'at the stables', supposedly because one of the Sultans, possibly Barghash, had some stables there, though no sign of them was visible in 1949. Soft turf swept up to a low cliff, covered with scrub, which overlooked a bay, an expanse of mud at low tide. Coconut palms inclined languidly in all directions in disorderly rows. Their fronds rattled overhead and turtle doves called softly in the green heat. Mazzizini was about three and a half miles out of town on the road to the aerodrome. You drove out through a splendid avenue of casuarinas, past the British sports club where white figures were leaping on the tennis courts, and past a rather attractive gaol, where other white figures with broad arrows on them were cutting grass with easy swinging movements of their arms. The tennis players and the grass cutters alike seemed perfectly happy and the laughter from the sports club was scarcely distinguishable from that from the prison. You drove on past native huts and through a herd of cattle sauntering unconcernedly along in charge of a black boy with a stick. Their hooves made a noise like rain on the road and their faces wore expressions of patient, unquestioning surprise. Then the mango trees, the casuarinas, the sweet almonds and the cassias, which covered the road with a gold carpet several times a year, gave way to the wide up-sweeping stretch of turf and the aisles of criss-crossed, leaning grey stems.

'All this,' said our guide, who was a government official, with a wave of his stick, 'will become a new housing estate. We plan to build about twenty-five houses for Europeans here.

Yours will be the first houses to go up.' He was speaking of the houses which the government were to build for the staff of our research unit. 'Of course we will have to clear a good deal of the bush and spray the place thoroughly. I believe the mosquitoes are pretty bad here. We'll make the road up and bring the water out. Doubtful if the supply will be very good. No head, you know. . . . No electric light yet, though you'll get it in time, I expect. No main drainage, of course. We'll build you a soak-pit, small one, you know. But you'll have to go easy on that sort of thing. Not too many baths, what!'

He laughed and waved his stick. My heart sank a little.

It is extraordinary how all over Africa suburbia keeps breaking in. Wherever Europeans live you find compact, tight little rows of houses standing shoulder to shoulder, almost touching, huddled together like frightened animals, as though afraid of the great inscrutable spaces all round them. They are like the brave advance guard of an army, carefully trained at home and now for the first time on reconnaissance against an invisible and unknown foe, whose weapons are the insect, time, decay and silence. Especially silence! Never yield to that terrible insidious silence that comes flooding in the instant you turn off the radio!

And so suburbia broke into our coconut grove where the turtle dove called by day and the cricket shrilled at night. In the course of months, for labour is a leisurely affair in Africa, a miniature Kingston By-pass village arose among the palm stems. Like its prototype at home it did not seem to have any particular plan or arrangement. The houses just occurred. They were not built in rows but staggered in an odd and, I am sure, subtle way. I gather that the idea was to give every one a view of the wide bay which lapped the base of the scrub-covered cliff, but the effect was that everyone's upper windows looked into the lavatory of the house next door and the suburban illusion was complete.

It was, however, a by-pass with a difference. It seemed, on a closer look at the houses, that it was an oriental by-pass, making a detour round Baghdad or Damascus, perhaps, but hardly round Kingston-on-Thames. This was because all modern buildings in Zanzibar had to pass certain rigorous tests, not, as you might suppose, concerned with frontages or cubic capacities or drains or damp-courses, but concerned with external appearance. This was not in itself a bad thing, but was a most unusual state of affairs, for as a rule it is the other way round and the appearance of the building is the least important consideration. It seems hard to strike a happy medium. In Zanzibar all plans for new buildings had to be vetted by the Chief Secretary, whose hobby was architecture. It was his no doubt excellent conception that all modern buildings in Zanzibar must conform to a style of architecture which he caused to be known as 'Neo-saracenic'. This was considered to be the appropriate manner for an Arab city. It involved the construction of maddeningly Moorish arches, of lattice-work balustrades and pointed architraves, of turrets, domes and cupolas reminiscent of old Baghdad. For these the Chief Secretary had an eye like a hawk and no plans were allowed to pass without them. Drastic internal deformities were often inflicted upon buildings in order to achieve more and larger and wider Moorish arches, more elaborate lattice-works, more fluted columns, domes and minarets. Thus the new Maternity Hospital, under the watchful eye of the Public Works Department, assumed the aspect of a Caliph's palace. A cinema near the docks seemed to have affinities with the Alhambra, while the new airport building seemed to have exchanged nods with the Great Mosque at Cairo. It was slightly spoiled, as a matter of fact, by a rectangular control tower which the young Air Control Officer tiresomely insisted it must have on top of it.

The first houses to be built in our coconut grove faced the sea on top of a considerable sandy rise. Their backs were turned upon the high road from which one approached them. From this aspect, except that they were white and had outside shutters, they might have been seen by the hundred in rows outside any town in England. They looked even more familiar and homely later on when washing was flapping on lines behind each one. But in front, what a surprise! For each had three low Moorish arches on the ground floor, leading on to a sort of verandah which could not be used for any special purpose because the Moorish arches, which gave access to it, were too low and the dividing pillars between them too thick. On the Moorish top of the arch you bumped your head if you were not careful and I myself could just walk upright through the dead-centre. On to this odd sort of loggia opened all the doors of the ground-floor rooms, a dining-room and another of unidentified function that led off it, a kitchen and a lavatory. At one end of this verandah stone stairs, unprotected by a door, led up to the floor above where there was a balcony, too narrow to be used conveniently for sitting, except in a row facing outwards, but provided with the requisite latticework balustrade. The balcony was over the ground-floor verandah and the doors of the three main rooms of the house, a sitting-room and two bedrooms, opened on to it, as did that of a bathroom. If you went out and left your house unoccupied there were thus eight doors to be safely locked with enormous brass keys attached to a piece of string. There was also a ninth, the back door to the kitchen, with another large and heavy key.

The rooms were quite square, with dead-white walls and cement floors, like little cells. Windows were rectangular gaps in the walls with no glass but with outside wooden shutters. Those on the ground floor were defended by grills of 'expanded metal' so that you looked out of them as through the bars of a cage. These guards had been put on as an afterthought and it was, as a result, impossible to close the shutters on the ground floor from the inside. There was no cupboard or storage space of any sort, but under the stairs there was an L-shaped space completely wasted, signifying nothing. The stairs themselves were too narrow for any but the smallest pieces of furniture to be taken up without knocking pieces out of the plaster walls. I thought it a horrible design for a house and said so loudly. Yet it had the Moorish arches in front and the latticework balustrades that made it, in the eyes of authority, all that could be desired.

The workmanship was as bad as the design. During the long rains the water came pouring through the sitting-room ceiling so that buckets and basins had to be, always ineffectually, disposed about the floor. During the year I lived in the house the kitchen ceiling fell down in showers of plaster three times. The garage, which was a sort of annexe stuck on to one end, kept threatening to become detached and to slide down the hill on its own. Great cracks kept appearing where it joined the house and reappeared whenever they were covered up. Many of the doors and window frames were second-hand, taken presumably from a demolished building. They were rough and ill-fitting and full of shot holes made by beetles. My bedroom doors had glass panels crudely daubed with white paint on which someone had scratched a rude picture. It was only by making a great fuss that I was able to have the paint and the picture removed. In smaller details the workmanship was equally bad. Door knobs and hinge plates, which ought to have been secured by, say, five screws, were clinging on for dear life by means of only three. Screws were driven home crooked with head protruding at an angle. Nails had been knocked in sideways or with their points showing through on the other side. Wood with knots and splits was to be seen everywhere. As is very often the case in Africa there were all the signs of slipshod work improperly supervised.

It was a rotten house, ugly, badly sited, badly designed and badly built. But it was mine and I loved it. I lived in it for a very happy year and when I left it, empty and forlorn, with the government furniture stacked up on end and all my possessions packed in crates, I wept.

I used to drive out to Mazzizini about once a week to watch the slow and painful growth of my house. It crept slowly from the scaffolding stage to the roof stage, to the fitting of doors and windows. The crowd of lazy ragamuffins, who were supposedly working on it, uncoiled at my approach from attitudes of ease and relaxation. For the duration of my unwelcome visit they reluctantly went through the motions of driving in screws, hammering nails, sawing wood and daubing plaster. I knew they would cease this activity immediately I was out of sight, like the living toys in the fairy tale which became immobilized at cock-crow. They were in the charge of a dear old gentleman in a large and dirty white solar topee, much too big for him. He was usually around somewhere when for some reason or other he was not attending hospital. The ragamuffins paid very little heed to him and he paid absolutely none to me. Sometimes I would point out something, or express a wish, as, for instance, a wish to have the rude scribbles removed from my bedroom door, a wish to have the waste space under the stairs partitioned off so as to make a store room, a wish to have a door knob fixed by all five screws instead of only three. But he only shook his head.

'You must see the Bwana Mkubwa,' he would say. 'He said it was to be like that.'

But the Bwana Mkubwa, the Great Lord, the government official who had waved his stick a long while ago in 1949 and had thus caused all this to happen, was an elusive figure, like all such bwanas, and difficult to get hold of. One gets the impression that there are a great many bwanas in East Africa whose function it is to drive from place to place, wave a stick and say—'Here, I think. Or would you prefer it there?' Occasionally, however, his visits to Mazzizini coincided with mine, and we would go at it with raised voices and angry gestures among the builders' rubble that looked as though it would never be cleared away, and the ragamuffins watched out of the corners of their eyes.

'I don't know what some of you young fellers want.' (I was younger of the two by a year.) 'D'you think we're going to build you Buckingham Palace? You don't know when you're lucky! Damned fine house that'll be when it's finished.'

The ragamuffins, galvanized into feverish activity by our arrival, grinned. Two Europeans having a heated argument is always fun, even if the subject and result of it are obscure. And when at last we drove away, I hot and exhausted but possibly having gained an inch or two, and the Bwana Mkubwa, ruffled but mainly victorious, to wave his stick over pastures new, the ragamuffins folded themselves up again on their shelves and in their niches and, with relief, composed themselves for slumber after so long a disturbance.

One of the eccentricities of the design and layout of this little suburbia in Africa was the fact that none of the houses was provided with servants' quarters. This was an unprecedented state of affairs, for all European houses in Kenya or Tanganyika are, as a matter of course, provided with a small annexe where the servants live. Each boy has at least one room with a kitchen, a tap and a lavatory. In somewhat inferior establishments kitchen, tap or lavatory or all three may be shared by two boys or more, and the result is constant bickering as to who has the right to use what and when, and who shall keep it clean, and who made the mess and why should I clear it up? In their quarters the boys have their plump, soft-eyed women-folk, sitting about in their bright kangas, and their babies toddling about all day in the dust. The master or mistress of the house seldom goes into the boys' quarters except to see that they are kept clean.

It never became at all clear why our houses at Mazzizini, nearly four miles from town, should, alone among European dwellings in almost the whole of Africa, be without these primary necessities. It was the shortage of building materials. It was the shortage of labour. It was the lack of water. It was the lack of money. The servants would not live in them if they had them, but would much prefer to live in town and walk or bicycle to and fro daily. Especially, I pointed out, in the pouring rain of the 'Masika', when, of course, they would simply never turn up. It was never the same reason twice running and one was merely left to conclude that there was, in fact, no reason that could be stated. All sorts of not very savoury reasons were, of course, adduced by Europeans and conveyed by means of dark hints.

I, however, was lucky, for immediately behind my house was a broken-down, square shed built of breeze slabs and roofed with dilapidated corrugated-iron sheets. It had been built as an ammunition store in the First World War and had been gently rotting there ever since. Now it was intended to knock it down since it was very unsightly and was generally considered to be of no further use. At the moment it contained bags of cement. It was divided into two small compartments, each of which had a rough cement floor, a barred unglazed window with broken shutters and a door. There was neither water tap nor sanitary arrangements. The roof leaked badly. Enormous spiders lived in it and there were rat runs round the outside. After a long and acrimonious argument it was conceded that one of the apartments in this desirable residence would do for my servant and the other for the servant of the house next door. A coat of lime inside and some tar on the roof were all that would be needed to make it a home from home.

'After all,' said the Bwana Mkubwa, 'we've got enough to do providing houses for Europeans. We don't reckon to have to provide houses for Africans as well!'

As my house drew near completion I began, with shame and anger and humiliation, to look for a tenant for this abode.

The thing to do, when looking for a servant, was to mention

the fact to Omar, the head boy at the club. He was an ex-soldier of the King's African Rifles and had seen service in the Western Desert during the war. Whenever I saw these fine upstanding Africans, with their broad shoulders and flashing smiles, serving as houseboys, waiters and pantry boys, I used to meditate on the degradation of the African race and think how much better off their ancestors were, naked on a wide plain with their bloodstained spears. Probably I was wrong. It is easy to sentimentalize and to dismiss the benefits that have come to them with their present way of life. Perhaps Omar and Shabani and the other disinherited warriors, padding about in the English Club with bare feet and white kanzu and round embroidered cap, serving whiskies to bwanas, felt no fury at all racing in their blood and no sickness for sky and space. Yet it is a fact that almost everywhere in Africa, in the Union, in Kenya, in Tanganyika, your houseboy is liable to be suddenly overwhelmed by an irresistible homesickness, a longing for his village and people which cannot be denied. He will say one day, 'Bwana, I go to-morrow to my people. I shall be away so many months. My friend will work for you.' And go he must.

He will return, but the odd thing is that he will often in his absence have forgotten all that he ever learnt of western ways and habits. I knew a European family who had a very skilled cook, carefully trained for years by the memsaab herself. He went home to his village for six months, and when he returned he could not cook at all and had to be taught all over again from the beginning. A friend of mine knew an African typist who worked in an office and could type accurately at a speed of 120 words a minute. He too went home and when he returned was observed typing slowly and painfully with one finger, in tears because he could not remember. Africa remains very near the surface and I saw illustrations of that strange and baffling fact not once but many times during my short stay in Zanzibar.

Until my house was built I had a bedroom in the house of some friends and ate at the club. When I told Omar over the bar that I wanted a houseboy he nodded and looked sagacious. In a few days' time a little man appeared in the usual long white smock-like kanzu and round embroidered cap. He agreed to work for me for a reduced wage until my house was ready. At

least that was what I understood, for he spoke no English and
my Swahili was rudimentary. His duties until then would be
to clean my room and do my laundry. He performed these
tasks efficiently for a week and then said his mother was ill
and needed to be looked after. His friend would come instead.

The mothers of houseboys are a remarkable race, and they
play an important part in the lives of European families in
Zanzibar. They are all of great age, no matter how young
their sons may be, and they are perpetually ailing. Many of
them live permanently at death's door without ever actually
passing through those grim portals. The filial devotion of their
sons is as remarkable as their chronic ill-health. It constantly
necessitates long spells off duty during which, one must suppose,
the son acts as nurse and tirelessly attends the bedside. There
is never anybody else in the family who could possibly act in
this capacity. But though the patient may be ill for weeks the
illness is never fatal. In course of time she recovers enough for
her son to resume his normal life and he is outraged if he finds
that his place has been taken in the meantime.

The friend, who duly turned up to take the place of the devoted
son, was a small neat figure in a very clean white kanzu. The
crown of his cap was squashed up into a peak by making three
dents in the sides with the fingers, a curious fashion that seemed
to prevail in Zanzibar. He was unusually dark skinned, almost
pure ebony, and did not show the coffee colour which many of
the coast Swahilis get from the Arabs. His lips were thin but
his nose was very negroid and spread all over his face when he
smiled. As time went on I found that this was not very often,
for he was unusually taciturn and impassive for an African.
His name was Saleh.

Saleh stayed with me for the whole of the rest of my stay in
Zanzibar. I only saw his friend once again, and that was when
Saleh and he came to me in the middle of the day, forming a
deputation of two, to explain that the reduced wages I was
paying Saleh were not enough because the friend was married.
This all seemed very complicated to me, but, without inquiring
further into the intricacies of the affair, I agreed to raise Saleh's
wages with a promise of a further increase if he proved satisfactory. I gave him the increase soon after moving into my
house and for that he did everything in the house, which was

not very much—my cooking, which was slight; my housekeeping, which was perfunctory; and my laundry, which was considerable. Saleh was a good and faithful servant during the year I lived in my house at Mazzizini. He was not over-energetic, but no one is in Zanzibar. He did not often do anything without being told and his cooking was rough and plain, though perfectly sufficient for me. But he was very honest and, for that reason, a pearl of great price. I could leave my house and go to sea for days and weeks at a time and find everything on my return exactly as I had left it. This was bad for me since I became careless, leaving money and silver lying about and unlocked. Saleh never touched alcohol. He was a strict Muslim and rigorously kept the fast of Ramadhan. He was a self-respecting, upright little man, but with a curious mask-like impassivity which I never really penetrated. I never knew what place I occupied in his regard, if any at all, but he was devoted to my Persian cat. For myself, I said good-bye to him at last with a heavy heart.

However, whatever Saleh thought of me he certainly liked his place with me. He had little to do, for I seldom entertained and am by nature somewhat solitary. I was often away for days together and then Saleh had nothing to do at all. His wages, I was told by all the memsaabs, were far too high. To which I would reply that it was not I who was paying wages which were too high, but they who were paying wages which were too low. 'You're spoiling the market,' they said.

It is the ambition of all houseboys to obtain a situation with a single man. It is a difficult ambition to achieve for on the whole British Colonial servants and commercials seem to be the marrying kind, and, so far as the servants are concerned, it is always the memsaab who 'wears the trousers'. This is a most understandable ambition in view of the way some British housewives behave towards their African servants, a kind of magnification of the manners and customs of Victorian mistresses in the days of £18 a year and no followers. The initial assumption with which you start off in regard to your houseboy is that he is your worst enemy, a thief, a cheat and a liar. If he does not steal all your sugar, your tea, your coffee, your soap and so on, it is only because of ceaseless vigilance on your part. The price of groceries is eternal vigilance. You must go about jingling keys incessantly, locking and unlocking, doling out little dribs of this and little drabs of that. I knew one lady who went so far as to deal out firewood two sticks at a time. You must supervise constantly and tirelessly, following your boy as he goes about his work from room to room with a continual barrage of orders and instructions and comments, usually delivered in tones of glacial contempt, as though he were half-witted and it were quite useless to expect him to do anything correctly. If you do not do this he will, of course, skimp his work. He must always be at hand for a summons at all hours of the day and until late at night, and any desire he may show for regular hours is only to be regarded as another sign of his determination not to work properly for his grossly inflated wage, which is usually about ninety shillings a month. Many European women make no attempt whatever to speak Swahili. One I knew had lived in Africa for twenty years and had in that time acquired two words of Swahili, one of them incorrect. She would shout after dinner 'Boy! *lete kahow*,' meaning 'Boy! *lete kahawa*— bring coffee!' Another, if addressed by her boy in his native tongue, would snap 'Don't you dare talk to me in that damned lingo!' Another, exasperated about something or other and meaning to tell her boy to go away, said '*Nakwenda*', which means 'I go'. When he still stood there, grinning in a puzzled way, she shouted in a fury, 'Look at that fool! I say "*Nakwenda*" and he just stands there grinning!'

I do not wish to convey that all memsaabs conduct their domestic affairs on these lines, or tyrannize in the dark and smoky caverns which the kitchens often are in those old houses. Many are gentle and kind and boys usually love to work in a house where there are children. They even enjoy working where there are lots of parties, for Africans are convivial and gregarious and love lots of people and noise. They love the spectacle of people enjoying themselves, and, since they are entirely without our particular form of self-consciousness, they see nothing odd in what to us might appear to be a loss of personal dignity. A British Resident, much loved in Zanzibar, once went to an African party. Next day he was filled with those doubts and self-questionings which are apt to assail us all, even Excellencies, after a party we feel we may have, perhaps, enjoyed rather too much. He dimly remembered dancing solo round the floor in the African manner with African movements. He made discreet inquiries in order to test reactions. He need not have worried. To his astonishment he found that his African hosts were all delighted. The Bwana Balozi was actually joining in their dances and enjoying himself. Astonishing and unprecedented spectacle!

At Mazzizini Saleh was king in my castle and reigned supreme. My kitchen was his kingdom. Knowing hardly anything about cooking I very seldom went in there. When I did I usually withdrew hastily before the spectacle of chaos it presented. For like most Africans Saleh's motto, so far as his own surroundings went, seemed to be 'No place for anything, and nothing in its place.' But nothing ever seemed to get lost and very little got broken. In this regard Saleh was exceptional for most Africans smash china and glass with magnificent disregard and abandon.

Housekeeping at Zanzibar was a simple business. There were only two or three provision merchants in the town and they provided their customers with books of chits. You wrote down an order on a chit, signed it and gave it to the houseboy who fetched the goods during his morning's marketing expedition. The butcher, one of a row of rather gruesome stalls in the market, and the charming Indian fruiterer, with whom I took coffee from a coffee seller whenever I paid my monthly bill, used the same system. European ladies used to tell me how I should be swindled by the tradesmen of Zanzibar and what elaborate precautions one must take not to be swindled. During the year I dealt with them I never found this to be true at all and took no precautions whatever. But then I never do anywhere.

I used to write out my orders for the day on the chits every morning after breakfast. I loathe housekeeping and dislike having to think about meals hours in advance, usually half expecting meals to arrive on the table by themselves, conjured out of the air. As a result of this lazy habit of mind I never could think of anything but steak for dinner, nearly always as tough as an old boot, or fish—a vague generic term covering anything with fins. For lunch I would for weeks have tinned tongue or ham and salad, until the hot season arrived and there was no more salad. Then I had tinned tongue or ham.

Saleh never had any ideas. African cooks never have. It is all the same to them what they cook and I suspect that they think our method of eating, with its innumerable plates and complicated tools, just a lot of finicky nonsense. Why can we not sit down to a bowl of rice like other and more sensible people? Every day, after Saleh had spent hours preparing my meal, laying the table, serving and washing up, he would squat down on the kitchen step with his own bowl of rice and meat or fish, which he had prepared at the same time as mine, and eat with his fingers, Arab fashion. A week or so before my house was ready and before I moved in, I went into conference with Saleh about what provisions I ought to lay in. It was an abortive conference for Saleh's mind was a blank on the subject. In any case the idea of laying in anything at all or making any provision for a possible future is quite alien to the African mind. His ebony features were an impassive and slightly puzzled mask, but presently a light dawned.

'Custard,' he pronounced.

The ever-present help in time of trouble, the universal standby, for cooks all over East Africa is 'custardi-bake', with 'flooti-salad' as an occasional alternative.

Every morning, after he had done his household chores, Saleh rode into town on a second-hand bicycle I had bought for his use, and did the marketing with the chits I had signed. When he first came to me he was unable to ride a bicycle, but with great determination he acquired this difficult art on the high road at Mazzizini. He climbed on and fell off every evening with his white kanzu tucked up round his knees. The market section of the little town was a gay and lively sight every forenoon when it was crowded with white-robed figures with baskets over their arms, houseboys doing their morning's marketing. This daily expedition is the part of his duties that your houseboy loves most of all. He bitterly resents it if he is prevented from making it and Saleh always went into town, even if he had only to buy a box of matches, and he stayed there all the morning. If, by some mischance, nothing was needed in the house he would invent something and take just as long getting it as if he had a long list. In town the houseboys met all their fraternity. When the shopping, which for me could seldom have occupied more than half an hour, was finished

EUROPEAN QUARTER

ARAB QUARTER

AFRICAN QUARTER—A WEDDING CELEBRATION

ON THE OUTSKIRTS

they would gossip and drink coffee. There was in Zanzibar, I believe, a 'European Servants' Association', which had been formed as a defensive measure against the more overbearing and tyrannous memsaabs. It had premises, though I never knew where, and the houseboys used to meet there after their shopping was finished every morning, drink coffee, and gossip about the families they worked for, while the more erudite of the company translated the English papers into Swahili.

Who would deny them these simple pleasures? Yet some people did try to prevent their boys from going marketing and scolded them if they took what seemed to be an unduly long time to buy a loaf or five eggs. Some even insisted on doing all the shopping themselves. It was said that 'scandal' was spread during these morning sessions. If scandal existed there is no doubt that this was one of the ways in which it was spread. But there were many others, and to prevent your houseboy from making his daily expedition into the town was certainly not the way to stop him talking. It was always surprising, and somewhat disconcerting, to be suddenly made aware of how much Africans in the town knew about one's affairs and one's actions. They often seemed to know far more than one knew oneself. Nearly all European employers had a nickname, not by any means always complimentary but always humorous and seldom spiteful. These nicknames, conferred by Africans, were usually based on some personal idiosyncrasy which tickled their fancy or sense of humour. One old gentleman, who was reputed to be rather careful in his habits and to look rather over-carefully after the shillings, was known as Bwana Sahani Moja (Mister One Plate) because he was said, falsely I believe, to have only one plate in the house which he used for all courses and all meals. Another gentleman, of the stick-waving fraternity, was known as Bwana Stand-About-and-Shout.

The Servants' Association was an entirely natural growth, a trade union which was formed quite spontaneously without any coaching from outside. No trade union representatives with English nineteenth-century Liberal ideas, incomprehensible to Africans, had been sent out from the United Kingdom in order to bring it into being. It had no class basis and called itself a 'Servants' Association', not an 'Association of Domestic Employees or Household Workers' or any other

E

bogus clap-trap. For fundamentally the African does not believe that all men are equal. He certainly does not feel the equal of his fellow Africans and does not hesitate to make it plain when he feels superior to them. The idea of equality is an indigestible one which he picks up as an unassimilated bolus with an European education. Nevertheless the Servants' Association was quite an effective body in a place as small as Zanzibar. It kept a blacklist on which were noted the names of unpopular employers. Those who acquired a bad reputation, or were scolding, shrewish, inconsiderate or mean, soon found it difficult to get servants at all. Although I must confess there were moments when I wondered whether Saleh was my servant or I was his, I was able, while he was with me, to regard other people's domestic troubles with philosophic calm and detachment.

Saleh did not react as violently to the idea of inhabiting the cement store as I had expected and feared. After an infinity of wearisome badgering and fussing, the inevitable concomitant of life under a Colonial Administration, I got some new window frames and shutters put in, and a lazy old gentleman came along with a tar-brush and made a terrible mess on the roof. Swept out and whitewashed inside, the cement store did not look too bad. As my house drew near completion Saleh moved his furniture in. It consisted of a low four-legged string bed and a mattress, a rush mat, a bowl and a conical wickerwork dish cover.

About the same time I moved my furniture and effects into the house, but this was a far more elaborate business. It showed how we have complicated our lives and burdened ourselves with apparatus for living. I wonder if we have much increased our happiness thereby.

When one goes visiting one's friends in Zanzibar one cannot help being struck by the fundamental sameness of their apartments. The 'lares and penates', of course, differ from house to house, for these are the froth and bubbles on life's stream which collect around everyone as he drifts along on its troubled or placid surface. But the fundamentals of all the houses or flats of European families, in Zanzibar as in any other small colony or protectorate, are much the same, the same furniture, the same fabrics and the same floor coverings. This is firstly because most of the European community consists of government servants who are supplied, as I was, with stock government furniture. Secondly, the choice of fabrics and floor coverings in the shops is very limited. In the Indian stores you can buy a narrow selection of curtain materials and chair covers which startle and amaze, but few which uplift the soul. Floor coverings are either rush mats or Persian rugs bought from the dhows. These are often very beautiful, but there is a sameness about them and they are becoming fewer since they are now very expensive, whereas, like so many other things, they were once very cheap.

English furniture does not last long in that humid climate and is expensive to ship out to Zanzibar. The wood absorbs moisture, buckles and bursts at the joints. It is also liable to attack by white ants and beetles. Beneficent government, therefore, provides its servants with furniture, made from local wood and, not always happily, from local designs. Unfortunately, and perhaps inevitably, it is not, in many cases, the kind of furniture that government servants would always choose to provide for themselves. Since the early part of this century the type of furniture produced by the Public Works Department for government officers has changed little. Slight modifications were introduced in Zanzibar in 1951 and there was a considerable improvement compared with the designs that had been in use for over fifty years. The general idea, however, remained very much the same. If the sideboards, bedsteads, wardrobes, chairs, sofas and wash-stands issued to me in 1951 were not quite the same as those which would have been issued in 1900, in the days of spine pads and solar topees, yet there was a very distinct family resemblance. Indeed some of the pieces seemed to have come down to us unchanged from a very remote era, like the horse-tails and the coelacanth. As a result, when one attends the sundowners that are a feature of the social life of the colony, certain familiar domestic objects continually obtrude themselves upon the consciousness. In Zanzibar, for instance, there was a rectangular revolving book-case of Victorian design, known to everyone as 'the birdcage', such as I had not seen since my early youth. My grandmother had one which I used to spin giddily on its axis until the books fell out. Those produced by the Public Works Department in

Zanzibar were large and ponderous and creaked when they
rotated. I was told that these interesting objects, not found
anywhere else so far as I know, are of German origin and date
from the early German occupation of what is now Tanganyika.
How they reached Zanzibar and survived there, like the giant
tortoise of Galapagos, I do not know, but it is possible that the
German Consulate, once a power in Zanzibar, had something
to do with it.

In the bedrooms there were also interesting survivals. There
was a dressing table with a mirror fixed between uprights by
means of butterfly screws. This was extremely redolent of sea-
side boarding houses. It was difficult to persuade the mirror,
by manipulation of the screws, to stay at the right angle. It
either gazed vacantly upwards at the ceiling or swung tipsily
forward. There was also a washstand with an upright back
portion and a complete set of white utensils, basin, ewer, soap
dish and chamber pot. Or so the book said at the page headed
'Furniture Issued to Government Officers'—'Pots, Chamber,
One.' But perhaps owing to the different manners and customs
which have become the rule since the reign of Edward VII, or
perhaps because of the stringency of the times, none of the
utensils came my way, though I received the washstand and
used it for purposes for which it was not intended.

Thus, in due course, I was able to look with pride upon my
rooms, furnished so far as the fundamentals were concerned.
Only such additions as I chose to make would distinguish them
from other people's rooms, would give them my stamp and
signature. The heavier and larger pieces of furniture went up
the narrow stone stairs with much grunting and sweating and
their corners carved large holes in the new plaster. The sofa
and armchairs arrived without the cushions they were supposed
to be provided with and it took more weeks of fussing and
bothering before I got them. But I had double my proper
ration of dining-room chairs and was hard pressed to know
where to put them all. My wardrobe door jammed with all
my clothes inside it and it was a day or two before the polite
little Indian carpenter could come and unjam it. Mosquito-
net frames were placed in the middle of the ceiling to cover
beds that stood against the wall. The basin and bath had no
plugs because they had been stolen. But when all these small

difficulties were overcome, I looked at my dwelling with pride
and wondered whether or not to give a housewarming. And
decided not to.

The house slowly began to acquire an inhabited look. I lived
in it for a year and was very happy, but there were certain
snags which are the accompaniment of life in Africa. Water,
for instance, was always a difficulty at Mazzizini. For although
my house was one of the highest in Zanzibar it stood only about
thirty feet above sea-level and the head of water in the town
supply was inadequate. For days together, therefore, I would
be quite dry and Saleh would have to fetch water from my
neighbour's well. This did not seem to worry him in the least.
Our western arrangements are not, on the whole, very efficient
in Africa and are subject to recurrent breakdowns, which the
African regards as a matter of course and takes in his stride.
I used to suspect that many of the benefits of our civilization
are little understood or appreciated by him.

'This beer is warm,' I remarked once to Omar in the club.

'*Ndio, Bwana*'—'Yes, it is so, sir.'

'Then why don't you keep it in the fridge?'

'In fridge all day, Bwana Mkubwa.'

'Is the fridge working?'

'No, not working, Bwana Mkubwa.'

A friend of mine, travelling on the East African Railway, put
his head out of the window during a halt and saw an old man
going along the track tapping the wheels.

'*Wafanyaje, Mzee*?'—'What are you doing, Old Man?'

'*Sijui, Bwana. Shauri ya Mzungu*'—'I dunno, sir. European
business.'

Similarly, when my water supply dried up and remained
dry for several days I went to the office and made a complaint.
A little elderly Indian like a gnome said he would come with me
and see what he could do. He examined all the hydrants along
the road to Mazzizini and at each one pronounced sagely that
there was no water. He went into several houses and came out
of each one with the satisfied air of a doctor who has made a
successful but difficult diagnosis.

'No,' he said, heavy with authority. 'There is no water.'

At my house he turned on the taps and listened to the dry
gurgling noises.

'You have no water, too,' he said.

'Damn it! Have you come all the way out here to tell me that? I told you I had no water.'

'I tell you what I will do,' he said, after much thought. The doctor was about to prescribe. 'I will have a meter fixed to the main in the garden. Then you will be able to tell when you have no water.'

I drove him back to town.

'Please slow down,' he said, pointing to a pedestrian in the distance ahead.

'Why?'

'That is my brother—a very rich man.'

Again, there was no electric light at Mazzizini and we all used paraffin pressure lamps. Mine frequently went wrong or the paraffin ran out, but Saleh was not in the least discomposed and cooked my dinner quite happily by the dim light of an oil lamp, or even of a candle. He cooked on a wood stove and used to go out on forays among the coconut trees collecting firewood, thus saving me a heavy expense. He would place a long baulk of timber in the stove so that one end was burning in the grate and the other projecting far out into the kitchen. As the burning end was consumed he moved the piece of wood gradually farther and farther into the grate. This was a common practice and saved chopping the wood. I even knew of one cook who brought home an immense pole which took several days to consume in this manner, beginning with the other end sticking out through the kitchen window.

2

The old primeval Africa was never very far from our little suburb among the coconut trees. It watched from the thick bush across the road beyond the swampy pond full of water lilies, where the frogs made such a din. It throbbed and chanted all night down by the shore. Every morning aged cowherds drove their hump-backed Indian cattle right across our plots of land regardless of what the government called 'quick-growing hedges', put in to mark boundary lines, and regardless too of our attempts at cultivation. In the evening they drove them slowly and deliberately back again. They and their ancestors had pastured their cattle on that soft turf for centuries, and pasture them they would, despite the rows of white pill-boxes the Europeans had put up. Sometimes I would look out of my window, or over my oriental balcony, and see cows trampling over my garden, nibbling or about to nibble the newly planted shrubs which I was nursing with such care. Nearby the cowherd would be standing, placidly looking on, leaning in an immemorial attitude upon his staff, often supporting himself on one leg like a stork, one leg bent with the sole of the foot pressed against the other knee. From my sitting-room window I could see my neighbour's well and pump under a cassia tree with big pods. Here all my African neighbours washed themselves and their clothes, cackled, gossiped and spread out brightly coloured kangas in the sun.

My African neighbours were few. Next to me, on the side away from the rest of the new houses in the row, was a much older house to which belonged the well and the pump. It was inhabited by a young Agricultural Officer and his wife and, like all the older houses in Zanzibar, had a large and solidly built annexe which contained quarters for African servants. The Agricultural Officer's cook and houseboy lived in these, each with several wives and many children. Across the high road about two hundred yards away was a little squat mud-and-thatch house which was the scene of domestic bliss that anyone might envy. A handsome African lived in it with his young wife and one tiny child aged about two. They kept a cow or two but I never knew if he had any other occupation. He seemed to be very poor and quite content. They used to wander over my quarter-acre plot of land collecting firewood, the young wife a splash of red or yellow against the green, tiny beside her large husband who had a face of great beauty and a calm, dignified bearing. The tiny baby tottered behind crowing to itself or, quite as often, shrieking with totally disregarded fury. Sometimes the girl wandered forth alone, singing as she went, graceful and light as a deer, her bundle of firewood on her head. She used to wash her baby under the pump where it stood naked under the stream of water, cooing with pleasure and flapping its arms, a tiny thing in shining ebony to put on your mantelpiece.

African babies pull at the heart strings. But perhaps my strangest African neighbour was the old lady with her cow. She was a watchman's wife (though I never knew just what her husband watched), and she lived in a small hut a little way away. She was the owner of a brown cow with a hump on its back and she was utterly devoted to it. She was its guardian and its slave. It was her whole life and the reason for her existence. It suited her, for reasons known only to herself, to tether it on my plot of land, perhaps only because she had always done so, had always tethered it there before the plot was anybody's in particular. And who was I anyway? She would arrive with her cow in the morning when the dew was still on the grass, talking to it, scolding, coaxing, upbraiding in a high, thin, shrill voice. She was an ugly old thing with a head covered in tiny, tight pellets of black woolly hair and a wizened face like a monkey. But she had a light springy walk like that of a young girl and her figure, broad-based and shapely, moved voluptuously under her kanga. Her arms and hands were delicate and slender. She would find a suitable spot on my piece of ground to tether her charge and there she would leave it until evening. At sundown she would come back, give it water to drink from the pump and throw water over its back, a routine that it found highly enjoyable, and lead it back to bed. She talked to it all the time in the same upbraiding, scolding tone. But it had a will of its own, and if its mistress were late fetching it in the evening or if she tethered it in a place which did not meet with its approval, it set up a dismal and lugubrious bellowing and continued until she appeared. Personally I thought it was a disagreeable and hostile old character. I made overtures to it once, but it lowered its head and made unfriendly movements with its horns. Sometimes it was tiresome and fractious and hornily obstinate, refusing to go where its mistress wanted to put it and bellowing in a discontented and querulous manner. Then she would give it long shrill lectures, tell it that it had no manners and generally give it a good talking to. She stood no nonsense. One day, however, she tethered it in a place which, while highly satisfactory to the cow, was not satisfactory to me. She had tied it to a young sweet-almond tree which it threatened to ring-bark by wandering round with its halter at full stretch. I asked her, politely enough, I thought,

in my halting Swahili, to take the old beast away and tie it
somewhere else. But this had a terrifying and unexpected
effect. She seemed to lose control of herself at the mere idea of
such an outrage. She ran furiously back and forth and up and
down the dust road that led to my house, screaming and
waving her arms and calling down all manner of curses (I suppose) on my head for an interfering upstart and an European
into the bargain. It was a long time before she could be paci-
fied—a task I left to my gardener. Thinking she might have a
stroke I went indoors and left him to it.

After a month or so a great event occurred. This was the
birth of a calf, which added to the old lady's cares but was also
a matter for great pride and joy, as though she had given birth
to it herself. If one asked politely after it, saying 'What news
of the calf?' she would launch into a long, shrill and incomprehensible dissertation, which one took to be about calves and
the production thereof. Now I had both the cow and the calf
tethered in my plot until she removed the calf for reasons, I
supposed, connected with the production of milk. Then the cow
bellowed all day. But one morning I was awakened rather earlier
than usual by bellowing noises of a most unusual kind, heard
against a background of laughter from the building labourers
who had just arrived at the still unfinished houses. I threw
open my shutters and saw an extraordinary and rather embarrassing sight. I seemed to be witnessing the sudden abandonment
of all dignity and restraint on the part of the mistress of the cow.
She was like someone suddenly overtaken by panic. Her calf
was galloping along the dust road trailing its halter, making
full tilt, one supposed, in what it thought was the direction of
its mother. Its mistress was sprinting after it with an agility
and endurance remarkable for her age. As she ran she was
uttering extraordinary bellowing sounds which were meant to
imitate the voice of the cow, but which instead sounded as
though she had gone out of her mind. She was waving her
arms above her head and clawing at the air. Her kanga had
fallen away, fluttering like a banner behind her, revealing her
large slack breasts swinging as she ran. All the ragamuffins
stopped work and roared with laughter with wide open mouths,
doubling themselves up and slapping their thighs at the sight
of the old lady's distress. No one attempted to help her or to

retrieve the calf. But at last, unaided, she overtook and recaptured it by throwing herself prostrate in the dust to grasp the halter. She picked herself up, rearranged her kanga, tucked away her breasts, and walked back along the road with her prisoner, her composure suddenly and miraculously restored. She was telling the calf exactly what she thought of it. The laughter she had aroused meant nothing to her whatever.

Some days later my gardener shook his head sadly. 'Soon,' he said, 'both cow and calf dead. They are to have the needle.' I had no idea what he meant, though I was presently to find out. I said I was sorry but secretly rather hoped he was right.

3

The site of my house was a place of enchanting beauty. Even the irruption of the new suburbia could not really spoil it. Once I had found a position where I was not looking at close range into the lavatory or the kitchen of the house next door, or at long range into the bedroom of the house opposite, I could take in at one glance a lovely sweep of bay over the tops of the palm trees that grew on the face of the cliff. Immediately opposite me at the foot of the cliff was a huge baobab tree with a vast girth of squat trunk and curiously foreshortened branches like those of a tree in an ancient print. It had large pendent fruits and cherry-like foliage that waxed and waned with the seasons. Strange superstitions attach to the baobab tree and Africans will never allow one to be cut down. They say that an evil spirit lives in every tree and will revenge himself for the loss of his home if the tree is destroyed. For this reason you see baobab trees dotted all over the sisal plantations on the coast of Kenya and Tanganyika, taking up valuable space but immune by reason of their strange powers. It is said that the devil once stalked through the country in a rage, tearing up trees and sticking them into the earth upside down. Ever since then the baobab has grown with its branches underground and its roots in the air. And indeed when the branches are bare of leaves—it is one of the few large deciduous trees on the coast—it looks very much like it.

To the left of my house the plumed shore of the bay curved round to end in a low headland where, in a clearing among very tall palms, there stood a little gazebo. Seen from a distance of about a mile it had a quite eighteenth-century look. It stood in the grounds of the old house which once belonged to Sir John Kirk. The house had passed into Indian ownership and the lovely grounds were forlorn and neglected, but some of the splendid trees which Kirk collected and planted there still remained. At night lights came and went in the little gazebo and rumour had it that strange parties went on there. Needless to say this tickled my curiosity and I used to gaze across the water at the lights coming and going like whip-poor-wills in the gazebo, and speculate darkly about what they could mean. I laid plots to get to know the proprietor. After some weeks of making myself elaborately agreeable I was asked by the owner to a party in the gazebo. 'Only just a few friends you know—and a little drink.' A wink accompanied the invitation and confirmed my worst suspicions. But on the evening appointed the six of us sat outside the gazebo, under an enormous moon, and made laborious conversation for three hours about the difficulty of English as compared with Kiswahili. Across the dark, still water I saw lights moving in my house and itched to know what Saleh could be up to.

About half-way round the bay was a small fishing village. In front of a gathering of thatched huts fine nets were hung up to dry and outrigger canoes were drawn up on the beach. Dark doings were also said to go on there since the village had a reputation for witchcraft. Whether or not there was any truth in this I never really found out, but the drums beat often in the village, sometimes until the small hours of the morning. I used to see the glimmer of fires, and a wild rhythmic chanting competed in the silver darkness with the shrill of crickets and was, in some strange way, disturbing and troubling.

The bay itself was very shallow. At high tide I could swim in water warm and thick like soup. At low tide the sea retreated for about a quarter of a mile, leaving a gleaming expanse of naked mud. Women wandered all over it, stooping about to dig for shell-fish and worms for use as bait, their garments tucked up about their knees. As usual with Africans you could hear their voices chattering and their laughter a long way off. All over these mud flats the fishermen had built their palisade fish traps, long fences made of slender stakes, which they moved from time to time. At the end of each palisade to seaward was some kind of enclosure into which the fish, coming up against the palisade, were finally guided.

Far away on the horizon were the hills of Africa, to me mysterious, unnamed and unknown. Sometimes they were hard and clear in outline and you could make out individual coconut palms along the distant shore. At other times veils of rain swept along the channel and hid them. The sun went down in glory behind them every day and after dark giant lightnings lit the entrails of the clouds.

During the month of May the rains came clattering through the palm fronds like a curtain of chain mail and my quarter acre, the road and the low-lying land beyond disappeared under a soupy flood. Saleh ran briskly about placing basins and buckets in appropriate places. Myriads of large hostile mosquitoes appeared and made life impossible outside a mosquito net after sunset. One either had to go out or go to bed. During the South-East Monsoon sudden storms swept in from the sea, bent the coconut trees and combed their stiff plumes downwards. A palm tree fell down outside my back door and narrowly missed Saleh's abode. The wind rushed through my house driving rain on to the balcony so that I had to arise in the middle of the night and drag mats, rugs and furniture to safety. One of the disadvantages of having no glass in the windows was that at this time of the year it became impossible to sit at a desk and write, or to leave any loose papers lying about. On more than one occasion the wind whipped them out of the window and scattered them broadcast over the garden.

But the nights had a soft, silver lustre, cool and fragrant. The moon rode through the tops of the palm trees and turned their fronds to steel. The shrilling of crickets, all around yet never to be located, intensified the rapt stillness in which the whole silver world seemed to be listening to the far-off rhythm of a drum. And after the rains countless myriads of fireflies turned the darkness into the likeness of the drop curtain in the transformation scene at a pantomime.

4

One of the ornaments of my establishment was my gardener, whose name was Mvita, the Warrior. He was an ex-policeman from the Tanganyika police force. When addressed he always stood to attention and snapped to a magnificent Guard's salute. Every morning, or almost every morning—for there were days when he evidently had more important things to attend to at home and failed to turn up—I would throw back my shutters and there, in the hot, glittering blue morning, was an Etruscan bronze bending over the tomatoes, or cutting grass with long, sweeping, easy strokes of the curved metal strip used for this purpose all over East Africa. When he saw me he would straighten up from his work, if any, salute smartly at attention, and say '*Jambo, Bwana Mkubwa—habari za kutwa?*'—'Greetings, sir. What news of the morning?' It happened that my bathroom window was of such a height and the bath so placed that when one stood up in the bath one was plainly visible from the outside—one of those little quirks of design that one gets used to in Africa. This did not in the least disconcert Mvita (or me) and he leapt to attention when he saw me standing stark naked and saluted as though I were dressed like a Field Marshal.

Mvita lived in a modest little thatched dwelling some way up the road towards the neighbouring village of Kiembe Samaki (Fish Corner). He went to and fro between the village and the town, and between his house and mine, on a bicycle, often with his wife perched on the carrier, heavily draped in her black bui-bui, as did all the other inhabitants of Kiembe Samaki and thousands of the less affluent citizens of Zanzibar. When he met me in my Morris Minor he gave me the usual military salute without falling off the bicycle, but his wife drew her bui-bui closer and hid her face behind her husband's back. Not without a sly glance first, however. Sometimes Mvita brought his son to help him work, or to help him to abstain from working, a small stripling with a bullet head, flashing teeth and large, soft eyes. Whenever the boy saw me his smile stretched from ear to ear like a cut melon because I sometimes gave him sweets.

Mvita was discovered for me by my neighbour, the Agricultural Officer, and I engaged him in the first fine careless
rapture of possessing a garden. I thought I should be able to
grow things and, when the rest of the British were hitting little
white pellets about the golf course, I should be engaged in the
most innocent of human pleasures. I was thus engaged, I
suppose, up to a point, but it was a heart-breaking business. I
reckoned without the primeval Africa which lurked in my
garden, above, beneath and around. It was beneath in the form
of innumerable virulent insects, centipedes, slugs and other
enemies. Things shrivelled up and withered away during a
single night. Cut-worms and woolly caterpillars ate the shoots
and leaves of anything that survived the attacks of the insects
underground. I planted flowering shrubs about the estate and
Bougainvillaeas along its edge, but the old lady's cow saw to
them. And above, in the tops of the coconut palms, sat hundreds of Indian crows, shrieking insults at me as I moved among
my beans and tomatoes, ready to swoop down like harpies
directly my back was turned. Yet perhaps the worst and
cruellest enemy was Mvita himself.

Mvita conceived that he had two primary duties, and it was
difficult to get him to perform any others. The first of these
was watering. He watered constantly and remorselessly. He
watered everything whether it needed it or not. Often I would
see him carrying out this duty cheerfully in the pouring rain.
It was a pleasant peaceful task which called for little thought
and not very much energy. The other duty, which he took
seriously, was that of cutting grass with those long, strong,
sweeping strokes, throwing up swaths of dead grass at the end
of each swing. These remained where they landed, on my
canna lilies, on the roof of my car, on the window ledges, on
the verandah. It was possible to cut grass with even less mental
process than was necessary for watering, as became very evident wherever Mvita had been around with his cutter. Everything that came in the way of those swinging strokes was ruthlessly mown down, cuttings planted in the hope that they would
one day be flowering bushes, seedlings which I thought might
presently delight the eye, pineapple plants which Mvita had
put in himself, creepers which I planted against the house in
the hope that they would one day clothe its nakedness and soften

its outlines. They all fell beneath his abhorred scythe, as pitiless as that of Time.

The cultivation of vegetables is carried on in Zanzibar, as I suppose it is all over East Africa, on the ridge-and-furrow principle. The soil is piled up into long straight ridges, the tops of which are raked smooth and flat so as to give beds of soil divided by furrows down which you walk, watching with pride and joy the springing of new life. I decided where I would have my vegetable patch and, one morning after breakfast, I instructed Mvita accordingly. He leapt to attention, saluted smartly and shouldered his '*jembe*' (a large heavy instrument like a hoe) as though it were a rifle. When I returned in the afternoon I found he had dug two and a half ridges in a position exactly opposite to where I had told him to put them. This, I decided, must be my fault. He had evidently misunderstood. But it could hardly be my fault that, instead of digging the ridges in a straight line, he had described for each one a separate and distinct S-bend. However, perhaps he was right, for later I found that the place where I had originally planned to grow my beans, my tomatoes and my enormous pumpkins became quite water-logged during the rains and bred only large black mosquitoes. At my request, when the floods had subsided, men looking like Martians came in their space ship, a battered P.W.D. lorry, and sprayed the good earth. After that it shone with an oily iridescence which poisoned everything, including all the Bougainvillaea cuttings which had escaped the old lady's cow.

There was, indeed, a strange caprice about most things that Mvita did. He did not seem able to plant or dig or hoe in a straight line. Nor did he ever plant or dig or hoe in the same place for long, but after a little would leave off and begin again somewhere else. When he cut grass he would do a little here one day and a little there the next. One of his favourite activities, after watering and cutting grass, was the making of bonfires. All household refuse had to be burnt because there were no sanitary arrangements in the new suburbia, so Mvita lit pyres constantly and with enthusiasm, but never in the same place twice, and soon my quarter acre was pock-marked with many round black scars. It was a long time before I could persuade him to consecrate a single spot for these sacrificial fires. Such rubbish as could not be burnt had to be buried. For burial also Mvita had his own technique. He would lightly scrape away a little surface earth and cover indestructible refuse with a thin layer of soil. The rite was also, like the lighting of fires, carried out in a different spot every time so that after a single shower of rain my garden sprouted old tins, potato peelings, banana skins, grape fruit and paw-paw rinds. Mvita's favourite occupation, which I think he loved above all, was cleaning my Morris, which he constantly did out of the real kindness of his heart without being ordered to. Unfortunately he often did it with a rag full of dust which he dropped on the ground from time to time and continued to use without shaking out the small stones and grit. Finally I had to implore him to stop.

I wonder if my pleasant, but at times trying, association with this charming and childlike person did not give me quite an insight into the African mind. To begin with I found that, except for the simplest tasks such as watering and cutting grass, to which he was accustomed, constant supervision was necessary down to the smallest detail. The most minute instructions, even when given by the Agricultural Officer next door in fluent Swahili, were almost invariably misunderstood and wrongly carried out. It was astonishing how many wrong ways of doing one simple task there seemed to be. If one deliberately thought out how to do things wrongly one would hardly achieve such masterpieces of incorrectness, such perfection of wrongness. Eventually I decided that here again I was up against the old untameable Africa. For Mvita was far from stupid and had a lot of strange lore at his finger-tips, and endeavoured to impart it to me. It was just that he was African and his ways were not our ways, which were ways he could not understand. His frown of distress and the depressed droop of his wide shoulders on finding that he had again done something the wrong way were perfectly genuine and made all instantly forgivable. Nor was he really lazy, as he often seemed to be, for though he sometimes found it inconvenient to turn up, usually at times most inconvenient to me, yet at other times I would be surprised to find him still pottering about long after his stipulated knocking-off time. And though at first I swore many times that it was the end and Mvita must go, yet long

before I left Zanzibar I had decided that I could never part
with him, at least until I was compelled to, and that life would
not be the same without him.

Unfortunately Saleh and Mvita did not hit it off very well
and loud-voiced altercations used to break out, involving tor-
rents of excited, high-pitched Swahili, and calling for my
embarrassed intervention. I seldom understood what it was all
about and often had to get my neighbour to translate. One
row was about a bucket. Mvita used a watering can and a
bucket on his watering tours around the estate and appro-
priated for this purpose one of those which Saleh used in the
kitchen, and which he considered to be his and sacrosanct. He
regarded the kitchen and everything in it as his exclusive
domain. Even I hardly dared intrude. Mvita's invasion of his
territory provoked a terrible uproar one day. Another was
brought on by Mvita's habit of walking into the kitchen, without so much as a by-your-leave or thank-you, in order to fill
Saleh's bucket from the tap at Saleh's sink. In the affair of the
bucket Mvita delivered an ultimatum to me. Either I would
provide him with his own bucket or he would leave. In the
matter of the sink Saleh said that either he had his kitchen to
himself or he would leave. I said that of course I would buy
Mvita a bucket and did so that same morning. If I had presented him with an imperial crown he could not have received
it with more delighted smiles or with greater pride. Saleh's
problem I solved by buying a length of rubber hose and acquir-
ing an old oil drum. The hose was fitted to the kitchen tap
from outside the window and the oil drum filled every few days,
so that Saleh's territory remained inviolate. Thereafter a curious,
unmelodious soft chanting in the kitchen told me that Saleh was
content. Thus, by solving these and many other small problems,
I was in a fair way to gaining the wisdom of Solomon.

Africans, indeed, have a strange way of attaching themselves to you so that before long you feel that they belong to
you. They bring their families who gossip on your doorstep.
They appropriate your utensils and perform their own domestic
chores on your premises. They cook their food, which is often
in fact yours, in your pots and on your fire and interminably
wash themselves and their voluminous gay garments in your
house with your soap. Your back premises are festive with them

hanging out to dry. All this is resented and sternly squashed by many Europeans as further evidence of the thievery and knavery of the African. But it is not so. In my house both Saleh and Mvita had full liberty and did practically as they liked. Saleh used my pots for his own cooking and, I have no doubt, used a certain amount of my groceries. I think he made a bit on the marketing too. I seemed to buy rather a lot of certain things, particularly eggs, marmalade and jam. Mvita also did his own and his family's washing in my time with my soap and lent my gardening tools around to my neighbours' boys. But they always came back and, on the whole, the loss to me from these various small clandestine operations was negligible. In return for them both Saleh and Mvita did me many small kindnesses. Although Saleh bought more eggs than I used, yet I always had eggs and at a lower price than other people when eggs were scarce, as they often were. Firewood was expensive in Zanzibar and, to save me from having to buy it and be swindled like other people, Saleh would wander forth about sunset every evening among the coconut trees to collect wood, a small white-robed figure among the grey trunks, singing un-musically to himself. Every week he took to his girl friend in Ngambo a load of my clothes on the back of his bicycle. They all came back carefully darned and mended. I paid an insignificant sum for this service and he rebuked me when I offered more, laughing and saying, 'Not necessary, not necessary!' I never saw the lady who did me this service, and only knew that she existed when Saleh insisted most emphatically that he must have a carrier on his bicycle. I guessed that it was not for carrying groceries. And Mvita, too, constantly rewarded me with small and sometimes rather embarrassing kindnesses. It irked him when my neighbour bought a lot of bushes and planted them in front of his verandah. Mvita pointed to them with indignation one morning and the following day appeared with a lot of young bushes, identical with my neighbour's, which I did not much want. I wondered uncomfortably where they had all come from. This competition had to come to an end when Mvita came back from a mysterious foray one day with a paw-paw tree about fifteen feet high in full fruit which he planted outside my back door. In all these things it was a matter of what the Chinese call 'face', but which the African calls '*heshima*', meaning honour or credit, which is really the same thing.

In these ways the African becomes part of your life and worms his way into your heart. I was told that they do, in fact, have a strange feeling of 'possessedness', of being something of yours and part of you, and that this is a survival from the days of slavery when they were, in fact, chattels—part of the household furniture. They were usually well enough treated by their masters and the horrors of the slave trade were perpetrated during the transportation by land and sea. But the present generation has not yet lost the sense of belonging to the household that its forefathers acquired when slaves.

In these and many other ways a newcomer and a novice can begin to understand what is really meant by the 'call of Africa'. It may be in part the vast landscapes with their clear, incredible distances, the sense of heaven and space. It may be the animal life and the joy of contributing to its destruction. It may be the easier, more free way of living. But it cannot be entirely, or even mainly, any of these things. Mostly the love of Africa is the love for her black people. During my short term on the coast I met a surprisingly large number of Europeans who felt for the African a sense both of love and duty and who found them, during a whole lifetime, as I did during one short year and a half, puzzling, exasperating, at times maddening, but always lovable.

Chapter Five

STRIFE

I

THE village of Kiembe Samaki, which means Fish Corner, was very much like any other on Zanzibar or Pemba islands, or indeed on the whole coastal strip of East Africa opposite to them. The small thatched houses stood around a space of beaten earth among the coconut palms and bananas. One or two huge mango trees overshadowed them. There was a shanty shop, kept by an Indian, which sold millet and maize, cigarettes, hair lotion, cheap dress lengths of brilliant colours, gent's belts, American-pattern ties of the loudest sort, coarse china, hurricane lamps and a few bright kangas hung out like banners. Some tables were arranged under a mango tree where the elders sat drinking coffee and watching the world go by on the high road. All around in the dust black babies tumbled, pye dogs yawned and scratched, while scrawny chickens ruffled what feathers they could boast of. Over all, at most hours of the day, a loud-speaker blared forth Indian and Arab music or even sometimes, somewhat incongruously, the familiar voice of the B.B.C. 'Well, it's a lovely day here at Lords. . . .' This was something new in the life of Kiembe Samaki.

A great deal that was new in the life of Kiembe Samaki had been happening lately, none of it very pleasant and all in the name of progress. On the whole it was not surprising that the inhabitants of this small village looked upon the benefits of western civilization with a somewhat jaundiced eye. They formed, it might be said, a pocket of resistance and the elders under the mango tree viewed with marked disfavour the busy traffic on the high road.

The village lay in the middle of the best cattle-grazing district in the two islands. Beneath myriads of coconut palms wide sweeps of pleasant turf spread out in all directions. Down these green aisles, between the stems of elephant grey, the herdsmen and boys had for generations driven their droves of hump-backed Indian cattle, uttering as they walked slowly behind them those strange inarticulate cries that the beasts seemed to understand. They sounded like 'Oi! Oi-yah!' The herdsmen's dogs, shaggy, sharp-nosed mongrels, ran round the cattle yapping at their heels. Sometimes the herdsman stood, leaning on his staff, in the attitude of a stork on one leg, deep in contemplation while his cattle grazed. Turtle doves called in the palm fronds.

Unfortunately these levels of turf were useful for other things than grazing cattle. Since the war the Government had seized some hundreds of acres in order to make an aerodrome. A huge swath had been cut through the coconut trees and a Neo-saracenic control station had arisen. Nowadays the great silver birds, 'Iringa Pioneer' and others, came roaring down over Kiembe Samaki every day, while Europeans and Indians in their motor-cars went rushing to and fro along the high road past the elders sitting under the mango tree. The elders accepted all this as 'progress', but they did not like it. The younger inhabitants, however, did not accept it. Now many more acres of good grazing land were being taken over in order to build rows of houses for Europeans. And when one drove one's cattle over the land, as one's father and forefathers had done for generations, newcomers, white men, ran out of the little white houses and shouted and threw stones at the beasts. It was a plot, the people of Kiembe Samaki clearly saw, to rob them of their livelihood.

Lately further evidence of the plot had come to light. This was the Government's decision, in July 1951, to give the needle to all the cattle in the area. This was the well-known White Man's Magic for getting rid of their enemies' herds. On pretence of curing them of some disease or other, which the White Man had invented, the Government rounded up cattle by the hundred. Then the tall European with the beard and the big hat came along with his helpers and stuck needles into the cattle so that they died. Some years ago this had been done most successfully in the Masai country and several thousand head of the people's cattle had been killed.

What had in fact happened was that a few cases of anthrax had been discovered among the cattle of the Kiembe Samaki district. On the recommendation of the Government Veterinary Officer, who had a beard and a large hat, a decree had been issued ordering all the cattle in the district to be driven to certain selected points in order to be inoculated against the disease. There was, of course, no danger whatever of any injury to the beasts, but unfortunately it was true that a few years ago the Government authorities in Kenya had inoculated the cattle of the Masai against a disease called rinderpest, using a serum obtained from Egypt. The serum was defective and thousands of head of cattle died after injection. This story spread far and wide over East Africa, by bush radio and bazaar rumour, and had not failed to reach Zanzibar, and finally Kiembe Samaki, much distorted. Hence it was that Mvita, looking very solemn and portentous, said to me one day, pointing to the old lady's cow and its calf, 'Soon they will be dead, for they are to have the needle.'

The Government Veterinary Officer was an Irishman. He had a fine presence and a beautiful brogue. He also wore a brown pointed beard and a 'wide-awake' hat. By day one often glimpsed him tearing through the town in a jeep, and in the evening, on the many social occasions when it was correct to wear evening dress in Zanzibar, he would wear a crimson cummerbund, instead of a black one, with a fringe hanging down like a sash. Some ladies wondered if this was quite the thing.

When the decree had been issued he drove in his jeep, with the Mudir, or Chief Arab Administrative Officer of the district, to Kiembe Samaki to hold a '*baraza*' in the village. He told the Headman of the village to get all the people together, and they came from all the little thatched dwellings among the coconut trees from all around as far away as Fumba and from Chukwani near Sultan Barghash's ruined baths. Old and young gathered under the mango tree in Kiembe Samaki, overflowing on to the road, a white-robed multitude, their dark faces, hands and feet in sharp contrast to their white kanzus and caps. The Arabs among them, swarthy and bearded, in coloured head cloths, stood about in little groups, talking among themselves. They were silent when the jeep drove up and the Vet., in his

wide hat, beard and bush shirt, got out. The white-robed
Mudir, a handsome, clean-shaven, dark-skinned man, got down
after him. The Headman came forward and greeted them,
bowing with both hands laid flat upon his breast.

I do not know what the Headman of Kiembe Samaki was
like for I was not present at that '*baraza*'. But I can picture him
well enough from my meetings with other Headmen in other
villages. If you drive out along the roads of Zanzibar to the
remoter parts of the island, forty miles or so north or south,
you find your road becoming narrower and narrower. It loses
its tarmac surface and peters out at last in a village very much
like Kiembe Samaki or any of the other villages along its course.
The old men are sitting in front of the houses or round the bole
of a big tree. Children, dogs and chickens tumble and scratch
and peck about in the dusty silence. One of the old men rises
and comes forward, bowing with his hands on his breast.
'*Karibu, Bwana Mkubwa!*'—literally 'Approach, Great Lord',
but meaning 'Welcome, sir'. If you have a lady with you he
takes no notice of her, for she has no right to be there, out of
doors in broad daylight and unveiled.

The Headman is old and wrinkled, his face deeply lined and
seamed like a shrunken gourd. He has no teeth, or only a few
yellow stumps. His hair is a little white wool and the whites
of his eyes are yellow. Nevertheless this old man has the un-
mistakable air of authority, as the natural head of his people,
and of the wisdom that the years bring. His manner, humble
yet full of dignity, leaves you in no doubt that he is an
aristocrat.

The Headman led the Vet. and the Mudir to the base of the
mango tree where they were surrounded by the silent throng.
It was the Mudir who spoke.

'My friends,' he said. 'I have called you here to-day to tell
you some news. Some of your cattle are sick with a very bad
sickness that may kill them. The other cattle in your herds may
catch this sickness and if they do they will die. In order to make
certain that no other cattle take this sickness from those that
are already sick, the Government has ordered that this part of
the island of Unguja be closed, and no cattle may come into it
from outside. Further it is ordered that all owners of cattle
shall bring them to the Bwana Doktari here at certain times and

at certain places, as will be made known to you, to be given medicine with the needle. This the Bwana Doktari will do himself and no harm of any kind shall come to your cattle by reason of the medicine. After your beasts have had the medicine they will be safe against the sickness. This is for your good and for no other cause and the Government ask your help through me, your Mudir.'

The Mudir and the Vet. walked back to the jeep through the crowd in dead silence. The Vet. shook hands with the Headman and the Mudir bowed and they drove away. Not until the last blue wisp of exhaust smoke had vanished in the heat shimmer above the tarmac was the silence broken. Then Kiembe Samaki buzzed like a nest of angry hornets.

What the Mudir had said sounded quite different in the ears of his audience from anything one might infer from his words. He had said that the Government had decided to kill their cattle with the needle as the Masai cattle had been killed. How could pricking them with a needle and squirting medicine into their flesh have any effect on sick beasts? It was doubtful, indeed, if any were sick. The deceit of the Government was plainly shown by the intention to inject beasts which were perfectly well. How could any medicine cure beasts of a sickness they hadn't yet got? The whole thing was a trick, and the Government wanted their land for Europeans to live on and the easiest way to get it was to make sure that there were no cattle to graze on it. Then the people of Kiembe Samaki, and of Fumba and Chukwani and the other villages round about, would have no means of livelihood, their homes would be broken up and they would have to go elsewhere. There would be a time for weeping. Woe! Woe to the people of Kiembe Samaki!

Zanzibar must be one of the most peaceful places in the world. It remains so for years together, a cheerful laziness resulting from the heat making quarrels really too difficult and exhausting. But every now and then something happens which touches off the old fire that smoulders in the Arab blood. Then that volatile, excitable temperament is apt suddenly to sweep the people off their feet. They see red and madness reigns for a brief space so that blood may easily be shed on such occasions. An official of the Clove Growers' Association, whose duty it was to weigh and check bags of cloves brought in by Arab growers from their plantations, told me how ugly situations could and did quite suddenly develop. A bag found short in weight, or faulty in some way and rejected, a small dispute about a matter of procedure, and there is growling. Soon clubs begin to be brandished and knives appear. He told me he had been through some tricky moments in the godowns but that the storm usually passed as quickly as it had come, as often as not ending in smiles and bows and promises of eternal friendship. Some years ago a young British Agricultural Officer had occasion to find fault with an Arab clove grower, with his crops or his methods (or, more probably, his lack of them) of cultivation. In the course of duty he reprimanded him. Whereupon the Arab seized a '*panga*' (literally, 'a sword'—but actually a heavy broad-bladed knife used for cutting undergrowth), whirled it round once or twice in the air and sliced off the Agricultural Officer's head at one blow. At the trial, however, he was genuinely distressed and said he could not imagine what could have come over him.

On the first day on which the Veterinary Officer went to Kiembe Samaki to give the cattle their medicine no one arrived with beasts for treatment and he sat waiting all day with his attendants. On the second day a few came and on the third a few more. In the end there remained seventeen cattle owners who had not brought their cattle to receive medicine and who, in spite of warnings, refused to do so. They were duly summoned to appear before the magistrate in the Neo-saracenic court-house a fortnight later.

This was the spark which touched off the smouldering fire of Arab wrath. It had been smouldering for several years in the hearts of the people of Kiembe Samaki and now something came over them quite suddenly and they knew not what. On the day the case came on they assembled in an angry, but quite orderly, crowd outside the courthouse, babbling excitedly. They sat on the low stone wall opposite to it and milled about in the road. I doubt if they really knew what they had come for or were at all certain what they meant to do.

2

The military band of His Highness the Sultan is provided
by the police force and is unique on the East Coast of Africa.
There is nothing else quite like it anywhere. On Monday
evenings it plays on the Maidan outside the House of Wonders,
and delights the black and brown multitude who loll and wander
and scuffle on the trampled grass. On other evenings the band
plays before the Sultan himself inside the palace and on Thurs-
days, by his special permission, it plays outside the English Club
for the benefit of members. This is a pleasant weekly social occasion and the members, as a compliment to the band and its
royal master, make something of a ceremony of it. 'Evening
dress is *de rigueur* on this occasion' says the book of the club rules,
although in these days of lowered standards and deteriorating
manners there is a tendency for this convention to be disregarded, like many others. Coats are discarded and some
bounders even appear without ties, but no one has yet had the
temerity to present himself in shorts when His Highness's band
is performing.

The balcony of the English Club overlooks the sea which
furnishes a sibilant background to the music. The band plays
under a circle of electric lights on a space of green above a low
sea wall with a parapet. It is a splash of light and colour, like
a large glowing flower, against the indigo of the sea and the
incessant far-off play of lightning above Africa. A crowd of
Africans and Indians, only their white clothes discernible in the
darkness, sits around on the parapet and on the grass listening
and applauding. The bandsmen wear white uniforms and red
sashes with high red tarbooshes on their heads. They look very
proud and fine in this uniform for the scarlet and the white,
with gilt shoulder letters and buttons, goes well with their dark
faces and white teeth. They play military marches and tally-ho!
sort of music, anything with a marked rhythm which they can
pump out with gusto. Sometimes they try their lungs, for this
is essentially an affair of brass and wind, at a little Gilbert and
Sullivan, or even something like *The Chocolate Soldier* or *Lilac
Time*, but these also somehow acquire a military tempo. At the

end of each piece the crowd standing about, and the British on the balcony with their whisky and soda, give a round of applause which is acknowledged by the bandmaster with a little bow.

The bandmaster, Captain Harold Hull of the Zanzibar Police Force, regarded this band with especial pride. When he arrived in Zanzibar twenty years ago from India he had got the players together, all young Africans then, though those that remain of the original lot are not so young now. He had argued and badgered the authorities for money to buy instruments and uniforms. He had begged and stolen rehearsal time. The arguing with authority was perhaps the hardest part of his task for there was at that time no precedent for a band and, in Government circles, one must always go on all fours from precedent to precedent in all things. The captain had himself individually trained each man to play the flute, the clarinet, the oboe, the cornet, the bugle and the drum. They had little idea of music at first but he brought them to it slowly and patiently. Now, while he did not pretend that they were first class, they could produce melodious enough noises and, what was more, they greatly enjoyed doing it. They had needed discipline at first, and Harold applied it, firmly, fairly, without harshness, as he had been trained to do. Some fell out, others joined, most stayed. Quite a few, whom I heard playing adroitly outside the English Club on Thursday evenings, had been in the band for many years. All of them adored Harold. It would be small exaggeration to say that they worshipped the ground he walked on. Africans, especially those of the tribes who join the army or the colonial police forces, are a military people. Contact with our civilization has, most unfortunately, sapped their vitality and in many ways degraded them. But the military ardour is not dead, and they revere and admire a soldier above all other men. But he must be a good soldier, and this their captain undoubtedly was.

Captain Harold Hull was a ranker officer, late of the Indian Army. At fifty-seven his broad shoulders were as flat as they had been when he was a private soldier in India thirty-five years ago. His clipped moustache was tinged with grey, but his blue eyes were clear as those of a boy and his hand was as steady. On the Sovereign's birthday, on Empire Day and on the

Sultan's birthday, his own bearing and that of the members of his platoon were acknowledged to be the smartest in the force and always had been so for twenty years. They always would be so, for if Harold began to feel that his platoon was in any way falling off he would blame himself and go back to Hampshire, where he came from as a rosy-cheeked boy of seventeen to fight the Kaiser's war. Harold had no politics, I think. Anyhow I never heard him express any views. His task was to serve the Queen, as his forefathers and other soldiers had served another queen. He had now been in the Zanzibar Police Force since the early thirties and had seen several commissioners come and go. For a long time the band and the armoury had been his special care and it would now have been hard to replace him in either. On the parade ground this was also true.

When Captain Hull conducted the band in the evenings on the Maidan or in the Sultan's palace or on the green in front of the English Club, he wore a white jacket with gleaming brass buttons, blue trousers with a scarlet stripe and a peaked cap with a red band. His boots shone with a gleam that only a well-trained officer's servant could give them. He looked exactly what he was—a soldier of a famous legion.

'Why, Captain!' said an American lady ecstatically. 'I'd like to take you and your bandsmen right back with me to the States. It'd certainly be a treat for the folks back home!'

On Thursday evenings the bandsmen, in their white uniforms and red tarbooshes, arrived on the green outside the English Club in a lorry and sat tuning up under the circle of lights. Harold sat on a chair in the shadow of the house until eight o'clock when the programme was timed to begin. One of the bandsmen placed a gilt programme-stand in the lounge of the club carrying a printed list of the evening's selections. At eight o'clock exactly Harold left his chair, walked into the circle of light and took his place at a small rostrum. The bandsmen, their instruments at the ready, stood up for a second and then sat down again. Harold tapped on the music stand in front of him and held his baton aloft. Eyes under red tarbooshes watched it over gleaming instruments. It remained poised for an instant and then swung them into *The Bluebells of Scotland*. Between the items on the programme he resumed his place in the shadows, remained there for three minutes and then walked into the luminous circle again to take them safely through *The Soldier's Dream of Home*. At the end of the programme the band played the Zanzibar National Anthem. Conversation on the club balcony was usually in full swing by then, suitably lubricated, and on the green below, the noise of it could be heard above the quieter moments of the band like the sound of birds quarrelling. It came raggedly to a stop at the first bars of the Sultan's anthem. This curious melody, composed by Sir Dan Godfrey and first played at St. James's Palace in the seventies of the last century, has quite a jolly beginning but seems to have no particular end. It is familiar enough to residents of Zanzibar but unfamiliar to strangers who, taking it for another item on the programme, continue to talk through it until hushed, admonished or shamed into silence. After this anthem there was a second's silence while all remained standing and strangers wondered vaguely what was coming next.

There followed the 'God Save . . .' which Harold always rendered in slow tempo so that it took on a somewhat dirge-like quality. And that ended the band programme for the evening, and the aviary on the balcony broke out into renewed but slowly diminishing clamour. The bandsmen took tea and a bun each at the club's expense, climbed into the lorry and were driven back to the police lines. The lights went out and the crowds on the green and the parapet faded away, except the few lovers and lingerers who always seemed to be there at any hour of any soft warm night. The only sound was the murmur and hiss of small waves.

When Harold's stalwart bandsmen were not playing in the band, or practising, they were policemen. They had, of course, undergone the same training as the rest of the force and, if need arose, would be employed to preserve law and order and to protect the lives and property of citizens. Their occupation as bandsmen was a supernumerary one and lapsed in favour of that of policemen in the event of any emergency. Yet for them personally it was their whole existence, which revolved around their captain as around the sun.

3

When the people of Kiembe Samaki, a hundred or so strong, assembled outside the courthouse the rumour spread swiftly down the narrow streets that something was afoot. The idle and the curious, of whom there always seemed to be a large number in Zanzibar, came padding from all directions on their bare feet. It was a Monday morning. Driving into town about nine o'clock I saw quite a large throng of people in white robes standing about in groups in the street, or sitting on the low wall opposite the courthouse. They looked harmless enough, and I saw several acquaintances among them with whom I exchanged the usual bows that are part of one's progress through the streets of the town. The sight of a crowd just here was nothing unusual when the court was in session, for there were always witnesses and others interested in the proceedings in the courtroom, and possibly an overflow of spectators unable to gain admission. Opposite the courthouse, in a fork between two roads, there was a low wall forming two sides of a triangular shrubbery. This was an old Arab burial ground. The yellow flowering shrubs that grew there had been long neglected and had become tall and leggy. It was a place for lovers by night and children's games by day. The low wall which bounded it was cut into recesses to receive those who sat and lounged there at all hours of the day, the idle, the garrulous, the expectant or the contemplative, who had polished the stone as smooth as ivory.

The case was due to open at ten o'clock. By that time the crowd in the street had enormously increased for many had come from the bazaars to see what it was all about. In the little town, where life was so uneventful and the hot days all so exactly alike, anything was welcome that gave life a slight additional interest and tongues something to wag about. By ten o'clock, therefore, the streets leading to the courthouse were filled with people and it was difficult, even in a motor-car, to push a way through them.

Somewhere in this crowd was young Ahmed, an acquaintance of mine, who had come to see the fun. He was an Arab, aged about eighteen, and he worked as a messenger in the Secretariat. He sat on a bench in the passage in the House of Wonders outside the room of the Secretary for Something or Other, wearing a red tarboosh and a white kanzu with the letters ZG embroidered on the left breast. When the Secretary for Something or Other had a file, or a package, or a letter to send to the Secretary for Something Else, or to some other Government department, he thumped on a bell on the desk in front of him. Then the Secretary for Something or Other's secretary came in and gave the file or package or letter to the chief clerk, a Goan, who gave it to another Goanese clerk, who gave it to an Arab clerk, who gave it to Ahmed. Ahmed took it with a little bow and then rang imperiously for the ancient lift. But the controller of so important and complex a mechanism would not answer a summons immediately. Nor would the bearer of important Government documents, marked in black letters ON HIS HIGHNESS'S SERVICE, so far lower himself as to descend by the stairway with the silver knobs on the banisters. A wait therefore ensued while the lift made a probably quite unnecessary journey up to the floor immediately below Ahmed and down again. Ahmed fumbled in the pocket of his shorts, under his kanzu, and found a cigarette, but he could not light it until he got outside the building, so he put it behind his ear. After a passage of arms with the lift man for not coming more quickly Ahmed ran down the wide steps between the big carved doors and the Portuguese cannon and into the glare of the hot sunshine.

Immediately outside the House of Wonders there stood an Information Service notice-board such as is to be found in prominent positions in all towns in the Colonies. From the photographs pinned on it, and changed at infrequent intervals, the citizens of Zanzibar could form an idea of what life was like in the United Kingdom and of what was going on in other parts of the Commonwealth. England, they were led to suppose, was a land of historic monuments, ruins and fancy-dress processions. Scotland was much the same, but the ruins were more ruinous and the fancy dresses more bizarre. I seldom saw anyone looking at these photographs, but on the dry beaten earth all around the notice-board, and around the umbrella-shaped flamboyants that overshadowed it, urchins of all ages and sizes and colours, and in every stage of raggedness, played at crap endlessly throughout the day with shrill shouts of enjoyment, with laughter and with fisticuffs. Here Ahmed always became delayed with his important documents under his arm, his book, which the recipient of the document would eventually sign, and a pencil behind his ear under the red tarboosh or else just stuck into his woolly hair. He had a number of friends among this jolly crowd. There was a flat-footed Indian boy whose ears stuck out like wings. He sometimes earned a shilling or two by washing motor-cars, but usually he sat about all day long on walls or on door-steps doing absolutely nothing at all. He constantly sat on the wall outside the courthouse and waved to me as I passed. 'I not work,' he told me once. 'My parents keep me. I not like work, very bad.' I thought he was a slightly backward boy of twelve, but was surprised to learn that he was twenty-one and had a wife and two children in Bombay. 'By and by my wife get work in Bombay. Then I go to live there,' he said. Since he wandered about aimlessly all day long he knew everything that was happening and I often found his detailed knowledge of the private lives of all Europeans, including mine, a trifle disconcerting. So it was he who first told Ahmed about the affair at the courthouse.

There was also Said, a handsome Arab boy, who was always to be seen wandering about the main street of the town when the mail boats were in. On these occasions he wore very startling shirts and a pair of tinted glasses. Tinted glasses, usually of the curved opaque kind, seem to be much in vogue with the young coloured people who, it seems, find that they enhance their dignity. Said used to tout for Indian shops and tried to persuade tourists to buy their elephants and inlaid coffee tables and brassware. If he got a chance he would whisper into the ears of the gentlemen of the party a brief recital of the charms and virtues of his sister, and watch lust, fear and shame fight for a moment on their faces. The sister was entirely imaginary for Said was not a native of Zanzibar at all, but a sister could be found easily enough if things went any further. Said, whose home was in Mombasa, was always about to depart for Nairobi where he had been promised a job as a houseboy and confidential servant, so he said, to a retired naval commander, if only he could get the money to pay the fare. He did go eventually, but only got as far as his native Mombasa where I ran into him in Salem Road. He was leaving for Nairobi in a day or two, he said. The commander had promised to send him part of the fare. All he had to do was to find the rest of it somehow.

Said also told Ahmed that something was going on outside the courthouse and, since Ahmed's large envelope was to be delivered to the Education Department, it would mean only a slight detour to go round by the courthouse and have a look at what was happening. The two boys decided to go together.

Ahmed had collected, during his wanderings round the town with important envelopes marked ON HIS HIGHNESS'S SERVICE, a lot of very advanced ideas. Some of these he had picked up from his crap-playing friends outside the House of Wonders. Others he got second-hand from his elder brother, Jumah, who was a motor mechanic in the P.W.D. yard. Jumah's ideas were extremely advanced. He had been to a technical training school in Mombasa for a year and finished the course with an excellent testimonial from the Chief Instructor, who said he was an exceptionally bright young man and had a remarkable aptitude with his hands. He should go far, the Chief Instructor said, and Jumah thought so too. When he came back to Zanzibar he was given a job in a higher grade and placed on the pensionable establishment. However, that did not satisfy Jumah who was aiming higher than that. Knowing that the Director of Public Works was only 'Acting' in that capacity, the directorship being in fact vacant, Jumah wrote a letter applying for the post of Director and enclosed a copy of the Chief Instructor's testimonial. After the usual delay the Government gravely replied that it was regretted that the post of Director of Public Works was not being filled at present and was in any case open only to officers in Division 1. He was, said the writer of this cold, unpromising communication, Jumah's obedient servant. Jumah was furious and carried this letter all over the town, into the Africa Bar, into the Central, into the Lusitania and into all the others where the boys gathered in the evening. He would whip it out of his pocket and wave it under people's noses until it became dirty and dog-eared, smudged and almost illegible. Jumah said he knew exactly why he had been turned down. It could not possibly be that he was not good enough for

F

the job. Look what the Chief Instructor had said! The Chief
Instructor's letter, by the time my turn came to hear all this,
was as soiled and grubby as that of Jumah's obedient servant.
No! It was obvious that the Government would never make
him Director of Public Works because he was coloured. All
the best jobs, he knew and everyone knew, were reserved for a
few overpaid parasites from Great Britain—'expatriate officers'
they were called—who drew an 'expatriation allowance' which
about doubled their salaries, already inflated far beyond what
any native-born Government servant could hope to earn by the
sweat of his brow in his own country. How could a hard-working
competent young man hope to better himself with this yoke
on the people's necks? It was 'colonialism', the newest of the
'isms' invented since the war. 'Zanzibar for the Zanzibaris!'
cried Jumah passionately, thumping his fist on the table and
upsetting my beer.

Ahmed lapped all this up and thoroughly agreed. He got
it all a little confused, however. Meeting me in the street one
day, with his usual bow and smile, he said:

'The Egyptians have the Atom Bomb, so now we'll be able
to turn the British out of Cairo!'

'They're not in Cairo. And who are "we" anyway?'

'Jumah says they'll be turned out of the whole of Africa soon,
and out of Zanzibar!'

'Well, he should know.'

'There's going to be a big revolution and all the Europeans
will be killed.'

'Including me?'

'Oh no, Doctor. I'll let you know when it's going to happen
so that you can get away in time.'

'Thanks! Oughtn't you to run along with that letter? It
looks very important.'

'Yes, I think it is. Very important letter. *Kwa heri*, Doctor.'

And now the revolution was indeed beginning outside the
courthouse. Ahmed must certainly be there, perhaps Jumah
would be there too. Some Europeans might be killed. The two
boys hastened their steps, laughing as though they were going
to a party.

4

The crowd outside the courthouse was far larger than the few askaris could control, a dense throng of people packing the narrow streets. It consisted largely of those who, like Ahmed and Said, had come merely to see the fun and had nothing whatever to do with the case. Nevertheless there was a small but vociferous nucleus among them. This core of trouble makers did not come from Kiembe Samaki and was not in the least interested in the wrongs, real or imaginary, of the simple and innocent people of that village, nor in the cause of the nineteen prisoners in the courthouse or of their friends who crowded in and around the court. They were interested in making trouble and were busy making it, persuading the crowd into an angry mood. They could be seen gathering the people together in little knots, in each of which someone was haranguing with much gesticulation. They were inducing in those who had nothing to do with the case, as well as those who had, a sense of wrong, of outrage, of wounded racial and religious pride. The temperature was rising. All sorts of grievances they had been scarcely aware of yesterday suddenly became enormously swollen and bloated. They putrefied in the sun of this hot morning.

It was odd, many thought afterwards, that the streets around the courthouse were not kept clear, but the police were in the difficulty which is inseparable from such occasions. For as yet the crowd was peaceful enough, only sullen and murmurous. It would have been hard to decide at any one moment that the time had arrived to clear the streets. If the police had acted too soon they could, and certainly would, have been accused of infringing the rights of peaceful citizens, peacefully and lawfully assembled. There were plenty of voices, in Zanzibar and elsewhere, which would have been raised on that theme and would have very much enjoyed the opportunity. On the other hand, later on, when the temperature of the crowd began to reach boiling point, some injudicious move by the police might have caused an avoidable explosion.

Excitement rose continuously during the hearing of the

summonses which took about two hours. The murmur of voices
kept rising to a roar and sinking again in waves of sound that
beat against the walls of the courthouse and the tall Arab houses
opposite, from the windows of which heads looked down with
interest and some apprehension upon the turmoil below. Doors
were barred and lower windows shuttered. As is often the case
the prisoners themselves, whom all the row was about, were
those who least wanted to have a row made about them.
They wanted to get this foolish and boring European nonsense
over and get back to their homes. Whenever the clamour
outside the court reached a crescendo the prisoners, sitting in a
row in the court with their police escorts, signalled through the
window of the courtroom to their over-enthusiastic supporters
in the street. By means of gestures and fingers on lips they
implored them to be quiet and to disperse. But it was in vain.
The crowd, growing steadily at its periphery, pressed around the
door of the courthouse, firmly shut and guarded by a few hard-
pressed policemen.

About half an hour before the court was due to rise, that is
about half-past eleven, the 'Black Maria' arrived to take the
prisoners, assuming they were convicted, from the courthouse
to the gaol.

The 'Black Maria' was a familiar enough sight in Zanzibar
for, in addition to taking prisoners to and from the courthouse
and the gaol, it also took parties of them out into the plantations
to work. It was painted blue. Its sides were open all round and
enclosed only by 'expanded metal' so that the vehicle was a box
cage. It always careered along at high speed, with the prisoners
inside it, in white prison uniforms with broad arrows, clinging
to the wire meshes and gazing out of their cage like captive
monkeys, as though the world outside were unfamiliar and new
to them. Two askaris, in khaki uniforms with rifles, sat next
to the door. One always felt, probably quite wrongly, that one
of the purposes of this open vehicle was to expose the prisoners
to their fellow citizens as objects of contempt or pity, like those
carts in the eighteenth century which used to go through the
streets of London with cargoes of whores, molls, pimps and
other unfortunate characters exposed to public obloquy. The
public, from a safe distance, used to throw rotten vegetables and
filth at them and shout insults. If this was indeed so the 'Blue

Maria' lamentably failed in its purpose. Nothing was ever thrown at the prisoners, but friendly greetings were sometimes shouted at them by their friends and admirers as they drove through the more populous quarters of the town. The less educated Africans, and many of the more educated ones, as well as Arabs and Indians, feel no shame at doing a spell in gaol. For the African it is no dishonour and one is often told, when engaging a houseboy or a gardener, that the applicant has done a two years' stretch and come away with so much of his sentence remitted for good conduct. And life in gaol is no hardship. On the contrary, the food is abundant, the beds are dry, hours are regular and work by no means too hard. For these reasons the captives were always cheerful as the 'Blue Maria' went bucketing through the countryside. Inside their swaying, bumping cage they sang 'John Brown's Body Lies A-moulder-in the Grave' and 'Way Down Upon the Swanee River' at the top of their voices and laughed and cheered so that you could hear the 'Blue Maria' coming a long way off.

The arrival of the 'Blue Maria' outside the courthouse had a provocative effect upon the crowd. There was an outburst of angry shouting when it appeared on the outskirts of the throng and a surge towards it as it tried to edge its way through the people up to the door of the courthouse.

At this moment more police arrived, armed with staves and shields. They dismounted from their lorry on the outskirts of the crowd and, forming a guard round the 'Blue Maria', began to escort it to the door, pushing and jostling to clear a path for it.

It may have been this pushing and jostling which started the trouble, for when one is jostled one tends to jostle back. The askaris with the shields and staves found themselves compelled to use them in order to force a path through the press of people. There was a lot of scuffling. It was very hot. Black faces gleamed with sweat and there was a smell of hot African bodies. Bare feet were stepped upon. People lost their balance and swayed and clutched at each other. Some fell under the feet of others and some shrill screams were heard. Tempers stretched and grew taut. Suddenly upon the roof of the courthouse, looking down upon the multitude in the street below, a tall, thin figure in a white kanzu appeared. Lifting his arms to heaven he cried in a high, thin voice above the uproar of the people:

'*Ni jihadi! Mnangojea nini?*—It's a Holy War! What are you waiting for?'

This was the terrible battle cry of Islam calling again after centuries in the usually peaceful streets of this British-administered city. Proud cities of Christendom had trembled at that cry and now, at the sound of the high, quavering voice, uttering the ancient call again, something snapped.

Ahmed and Said arrived on the scene just at this point and found to their delight that the revolution really had begun. In the middle of the white-robed mob angry black faces could be seen with hands and sticks upraised. A nucleus of the crowd round the 'Blue Maria' near the courthouse door was swaying backwards and forwards and shouting, with khaki figures jammed in the midst of it. Voices, hoarse with anger, kept up the shout—'*Ni jihadi!*—It's a Holy War!' The two boys had to push and shove their way forward in order to see better. In doing so they were forced by the swaying of the crowd first on to the low wall which enclosed the shrubbery in the Arab burial ground opposite the courthouse, and finally over it. The shrubbery was by this time full of people busily hacking off branches from the overgrown bushes, stripping them and making them into weapons which they handed over the wall to the crowd.

The Zanzibar Police Force is the only one in East Africa which still goes bare-foot. Until recently the Uganda force was also bare-foot, but a year or so ago it was decided to put all the Uganda askaris into boots. For a long while they were unable to walk in them and, when marching, carried their boots slung round their necks. But what the Zanzibar policemen gained in foot comfort they on occasions lost in others ways, as now, for instance. For the crowd, finding that not much could be done unarmed against askaris armed with staves and riot shields, soon discovered that bare shins and feet are extremely vulnerable. With the sticks cut from the shrubbery they whacked the askaris round the shins, feet and ankles. This was brilliantly successful and infuriated the askaris, who laid about them with their staves. More of the crowd leapt over the wall into the shrubbery and cut off branches which they stripped and made

into staves longer and more flexible than those which the police
carried, excellent for the whacking of bare shins. They passed
them into the crowd over the wall.

This seemed a bright idea to Ahmed and Said. They, finding themselves in the shrubbery whether they wanted to be
there or not, seized hold of the tough green branches and bent
them down to the ground. But since they were green they did
not snap as easily as might have been expected. Ahmed,
wrestling with his branch, flung aside the large and important
Government envelope and the receipt book he was carrying in
order to have two hands free, and placed one foot on the bent
branch. He never saw his receipt book again, and whoever it
was to whom the envelope was addressed never received it.
For as Ahmed was bending down, with beads of sweat running
down his brown forehead and his face contorted with effort,
he suddenly felt himself seized roughly by the seat of his shorts
and the collar of his kanzu. In a second his arms were pinioned
and in another he was being pushed through the jostling crowd.
The rest of the revolution he viewed rather sadly through his
tears from inside a police van round the corner, guarded
by steel-helmeted askaris. His part in it was over, as indeed
was his part in anything for a term of several months. His
companion, Said, however, who had not been too busy to
notice the police squad enter the burial ground to clear it,
had wisely vanished and, while Ahmed was being hustled away
protesting, was walking away from the scene of the battle down
the narrow alleyway of Sokomahogo Street, with haste but
with the best possible air of innocence and unconcern, rather
as one walks in a field away from a bull whose intentions are
doubtful, with dignity but not without an occasional backward
glance.

As more police arrived several more of the crowd were
arrested in addition to Ahmed and bundled unceremoniously
into the van where, like Ahmed, they immediately became very
meek and humble and kept protesting that they never meant
any harm. As for poor Ahmed, the tears were streaming down
his face as he begged the impassive askaris to let him out. The
revolution, so far as he was concerned, had not gone according
to plan.

The proceedings in court lasted about two hours. They

resulted in sixteen of the nineteen prisoners receiving each a sentence of six weeks' hard labour. The other three were discharged. The sentences did not appear to worry the guilty prisoners very much. Nobody minds going to prison and, in any case, what is six weeks? Meanwhile they were important figures and their '*heshima*' or 'face' was vastly increased.

Almost on the stroke of noon, eleven of the convicted prisoners filed out of the main door into the hot sunshine. They were handcuffed and chained together and guarded by askaris. They climbed quickly into the 'Blue Maria' and, with their escorts, filled it completely. The other five, for whom there was no room in the 'Blue Maria', remained inside the courthouse to be brought on later. As the prisoners came out of the courthouse door they were greeted by a roar from the crowd, through which another wave of excitement ran like wind through standing corn. The wave seemed to break over and for a moment engulf the 'Blue Maria' as though it were a small ship in a turbulent sea. There was a mêlée round it, a lot of shouting and more whacking of shins. In the middle of it the driver managed to start up and, almost before the doors of 'expanded metal' had closed upon the prisoners and their escort inside, he launched his vehicle through the angry, tossing sea of white robes and black or swarthy faces. He got clear of the crowd, but with four or five figures still clinging like remoras to the forepart of the 'Blue Maria'. With great persistence and pluck, the sweat streaming down his face and a wild look in his eye, he drove off at a fine speed, though unsteadily on a very swerving course, down the avenue of casuarina trees which leads from the courthouse to the gaol. The 'Blue Maria' lurched and rocketed from one side of the road to the other as though the driver were drunk. Clinging on with one arm and one foot his unwanted passengers were buffeting the driver about the head and trying to wrench his hands from the steering wheel, so far with no success. They cursed and shouted as the van rocked down the road.

Just before the gallant 'Blue Maria' had got under way several other motor-cars, jammed full of people, with some sitting on the wings and others on the bonnet, had raced screeching out of side streets near the courthouse and made off at high speed up the road in the direction of the gaol. No one knew to whom these motor-cars belonged, nor what became of them afterwards. No one, strangely enough, noticed their numbers. But at the inquiry into the trouble, which took place when it was over, the fact that these motor-cars must have been waiting in the side streets, ready for their part in the day's work, was held as evidence that the affair was not merely an outburst of popular indignation, but had been thought out and planned beforehand to a considerable extent and with a certain amount of skill. But by whom? There was never any answer to that question, but whoever it was seemed to have had previous experience in the gentle art of arranging riots.

The road from the courthouse to the gaol runs in a 'dog's leg' through a fine avenue of old casuarina trees with the golf course on one side and the wide green parade ground on the other. Shortly before the gaol it forks, the right-hand branch leading to the gaol and then on, past the gaol's pleasant garden of bougainvillaeas and canna lilies, to Mazzizini and Kiembe Samaki, the left-hand branch leading through groves of coconut trees to the back of the town and Ngambo. A green space with coconut trees lies in the angle between these two branches. It was on the right-hand fork, leading to the gaol, that the mysterious motor-cars deposited the ringleaders and trouble makers, in a strategic position to ambush the 'Blue Maria' when it arrived. Then they disappeared and were never seen again. Meanwhile another large crowd of the idle and inquisitive had also been collecting here for some time. They were late comers, who, attracted by exciting rumours of trouble, had not been able to reach the scene in time to get a close-up view of the courthouse but judged that the gaol would be the next centre of attraction and made their way there as fast as they could.

The brave driver of the 'Blue Maria' managed to get as far as the fork in the road in spite of the determined efforts of his unwelcome passengers to stop him. One of them had by this time succeeded in opening the bonnet. At the fork the driver saw that his way by the direct road to the gaol was barred by a large and evidently hostile crowd. He swerved left into the other branch, meaning to get to the gaol by a round-about route. But this was as far as he got. With a shout of triumph the man on the bonnet tore at the innards of the engine and it stopped. Though I never heard what it was he did I suppose he must have disconnected the ignition leads, or perhaps damaged the throttle lever. At the same moment another man at last wrenched the steering wheel from the driver's hands and the 'Blue Maria' lurched drunkenly into the ditch. The crowd roared towards it across the waste ground in the angle between the two roads. They wrenched open the doors and pinned down the escorting policemen. The prisoners escaped, disappearing into the crowd and into the jumble of native houses nearby. It was never, I think, explained how they escaped from their handcuffs and their chains.

This was a resounding success for the enemy who let out a great shout of triumph. But while the rebels were achieving this remarkable feat their backs were turned to the right-hand road which leads to the gaol. There was a straggling crowd there, but it consisted mainly of spectators who enjoyed battles as long as they were not involved in them. During these few minutes, therefore, the road to the gaol was clear of hostile forces so that the second police van, a 'utility' truck driven by a British police officer, was able to make a comparatively unhindered dash towards the prison with the remaining five convicted prisoners. Though the people on the road near the gaol only gaped as it approached, yet they impeded its progress and forced it to slow down. It arrived unmolested at the heavy double doors of the prison, though none too soon. For the trouble makers, busy with the 'Blue Maria', saw the 'utility' van streak along the road to the gaol. They turned and raced back across the triangular strip of waste ground and charged up the road after the van in the direction of the gaol, a disorderly rabble, drunk with easy victory, waving sticks and shouting 'Get them out! Get them out!' When the van reached the entrance to the prison driveway its pursuers had almost caught up with it.

Captain Harold Hull was there, waiting to receive the 'Blue Maria' with its load. He had a force of policemen, about sixteen men with batons, in the driveway guarding the prison door. Another small posse, consisting of two buglers and four bandsmen, was posted behind some outbuildings at the side of the main building, concealed by bushes. These boys were armed with four rifles and five rounds of ammunition each, but would willingly have exchanged them for clarinets and oboes with which they were much more familiar. Instead of the 'Blue Maria', Harold saw the 'utility' van turn into the drive with a whooping crowd following it. They were by now intoxicated with that curious rage which is born of so little but grows by what it feeds on, a dangerous hysteria which afflicts Arab peoples and drives them on so often to deeds of blood.

When the van arrived at the entrance to the prison drive, grinding through the throng, the driver suddenly accelerated and raced up to the main doors at a fine speed, but with some indignity to the passengers who were thrown on top of one another. Harold opened the doors and the van drove in, followed by the sixteen policemen. Once the van was inside the prison walls Harold began to close the doors, large heavy wooden gates studded with nails. Hitherto the crowd had treated the gardens and the drive as a kind of Tom Tiddler's ground and left it clear, but at this moment the crowd swept up the drive behind the van and came up against the gates just as they shut, baulking it of its prey. But it had Harold at its mercy, outside the gates and alone. He had been unable to get inside in time.

The crowd had been shouting 'We'll get them out or die.' Now, increasing in volume, was heard another cry:

'The European! The European! Kill the European!'

Harold was on the ground and they were tearing at his uniform.

'A knife!' said a voice. Other voices said 'A knife! A knife! Kill the European!'

The faces, sweating and distorted with fury, above Harold were scarred with tribal marks across the cheeks. For the first time that day there was the glint of steel. Someone had a knife out.

The askaris in the shrubbery at the side of the main building saw this. They saw the big curved knife pass from hand to hand through the crowd in the middle of which, on the ground, they saw to their horror the captain whom they loved. The bandsmen came out of their hidden position, behind the out-buildings and the shrubbery, into the driveway and faced the mob. They raised their rifles and fired into the crowd which was trampling over the garden. The shots rang out one after the other, sharp cracks above the hoarse shouting, the sound of scuffling and the laboured breathing. No one gave any order. The askaris acted on the impulse of loyalty to their captain who, they could see, was in danger of his life. Had they not fired when they did he would certainly have been either killed outright or mutilated in an ancient and terrible manner and bled to death.

The crowd broke instantly and fled, a wide fan of white-robed figures fleeing away across the main road between the trunks of the coconut palms, under the mango trees, through the tangled underbrush to the sea, which shone blue and tranquil in the distance. The air was filled with acrid smoke drifting slowly away. Harold was lying insensible on the asphalt before the prison gate. A big negro was lying near him dead. About a dozen other crumpled heaps were lying around in various places in the driveway and against the prison wall. Three of them were dead, killed instantly. Two more died of wounds within twenty-four hours. 'We'll get them out or die!' they had shouted, and they had died. A great crowd had collected to see what would happen, and, as is so often the case when great crowds collect for this purpose, death had happened; and in surprise and terror the crowd was fleeing from it through the still heat of noon.

5

The road from Zanzibar to Mazzizini, on which these sad events took place, is joined by another just beyond the gaol. This second road comes from Ngambo and the African quarter, past the police lines and the football pitch and runs beside the wall of the gaol, which stands in the angle formed by the junction of the two roads. The gaol is thus in a triangle of which this road is the base, and the fork where the 'Blue Maria' was ditched is the apex. For some reason I took this road to get from the club to my house at lunch time that day. The two roads join on a sharp upward slope and one has to slow down. Lorry drivers, feeling safe in their juggernauts, rarely do slow down but take the awkward curve on the wrong side, which makes slowing down doubly important for others. I slowed down that morning and then stopped in amazement. A great crowd of people was running away from me through the undergrowth on the other side of the main road. I thought at first that, in my little motor-car, I had caused some sudden panic and that they were all running away from me. Then I saw that this was not so. A line of police with rifles was advancing across the road at a slow walk. What looked like bundles of washing were lying in the prison drive and against the prison wall.

When I arrived at my house my neighbour, the young Agricultural Officer, and his wife met me. They seemed alarmed.

'We're moving into town after lunch,' he said. 'Things are looking pretty ugly. More trouble is expected to-night, especially in this area. All women and children living in the country districts have been advised to get into town. They're forming a special constabulary and they want all European males to report at the police lines this evening. I think it would be a good idea if we went along together.'

'What do you think is going to happen?'

'Goodness knows. Anything may happen when these people's blood is up. It's rumoured they've sworn vengeance for the casualties this morning. There are meetings going on all over Ngambo calling for a "*jihad*". You know what that means. I'm sending my wife into town.'

At that time my house was the only one as yet built on the estate, and my neighbour's and mine were the only two European dwellings for some distance around. They suddenly seemed very lonely. I thought of the drums I had heard every night throbbing down on the shore in the fishermen's village only a mile away.

Some Europeans laughed at all this and refused to move, though most of those with women and children sent them into town. Those who stayed in their houses out in the dark countryside, where the scream of crickets and the distant pulse of drums were the only sounds which broke the silence that seemed to press in like a tide, appear now to have been very brave and calm, but at that time they seemed just foolish. For it must be remembered that, in an African and Asian community of about 120,000 in Zanzibar town and island, there were only some 180 Europeans, including women and children. Horrible things had happened in this island in the past. They might easily happen again. Many of the Europeans, also, were scattered

about the island, on agricultural estates and out-stations, so
that, in the neighbourhood of the town itself, there were only
about sixty or seventy European males upon whom, in the very
last resort, the maintenance of law and order depended. For
how far could the African police force be depended upon if their
wives and children were subjected to intimidation? And how
much support could be expected from the Indians if the Arabs
really started to run amok?

In the police lines that night it seemed that there was a war
on. The askaris' quarters consisted of long, low, one-storeyed
buildings arranged on three sides of a square. The fourth side
was open and approached by a road. The low buildings were
dormitories, and through the end doors and the unglazed
windows, the shutters of which were thrown back, I could see
row upon row of hard little beds, each with a blanket neatly
rolled at the foot. But no one on this night of emergency was
going to bed. The askaris were drawn up by companies in the
square with steel helmets and rifles. Words of command were
shouted to and fro and there was the constant pad of bare feet.
In the square and in the road dozens of lorries waited. At
intervals a company of askaris would march off, board two or
three lorries and grind away down the hill into the darkness.
Other lorries were continually arriving to discharge their loads
of askaris who had just come off patrol. They squatted down on
their hams on the verandahs of the buildings. Their cigarettes
glowed in the darkness.

Most of my male acquaintances in Zanzibar were gathered
together in a small room which looked like a school classroom
with desks, benches and a blackboard. Each man had a rifle
and a steel helmet. A police officer, who appeared to be in
charge, took my name and issued me with a helmet, a rifle,
five rounds of ammunition and an arm-band. The helmet was
one of the old-fashioned kind, like a soup plate. I did not say
that even during the war I could never make one of these things
sit on my head properly. I supposed I could remember how to
load the rifle but was not very sure.

Everybody was smoking cigarettes and talking about what
was now known as 'the riot' and its possible repercussions and
consequences. The police officer said it was believed there was
to be more trouble that night. All the plain clothes police were

out and they reported a very ugly feeling in the town, especially in the Arab quarter. In Ngambo meetings were being held at which inflammatory speeches were being made. There were calls for a Holy War. The drums were active that night, and if you went and stood a little way off in the velvet darkness you could hear, beyond the round shapes of great trees which blotted out the stars, the steady and meaningful rhythm. I wondered what it meant, that old and angry sound. I thought of *King Solomon's Mines* and *Nada the Lily* which I had read so long ago.

The police officer was very depressed. He talked sitting on a bench, pulling at a cigarette which he held cupped in his hand between his knees. What he said was not pleasant to listen to and full of bitterness. It was the sort of thing one hears very often from many people in executive and administrative positions in the colonies. It conveyed a sense of frustration, defeat and distrust.

'Well, there's one thing we can be quite certain about,' he was saying. 'Whoever else gets the sticky end as a result of this, we, the police, most certainly will. I reckon I might just as well hand in my chips now. If we act too soon in a show like this, there's the hell of a scream—interfering with the rights of citizens! No one knows or cares how many lives may have been saved by preventing a riot from coming to a head. But if we act too late there's another howl raised—"Why didn't the police take steps before? What do we pay them for?" There'll be an inquiry into all this, of course. Two or three silly asses will come out from home, completely ignorant of Africa or of Africans or of local conditions. They'll hear a lot of so-called witnesses. Hardly any of the witnesses will be telling the truth, of course. Some of them weren't even present at the time. Those that were didn't see what happened. That won't prevent them from spinning wonderful yarns, all pointing to the brutal, bloodthirsty conduct of the police. Some, of course, will have been bribed and coached. In due course a long, wordy report will be issued saying, in so many words, that the police were at fault. Either they shouldn't have done what they did when they did it, or they ought to have done something they didn't do. If they did it early, they ought to have done it later. If they did it later, they ought to have done it earlier. It'll be all very wise after the event and somebody will have to be sacrificed for not being quite so omniscient before it. It's not hard to guess who that'll be. The trouble is that there are no senior officers left now in the Colonial Police who know how to deal with a riotous assembly. All those who have ever had any occasion to deal with one have been sacked. Every officer in the force to-day prays that he'll never have the bad luck to deal with a riot because it'll mean the end of his career. To-day we've had that bit of bad luck in Zanzibar. Can't help it. Well, I suppose I'd better go and see what's happening outside.' He clumped out into the night.

Although what he said undoubtedly contains the germ of truth, he was, in this particular instance, quite wrong. There was an inquiry but it was conducted by Sir John Milner Gray, the distinguished Chief Justice of Zanzibar, who had lived in the protectorate for many years. His report completely exonerated the police. Indeed it commended them for the promptness with which they dealt with an ugly situation.

Nothing happened that night after all. When the sky beyond the dark shapes of the mango trees began to pale and, the drums having ceased, the cocks crew in all the back alleys of Ngambo, we wearily dispersed. Another lovely day of the North-East Monsoon dawned warm and clear, and Zanzibar was herself again, cheerful, friendly, smelly. During the fore-noon we handed in our rifles and helmets at the central police station behind the House of Wonders. All the special constabu-lary, who had voluntarily enrolled for the preservation of law and order in the town, were there and it was encouraging to see how many young Indians and Arabs had answered the call. But to-day law and order were not in danger and laughter was in the air. Cheerful, bare-footed, white-robed crowds had gathered outside the House of Wonders to greet their brave defenders who had never fired a shot. Said was there and the flat-footed Indian boy, but, alas, not Ahmed whom I never saw again. The sight of familiar figures armed with rifles and steel helmets seemed to everyone to be immensely entertaining.

'*Jambo, Bwana!*' said voices in the crowd when I appeared. This is the usual Swahili greeting, but is really a question mean-ing, literally, 'Any worries?'

'*Sijambo, Mabwana,*' I replied. 'There are no worries, gentlemen.'

Chapter Six

FAST AND FESTIVAL

I

I USED to take lessons in Kiswahili two or three times a week from a young Arab schoolmaster. He was a slight, dark-skinned man with grave and courtly manners and a most pleasant smile. We used to meet at the Public Library and, on the first occasion, not knowing him by sight, I waited among the old newspapers and magazines and the book cases (there was one mysteriously labelled 'Literature') for about twenty minutes wondering whether he was going to turn up or not. Just as I had decided he was not and was about to leave, he emerged suddenly from behind a copy of *The Weekly Times* and came towards me, a slim figure in the usual long white kanzu and round embroidered cap. He had been studying me from under cover of *The Times* when my back was turned. We bowed, bowed each other out of the library, into my Morris, up my stairs and finally into my sitting-room. We sipped iced, fizzy lemonade and wrestled for an hour with 'po', 'mo' and 'ko' and 'place as a subject'. Then we bowed each other down the stairs and into my car again and I drove him back to town. I always dropped him at the little shabby, square mosque that overlooked the mud flats near the creek, for it was the sunset hour of prayer. The authorities, whoever they may be, had long had their eyes on that mosque and wanted to remove it because it was not a very lovely object and it spoilt the nice modern line of the esplanade which, otherwise, would have been a credit to Weston-super-Mare. But the Waqf Committee, who looked after all the mosques and maintained them (though only just), would not allow the little mosque to be disturbed because it was where the people prayed, and had prayed for fifty years or more. I dropped my friend there each evening

145

and he joined the throng of men, for women do not enter the mosques, washing their feet and their arms, downward from the elbow, before going in to say their prayers.

'Pray for me, Abdulla,' I said one evening, when I knew him better.

'Certainly,' he replied gravely. 'But do you not pray yourself?'

'Sometimes,' I said, 'but my smoke blows sideways.'

He smiled and left me feeling that I had said something unpardonably sententious.

Five times a day all over Zanzibar, as is enjoined upon all the Faithful, the small prayers of humble people rise to Heaven. Together they must make one very big one. At dawn, if I were up, I used to see the fishermen by their nets upon the shore in front of their village, having first washed themselves in the sea, spread out their mats and kneel facing Mecca, the Holy City, the Navel of the World. Part of their prayers they said standing with heads bowed and hands folded in front of them. Another part they said kneeling with their foreheads touching the ground. Every morning my neighbour in the little house across the road said his prayers before his front door, kneeling towards Mecca in the sunshine. At noon every day I saw the people going into the mosques, casting off their shoes and washing themselves before entering. In the evening, before Saleh began to prepare my supper, he spread his mat upon the floor of the cement store which Allah had provided for him for a house and, bowing himself to the ground, gave thanks.

The Koran only enjoins prayer four times a day, but strict Moslems pray five times, at dawn, at noon, just before sunset, just after sunset and before going to sleep. Some people in Zanzibar, I noticed, seemed to be even stricter and more meticulous than this and prayed at all sorts of odd times. Two old Arab sailors in our ship, who came from the Hadhramuth and were a couple of engaging old scoundrels, prayed furiously whenever there seemed to be a danger of a job of work appearing. At length life for them became an almost constant state of prayer, a continuous retreat.

There is no god but God and Mohammed is His prophet. He rules in Heaven with His Angels, who are sexless, assisted by Jinns, who may be male or female and were created from fire.

Good and evil are foreordained and the will of Allah is immu-
table. The world 'Islam' itself means 'submission to the will
of God and obedience to His laws'. To this belief in predes-
tination the Arab owes his fatalistic outlook, his fecklessness
and lack of thought for the morrow, his bravery in war. Since
all things, including the hour and manner of death, are the
will of Allah and foreordained, why seek to change or to
avoid them? God is great.

The Prophet, on whom be peace, lived in the seventh century
A.D. and exhorted his fellow citizens of Mecca to turn back
from paganism to the God of Abraham. The divine message
of the Koran was revealed to him during lonely vigils on Mt.
Hira, outside the town, when he used to wrap himself in a
blanket and sweat profusely. Some say he had epileptic fits
on these occasions. At length he was driven from Mecca by
his enemies and, at the age of about fifty-three, he migrated to
Medina with his followers. This migration is known as the
Hijra and occurred on the Jewish Day of Atonement. In the
Mohammedan calendar dates are reckoned from the Hijra, as
in ours they are reckoned from the birth of Christ, and are
written thus, 100 A.H.—which means 'one hundred Anno
Hegirae'. The Mohammedan year consists of twelve lunar
months of twenty-eight to thirty days each, making 354 days.

After the Hijra, at Medina, the Prophet changed from a
revealer of the laws of God into a political and military leader
of the most ruthless and despotic type. He revenged himself
upon the city of Mecca, raiding the caravans of his own tribe,
the Kuraish, and eventually conquering the city. He brought
all the peoples of Arabia under his spiritual and military dominion and preached that it was the duty of the Faithful to convert
the whole world to Islam by the sword. He died in A.D. 632
of a fever in the arms of his favourite wife.

Before he died the Prophet said, 'O people! When I am gone,
see that ye fall not apart, killing one another.' But he failed to
name his successor, and over that very question, upon whom
the mantle of the Prophet might be said to have fallen, the
Faithful have been divided all these centuries, and have killed
one another upon very many and bloody occasions.

There are to-day three principal sects of Mohammedans, the
Sunnis, the Shiites and the Khawarij. They differ from one

another mainly in the views they hold as to who was the rightful Caliph, or substitute for the Prophet, and as to the manner in which he should be chosen.

The Sunnis are the orthodox Moslems. Their name is derived from the word '*Sunna*', a path, for they believe themselves to be the followers of the path, the traditionalists. They number somewhat less than half the total 235,000,000 Moslems in the world. They believe that the office of Caliph can be conferred by election upon any suitable candidate of the Prophet's tribe, the Kuraish. He must, however, be a man of unblemished character, learned in the law and of sufficient driving power and ability to conduct a Holy War. They acknowledge as the first Caliph the Prophet's friend and confidant, Abu-Bakr. The second, Umar, was named by Abu-Bakr, and the two succeeding ones, Uthman and Ali, were elected. Ali was the cousin and son-in-law of the Prophet, husband of his second daughter, Fatimah, by the first wife, of whom there were two in addition to many concubines. The Sunnis reverence not only the Koran but also certain unwritten traditions, the *Hadithi*—which is an Arabic word meaning 'a story'—which have been handed down with the Faith. They claim, as do all sects in all religions, that they alone know the revealed truth and they alone are saved. Nearly all the Arabs and Swahilis in Zanzibar are Sunnis, and they subscribe to the Shafite code of law, one of the four codes of Sunni law and that which is held in Egypt.

While the Arabs and Swahilis in Zanzibar are Sunni Moslems, the Indians are Shiites and belong to the Khoja and Bohora tribes who migrated to East Africa in the middle of the nineteenth century from Cutch, Surat and Bombay. There are also some Hindus, known as Banians. Indeed the Khojas and Bohoras are comparatively recently converted to Islam from Hinduism.

The Shiites are a smaller sect of Moslems than the Sunnis and they also consider themselves to be living in the light of the revealed truth and to be exclusively saved. They were for centuries regarded with loathing and contempt by the Sunnis, who do not, even now, look upon these heretics with too kindly an eye. The Shiites broke away from the main body of the Faithful in the seventh century and founded a dynasty of

Caliphs who ruled in fabulous splendour at Baghdad. The great Haroun-al-Raschid, A.D. 786–809, was the most famous of these and the Shiite faith has been the official creed of Persia ever since. The Shiites hold that the office of Caliph is God-given and cannot be conferred by man. When the Prophet entered into Paradise his divine power passed to his descendants. The first rightful Caliph was therefore the Prophet's son-in-law, Ali, and the first three Caliphs recognized by the Sunnis were accordingly usurpers. The Shiites prefer to think of their Caliph not so much as a substitute for the Prophet, as the title implies, nor as having any temporal power as most of the Caliphs had, but rather as an Imam or giver and interpreter of the law of God. They number to-day about 12,000,000 people and include most of the Indians of East Africa and many also in India and Pakistan.

The Shiites, however, though agreed that the descendants of Ali were the rightful Caliphs, soon split over the question *which* of the descendants of Ali were in fact the rightful Caliphs. There are in Zanzibar, as in East Africa generally, two principal sects which differ on this vexed subject, the Ithna'ashariyah and the Ismaelis. The former sect, known as the Ithnasheri or 'Twelvers', accept as Imams twelve of the direct descendants of Ali and say that the twelfth, who was named Mohammed like the Prophet himself, disappeared about A.D. 874 but is still living and will one day return to convert the whole world to the Shiite faith. The Ismaelis, on the other hand, only acknowledge seven of these descendants of Ali, and for that reason are known as the 'Seveners'. They hold that the seventh Imam was one Ismael-ibn-Jafar, rather than his brother Musa-as-Kazim who is acknowledged by the Twelvers. His descendants, rather than those of his brother, were thus the rightful Caliphs, and the office has descended in unbroken succession down to His Highness the Aga Khan, who is the rightful Imam to-day and the head of the Ismaeli sect everywhere, since he is the descendant of Ismael-ibn-Jafar and through him of Ali and Fatimah. Upon him has descended the superhuman power of the Prophet so that he can not only interpret the laws of God and foretell the future, but has other attributes and powers no less mysterious and, in many respects, no less valuable. Since Moslems may not take alcohol it happens that whenever His

Highness takes a glass of champagne or a whisky and soda, as
he occasionally does, the obnoxious fluid turns to water at the
instant of passing his lips. Furthermore his superhuman powers
are imparted in a lesser degree to his inanimate possessions
which become objects of value and of veneration to the Faithful like sacred relics. A tithe of the incomes of the Faithful is
given to the Aga Khan for him to put to whatsoever use he may
think fit, with the result that his charities are as vast as his
personal fortune. The jubilee of His Highness's accession to
the Imamate is periodically celebrated by the famous ceremonial weighings against a precious metal or gems. On the
twenty-fifth jubilee His Highness was weighed against silver
and on the fiftieth against gold. Since then the ceremonies
have taken place every tenth year in one or more populous
centre of the Ismaeli sect. The sixtieth jubilee was celebrated
in 1946 both in Nairobi and Bombay and the medium used was
diamonds. After the weighing the packages of gold, silver or
precious stones are publicly auctioned among the vast crowd
of the Faithful who look on with awe and admiration. They
fetch enormous sums, but the buyers do not receive them.
They each gain instead a place in Paradise. At the Nairobi
ceremony the total gate for admission to Paradise amounted to
£400,000, and the diamonds were flown back to Hatton
Garden to the merchants who had lent them for the occasion.
This vast entrance fee is handed to the Aga Khan who, having
consented to receive it, indicates his wish that it should be used
for charitable purposes within, and for the benefit of, the
Ismaeli sect all over the world. As his administering Committee thinks fit it is used for the foundation of scholarships
and assurance funds, the endowment of schools and hospitals
or the financing of private individual industry. The seventieth
jubilee was celebrated in Karachi and in Cairo. Platinum
was the medium used. The next celebration will probably be
in Rangoon but the medium has not been decided. It depends
on the prices of these expensive commodities on the world
markets. The most highly priced metal obtainable is always
chosen.

The Ismaelis believe that God is neither existent nor non-
existent, neither omnipotent nor powerless, since He Himself is
the Creator of all things, even of all names and attributes.

They make up about one-sixth of the Asian population of East Africa and are the richest and most prosperous of the Moslems. They wear fore-and-aft caps of black or grey astrakhan and their shirts outside their trousers, and give liberally to the Aga Khan's charities, so that Heaven must be full of them. Yet they keep enough for themselves to provide for large shiny motor-cars and for heavy ornaments to hang on their wives. Outside the town of Zanzibar they have a very exclusive and well-appointed club, terms for some reason usually only applied to the British sports club just across the road which deserves them far less.

Besides the Sunnis and the Shiites there is a third main division of Moslems known as the Khawarij. They maintain that the divinely appointed dynasty of the Caliphate came to an end when Hussein, second son of Ali and Fatimah, was murdered at Kerbala. Anyone, therefore, might thereafter become Caliph by election whom the Faithful might consider fit for office, even though he be the humblest among them, even a black slave. The Arabs in the eastern part of Arabia and of Oman belong to this sect, which is again split into several subdivisions. To one of these, known as the Ibadhi, belong the Sultan of Zanzibar and his family. The Ibadhi are very puritanical and frown upon all worldly display, which accounts for the simplicity of the Sultan's household and for his unostentatious manner of life.

Upon all Moslems, no matter what sect or sub-sect they may subscribe to, are enjoined five duties. They must pray five times daily, facing Mecca. They must say the creed at least once in a lifetime aloud and correctly, with full understanding and belief. They must give legal alms. They must make the pilgrimage, or Haj, to Mecca at least once in a lifetime in order to pray at the Kabah, the holiest place on earth. Finally all except the sick, or those making a journey of more than three days, pregnant or nursing women, or children under the age of puberty, must keep as a fast the ninth month of the Mohammedan year, the month of Ramadhan.

The word Ramadhan means literally 'burning', either because the fast burns away the sins of man or because, before the lunar month was adopted, the ninth month always occurred in the hot season. Since, however, the Mohammedan calendar does not quite coincide with the Christian, or intercalary one, the month of Ramadhan changes its position in the Christian cycle by a few days or weeks each year and thus, in the course of time, falls in all seasons. In 1949, when I paid a short visit to Zanzibar, it began early in July. When I was in Zanzibar in 1951 Ramadhan occurred in the month of June. In 1952 it began late in May. Thus in these years it was occurring in the cool season but was getting progressively earlier.

At the beginning of the ninth month the Sultan goes up to say his prayers, with his spiritual advisers, on the roof of his palace. The fast begins when he first sees the new moon, but it may begin if and when any one of the Faithful sees it before him, though I do not think this ever happens. A curious exaltation, a sense of expectancy, is in the air during these few days as though with the new moon some sign from Heaven might occur, some manifestation of divine power. People can be seen at sunset gazing skyward and talking excitedly in little groups. When the Sultan first sights the new moon the saluting guns are fired on the Maidan, announcing to the Faithful that the holy month of Ramadhan has begun. During that month they must fast throughout the daylight hours, from the moment when a white thread becomes distinguishable from a black one until a black and a white thread are again indistinguishable. No food or drink may pass their lips during these hours, and by strict believers not even the spittle may be swallowed. One notices with surprise in Zanzibar how many strict believers there seem to be.

During the month of Ramadhan the gates of Paradise are open and those of hell are closed, while the devils are chained by the leg. Those who keep the fast may enter by the eighth gate of Paradise, called Raiyan, cleansed of all their venial sins. Throughout the last ten days and nights of the fast devout Moslems seclude themselves in the Mosques and abstain from all worldly intercourse or conversation. For one of these last ten nights of Ramadhan is the Night of Power. Only the Prophet himself knows exactly when this night is, but it is believed to happen on about the 27th of the month. It is the night when the Koran came down entire in one volume to the lowest or seventh Heaven, to be revealed by the Angel Gabriel in portions as occasion demanded. On this night the whole plant and animal kingdom bows down in humble adoration before God and the sea loses its bitterness for one second of time and becomes fresh.

The fast, as observed at any rate in Zanzibar, can hardly be as rigorous as the Prophet intended when he summoned his followers to observe it. For, while no food or drink is taken during the prescribed daylight hours, yet as soon as darkness falls the people go from house to house visiting their friends, eating at each house of call a large and satisfying meal. Most of every night of the month is turned into day and spent chattering gaily and eating, though no alcohol is taken even by those less strict Moslems who take it at other times. About three o'clock in the morning we infidels, kept awake by the unwonted coming and going, the voices and laughter in the streets, can hear the high quavering call of the *Muadhin* in the nearby mosque calling to the people a warning to eat for the last time, for the dawn approaches. Thus, as a result of spending each night in these agreeable religious exercises, none of the Faithful is really in a fit state to work next day, nor on any day during the month of Ramadhan. As the month advances the pace of life in Zanzibar becomes slower and slower and the tempers of European employers shorter and shorter. Towards the end of the month it is almost impossible to get any work done by anyone. '*Nimefunga Ramadhani*—I am keeping Ramadhan' is always the excuse. Literally it means, with truth, 'I have shut down Ramadhan', and it is held to be perfectly valid as an excuse in native eyes at any rate, for all the inaction and inertia that accompany the fast. It is given with a pious and injured air, as by one suffering under a gross injustice. The fact is, however, that the general debility and hopelessness of almost everyone during the holy month are due far less to the rigours of pious observance than to a general lack of sleep throughout the community brought about by nights of carousal. Infidels heave a sigh of relief when it is over.

At the end of Ramadhan the Sultan goes up once more to the roof of his palace and, when he again sights the new moon, the guns are fired on the Maidan to tell the Faithful that the fast is ended. The following day is the celebration of Id-el-Fitr, the great day of thanksgiving and rejoicing that comes at the end of the fast. The devout go to the mosques and hear prayers and orations by the Imams. Then, for the rest of the day and far into the night, there is feasting and rejoicing.

Id-el-Fitr is celebrated by Moslems in rather the same way as Christmas is celebrated by Christians, and seems to arouse in them similar feelings. There is the exchange of presents and a similar rather vague atmosphere of goodwill. In Zanzibar the European section of the community is permitted to participate in both these occasions of general rejoicing, though somewhat one-sidedly. On this great day it is the custom to greet your Arab or Swahili acquaintances with the words '*Id mbarak*', roughly 'a blessing on your feast'. Your servants in your house and your club are given small presents, and do not fail to jog your memory if they are not obviously forthcoming. They will remind you, with a broad grin as they hand you the potatoes at luncheon, that to-day is their Big Day, their *Siku Kuu*. Can the bwana possibly have forgotten? But if you imagine that your offerings at Id-el-Fitr absolve you from all further obligations you will be greatly mistaken. For at Christmas, as they hand you your cold mince pie or club Christmas pudding in the noonday heat, they whisper hoarsely that this is your Big Day, your *Siku Kuu*. Surely the bwana will not forget his friends on such a day?

In accordance with this agreeable custom I gave Saleh a new kanzu as a present on Id-el-Fitr. The ceremony of buying it took up the whole morning following the feast day, when he took me to the street of the sewing machines, going importantly, like a bee from flower to flower, from one little shop to another. Outside each one woolly heads were bent over machines and black hands turned busily as though no celebrations had ever interrupted their clatter. Saleh bargained at each one at great length in rapid Swahili, with exclamations of disgust, gestures of scorn and every sign of indignation. All this was to save me a few shillings. Outraged dignity and contempt in every glance and movement, he stalked out of the street of sewing machines, with me, head and shoulders taller, at his heels wondering what it was all about. He could get the material two shillings cheaper at Ngambo, it appeared. So we went up there and clinched a bargain at last, to the sound of many loud-speakers and surrounded by a crowd of little boys, grinning and jumping with pleasure. Then Saleh bowed, thanked me and said he was going about his own business, and left me in the hot dusty street.

On Id-el-Fitr the big green space, surrounded by trees near the golf links, which is used as a parade ground on formal occasions and as a playground on all others, is the scene of public rejoicing to the beat of drums and, after sunset, the glare of many paraffin lamps. By daylight the Arabs from the dhows perform their extraordinary sword dances, passing and lunging at each other with heavy, broad-bladed weapons. They leap and duck and turn and twist over and beneath their sweeping blades with astonishing agility to the sound of a single drum beat. As they leap and cavort they utter unmusical, animal-sounding grunts. These dances are very ancient, I was told, and there seems to be something dark and savage about them. There is no music or lightness or rejoicing in them. They express the lust to fight, to kill, which, it seems, is not very far below the surface of these fierce natures. Little would be needed, I felt, to turn these feints into reality. If one of the dancers leapt too low over the circular sweep of a sword, or ducked too late beneath one, blood would flow but the dance would go on without a pause, with greater zest and more frantic leaps, with louder and more animal grunts.

All round the big tree-girt space there are booths and stalls, over which the hurricane lamps blossom after sunset like garish flowers. Mechanical music blares from the roundabouts and drums beat continuously, summoning the Africans to spend their cents. Crowds, mostly of young men and boys, gather round the stalls, most of which have been set up by the principal Indian shops in the town, and which sell much the same junk as on ordinary days but at slightly higher prices. The lights gleam on teeth and eyes, on black or brown throats and arms, on hands outstretched, pink palms upwards offering money. They buy curious, sweet, pink and orange drinks, sweets, belts, ties, and trashy ornaments because they feel they must enjoy themselves and this, surely, must be how it is done. Their cents clink into the tills of ruthless Indians, who turn everything and every occasion into profit. Farther off, away from the stalls, the little, tired family parties wander about. They watch the dances until they cease, and then they sit on the grass and chatter together in the darkness. They have come out from their

narrow overcrowded streets, or into town by donkey cart, to
see the fun. They have dressed themselves up for the occasion
and the Indian children are like little painted dolls, their eyes
heavily darkened, their hair flattened and plastered down with
oil. In their brilliantly coloured silk tunics and trousers and
glittering head-dresses, worked with silver and gold thread, they
look like sacrificial victims. Enjoyment seems to be the last
thing they are dressed for. The Arab children may have gaily
coloured head cloths and many have curved daggers at their
waists that seem almost as big as themselves. As on all occasions of public rejoicing there is a strange, slightly melancholy
undercurrent, as though mysteriously the fun were not quite
so much fun as it was meant to be. As darkness comes on the
gorgeous best clothes become oppressive, the little painted boys
and girls grow tired and fretful, and look wan and old in the
glare of the lights. Through the throng around the stalls, and
among the little groups of people islanded upon the dark grass,
the more sophisticated and westernized Indians and Arabs, and
string of Goanese boys and girls, walk with arrogant and scorn-
ful assurance, the latter with seductive gait and very up-to-
date giggles, dressed in the fashions learnt from the cinema
whose front is ablaze over yonder. Some of the young men sit
in their shiny motor-cars and toot as the strings of girls go past.

But there were almost no Europeans to be seen, except myself
and one or two others, who were generally regarded as slightly
odd. With that unlovable aloofness characteristic of them in the
places they govern, the British remained indoors or attended a
rigorously exclusive dance all on their own in their club, as
though this occasion of national rejoicing had nothing whatever
to do with them. Until sunset they played their usual golf on
the opposite side of the road to all the busy stalls, the loud-
speakers and the drums, and then went home to dinner without
so much as a sideways glance. It was Id-el-Fitr or something.
One could hardly hear oneself speak.

We, the rather odd ones, left the parade ground, tired of the
sad merry-making, and went up to the African quarter, to
Ngambo, to see if we could find a '*ngoma*', or dance, going on
anywhere. It seemed that there must be plenty of them for,
as the beat of drums on the parade ground grew less, it was
replaced by others which grew louder and more compelling as

we approached. The sounds came from several directions like opposing waves beating against one another, and soon we saw that there were several dances going on at once.

They were very different, these African dances, from those of the Arabs. At one of them I stood watching in amazement for nearly an hour. In the middle of a space of beaten earth, surrounded by one-storeyed mud and thatch houses, there stood a big spreading mango tree. This space had been fenced round by wire and was brightly lit by hurricane lamps slung on poles and from the branches of the tree. With their backs against the bole of the tree sat two young negroes beating out a monotonous rhythm on drums held between their knees. The throbbing pulse-beat they made, like that of a loud, over-worked heart, never varied. It seemed to get inside your head. On the crowd that thronged outside the circle of wire it had a disturbing, exciting effect so that no one could stand still. All were bobbing and shifting in some kind of movement in time to the drums. But even more exciting, apparently, was the effect on the grotesque company performing inside the wire.

The space inside the wire was filled with Africans. They came and went, entering and leaving by a narrow gate on the other side of the enclosure. Each one paid a small sum, a cent or two, to go in. The dancing company consisted mainly of young men and boys, though there were a few older men, but no women. They all seemed to be in an advanced stage of intoxication, drunk, not with alcohol but with rhythm. In time to the beat of the drums they twisted and leapt and capered. They stamped and shuffled their feet and rotated their buttocks and twitched every movable muscle under their shining skins. They threw up their arms and waved their hands. They gleamed with sweat and rivulets ran down their bare torsos, for nearly all were naked to the waist, and their lower garments clung damply to their flanks. Some repeated the same movements over and over again, others improvised new ones. Some danced in twos and threes and others singly, but it seemed to be a highly individual performance and everyone expressed himself by whatever movements and contortions he thought most appropriate. Some remained for a long time rooted to one spot, going through one set of movements only. Others rushed about over the beaten earth, leapt into the air and twirled about or stamped their feet. The whites of their eyes shone in the lamplight and a haze of grey dust rose like a mist, made haloes round the lights and hung in the branches of the tree.

Two boys near where I was standing were doing a curious private dance together, unconscious of anything but the drum beat. With legs apart and knees bent they held their tough bodies parallel with the ground, swaying rhythmically from side to side and twitching their right shoulders. The movements of each kept exact time with the drum beat and with those of the other and they swayed together as one, side by side with their shoulders almost, but not quite, touching. As I stood there watching them their rhythmic movements did not change or falter for perhaps ten minutes. Then a friend approached on the outside of the wire fence and spoke to one of the pair through it. Their swaying dance stopped while one of the pair carried on a conversation through the wire, straightening himself from his crouching posture. His partner, however, remained bent in the dancing position but motionless, like a machine suddenly stopped in full swing by an application of the brakes. Soon an expression of impatience came over his sweat-streaked face. Obviously this was waste of time. He tapped his partner peremptorily on the shoulder, and he immediately broke off his conversation through the wire and together, bent double once more, they resumed their extraordinary swaying and twitching in time to the drums, lost once more to all the world, in a trance of enjoyment and abandonment to rhythm.

Another strapping negro, streaming with sweat and naked to the waist, was making the circuit of the enclosure and passed me two or three times while I stood watching the swaying pair. He was revolving, as he went, on his own axis like a planet in its orbit and flinging up his great arms in time to the drums. Every second or so, while revolving, he swept his two arms down to the ground and scooped up handfuls of dust which he poured all over his head and his upturned face until his hair, head and streaked torso were grey. As he whirled and capered, saliva dribbled from his mouth.

Most astonishing of all the throng, perhaps, was a company of six lean, gaunt figures who, holding out their tattered nether garments like little girls at a dancing class, shuffled with mincing step and effeminate gestures hand in hand one behind the other across the dancing floor. They passed repeatedly back and forth like the chorus of some outrageous ballet.

All the dancers were utterly unconscious of each other and of the ring of spectators, of anything, indeed, but the pulse beat of the drums. With this they were obviously quite drunk and obsessed. It evidently gripped something deep down inside them which could neither be understood nor explained.

There were other dances going on elsewhere, though none was quite so extraordinary as the first. In one place, also in an open space by a mango tree, a large circle of several hundred boys was slowly rotating clockwise. Shoulder to shoulder and hand in hand they shuffled slowly round sideways to the rhythm of another drum. There seemed to be no beginning and no end to the dance, nor did it seem to express anything at all.

Farther on, in the middle of a wide dusty street, a dance was taking place in which both sexes took part, to a similar rhythm and under a similar fog of rising dust that filled the throat and eyes and half obscured the lamps that hung above encircled by moths. Here a big ring of boys and men rotated in one direction, while another ring of women rotated inside it in the other. Both the men and the women, shuffling round one behind the other in their respective circles, made continuous and highly suggestive rhythmic movements with their hips in time to the drums. There were many children of both sexes. They went round grinning broadly, making the same odd movements with the lower parts of their bodies as their elders, and falling in and out of the circle as the fancy took them. Many of the adults, however, especially the women, went round with prim expressions of the utmost propriety, others with an air of aloof boredom not very different from that to be observed in the more expensive resorts in London. Neither seemed very much in keeping with the highly indecent movements which were going on lower down. Occasionally a man would detach himself from the outer circle, or from the crowd of spectators who stood around, and claim the attention of one of the women. She would then break out of the rotating crocodile and take up a position outside the circle opposite the man who had chosen her. The pair would then continue on their own to perform the same strange, sexual rhythm opposite to one another but never touching. The girl would preserve the same expression of sophisticated boredom or prim propriety as though she were displaying herself in the advertisement pages of a fashion magazine. After a time the pair would part, the woman rejoining the circle and the man rejoining his or vanishing into the crowd. There was a continual coming and going of dancers joining and falling out, but what was odd was the air of extreme respectability which was rigorously preserved. Though the dance appeared at first sight highly suggestive and salacious, it seemed to have no particular denouement, no beginning and no end and not much purpose. Like the others it just went on and on.

Dust and the smell of sweat filled the nostrils. The tempo seemed to increase, the gestures within the circle of wire to become wilder and the drums to beat louder and faster. But this may have been only the intoxication in the air going to my head. It must have been that, but there must have been haughty and cold-blooded people somewhere in authority for something suddenly happened and it all stopped. Was this not a British Protectorate? The Governess suddenly clapped her hands, as she does, though somewhat earlier in the proceedings, in her native country. 'To bed with you!' she cried. The drums stopped. The hurricane lanterns went out, the dust slowly settled, policemen appeared. The crowds began to stream away. It was over for another year. In perfect sobriety, but covered in dust from head to foot, the big negro, who five minutes ago had been in an esctasy of intoxication, was walking quietly home as if returning from a solitary visit to the cinema. The two boys, who had been swaying from the hips, bent almost double, for the last two hours, were strolling away hand in hand, smoking cigarettes and obviously feeling fulfilled and satisfied. On the parade ground, too, the crowds were dispersing slowly and one by one the hurricane lamps were going out. The family parties were towing their fretful children home. The stalls were shutting up. But the dance at the English Club was only just getting under way and, from the sounds that floated down to the sea front, one could surmise that a Paul Jones was in progress.

THE COAST NEAR UNGUJA KUU

"OLDER THAN THE FAITH"

MY HOUSE NEAR MAZZIZINI

DAR-ES-SALAAM

2

My companion on this and many other curious expeditions I shall call Victor, because that was not his name. He was a retired Colonial policeman who, after nearly thirty years in the service, had settled down in Zanzibar. He was one of those men into whose blood Africa has injected some virus of her own so that, while they speak of her always with distaste, as though their years of service had been one long penance, yet they cannot bring themselves to part from her. It is as though they had been injected with a permanent itch. So now my stout amiable friend, having looked forward during most of his active life to a well-earned retirement in England, found himself chained to Africa by some unbreakable spiritual bond. One knew that he would not really be happy anywhere else, under less sunny skies, among less violent colours and less strident noises, among pale faces from which those broad white smiles were absent. He had settled down, with his pipe and his eye-glass, to the congenial occupation of watching the game from the touch line, laughing immoderately. His rotund figure, radiating geniality, was a familiar feature of the landscape in Zanzibar and was to be encountered in all sorts of unfamiliar corners. Victor and I took a stroll round the town on many evenings and our progress soon began to resemble that of royalty, so many were the bows, exchanged with hand on breast, the greetings and the smiles. The old gentleman who kept a durian stall on the corner bowed politely every evening, asked after our health and offered us slices of his disgusting fruits. We became well-known to the old tailor, who sat all day long cross-legged on his bench in fusty pyjamas while six pale young Indians, like etiolated plants, plied six sewing machines with hands that fluttered like moths. Fly-blown pictures of what the elegant male was supposed to have aspired to look like in the middle twenties adorned the walls. He would run you up a well-made suit in two days. Well, perhaps in three days, or, say, five. Next week, ready, sir. Wednesday, finish. Friday, you come, finish, promise. In the end one found he had been gestating one's suit for over a month. But it was a good one. We called on the little

G

bald-headed cobbler and his mates, who sat on the floor of their dark cell-like shop hour after hour in that extraordinary oriental attitude, with the thighs at right-angles to the body and one foot resting on the other calf, as Buddha sits and smiles upon the world. The little man would draw a pencil round your foot with one swift motion, after explaining that he was too busy to do anything for you at all, and make you a pair of sandals from the outline. Mine, I regret to say and never had the nerve to tell him, were too small. The ivory carver and the worker in silver both knew us and welcomed us into their shops. Coming out at last into what was left of the daylight we would meet young Salim on the Maidan exercising his Alsatian dog or his sports car. He was one of the gay young men about Zanzibar, always impeccably dressed in London clothes with suede shoes and ties from the Burlington Arcade. The sports car, presumably, was for prestige purposes, for there was nowhere in Zanzibar Island where one could go in it.

Many others greeted us on our walks. There was 'Bombay', for instance, who was a Government Guide and wore a metal badge when on duty, stamped with the words 'Guide No. 1'. I never found out whether Guides Numbers 2 and 3, or even 4, existed. At any rate, during eighteen months in Zanzibar, I never met them. But Guide No. 1 was constantly to be met with, especially when the mail boats were in. He invited the red-faced, sweating, camera-clicking tourists to allow themselves to be conducted round the sights under his guidance. Most of them looked both embarrassed and alarmed when he approached them, obviously fearing that suggestions were about to be made which would have to be indignantly repudiated—in front of female relatives, anyhow, and those rather nice people at the next table. Others obviously thought that some oriental sleight of hand was about to take place which would magically transfer from them to Bombay, money, wrist-watch, fountain pen, reticule, passport and travel tickets. But, in fact, as I got to know, Bombay was a dear old man, an honest and rather tragic old Arab sailor. He had excellent manners and was the soul of tact. Nothing out of place would ever have been said. Bombay was a 'Sidi boy', that is to say, a survivor of a large number of Arab and African ratings taken on as firemen and stokers in His Majesty's ships before and during the First

World War. They were called 'Sidi boys' by the navy because
they were subjects of the Seyyid, as the Sultan is known in his
dominions. There were several of them still surviving in Zanzibar when I was there. They were distinguished by that certain
something beneath their dark skins which everywhere marks
the old-style naval rating, directness, sophistication, self-pride.
They were also distinguished by the fluency with which they
spoke English, frequently with a broad cockney accent. It is
recorded that an Englishman once called at a friend's house
and was met at the door by his coal-black cook who said:

'Back in a jiffy, sir. Jest gorn dahn the road fer a ball o'
chalk!'

All the 'Sidi boys' drew a small pension from the Admiralty
and all were immensely proud of their arduous years in the
navy. To listen to old Bombay describing his service in the hot
stokeholds of coal-burning ships, and speaking of the Royal
Navy as though he were part of it, was a moving experience and
brought a lump into the throat.

Besides his fluent English, Bombay spoke passable French and
German, as well as his native Kiswahili and Arabic. He had a
working knowledge of the less attractive seaport towns of Great
Britain, France and Germany. Physically he was the remains
of a fine man and even now had immensely broad shoulders
and the remains of what had once been a powerful physique.
But he was getting old and so rheumatic that he walked with
difficulty with a big stick. He found it increasingly hard, with
his lame leg and stick, to do all the walking that being Guide
No. 1 required, pointing out the House of Wonders, the Sultan's
Palace, the Fort, the British Residency and the War Memorial
Museum and waiting while the cameras clicked. It was very
tiring. If he met you in the street while he was conducting a
party he would greet you loudly so that his clients could hear, a
kind of testimonial *en passant*.

'Good morning, sir. How are you to-day?'

But when you met him later on, when he had got rid of them,
he would say:

'A tiring day to-day, sir. A tiring day. Trade bad, too. They
don't want to spend the money nowadays. Well, thank you,
sir. You're very kind. *Asanta sana*.'

I am afraid that Bombay and his like, such as 'gully-gully'

men and pedlars, do not see humanity at its best. Fear, suspicion and meanness, often clothed in a rude and blustering
manner, must be the human characteristics that show themselves most often. It was surprising, I used to think, that
Bombay remained as gentle and honest as he did and that at
the end of his tiring and not very profitable day he could regard
with humour and relish the less attractive foibles of his patrons.

The Metropolis Hotel and Bar was often the place where our
evening strolls ended up. Bombay showed me the way there
on my first visit but when, subsequently, I tried to make my
way there alone I seemed to have lost the place. That was easy
enough in that maze of narrow streets, for all I could remember
of the whereabouts of the Metropolis was that to get to it you
passed an antique shop which had a sign over the door announcing 'Curiousities'. The 'curiousities' consisted of Arab coffee-
pots and brassware and very beautiful camphor-wood chests,
inlaid with brass, at very beautiful prices. I admired and came
away, and then lost 'Curiousities' and could not find it again
for weeks. Suddenly one forenoon when I was shopping, my
eye caught the word down a side street. I dived down it and
found, a little farther on, a faded sign which read 'Metropolis
Hotel and Bar'. I went inside, but there was no one there for it
was hot high noon. Only Scolastico Costa was dozing behind
the bar over his dog-eared and, to all but himself incomprehensible, account book. Even the radio was silent.

The Metropolis was one of the five pubs of Zanzibar, but the
most fashionable. This was a small number for the size of the
population because it is a Mohammedan community, and,
strictly, drinking is not allowed in it at all. Outwardly pro-
hibition was the rule. But there were many races and creeds
in the town to whom alcohol was not forbidden so that the pro-
hibition rule was relaxed in their favour. Nevertheless it was
necessary to obtain a licence to consume alcohol, or to be consumed by it. This might be a full licence, entitling the holder
to the worst excesses and permitting the consumption of spirits,
or it might be a partial one, permitting the holder to purchase
only the less expensive form of headache, such as is obtained by
drinking beer only. Europeans had no difficulty in obtaining a
licence for the most excruciating forms of hang-over. It was a
little red, pasteboard folder, very much like a motor driver's

licence at home. You got it with smiles and rather obvious jokes from a polite Indian clerk in the Municipal Office. But for a Mohammedan it was supposed to be impossible to obtain one. It was not impossible, however, for many of the clientele of the Metropolis were Moslems and all had full licences. Yet I often saw others turned away with a great show of strictness because they had none. I never discovered the secret, chiefly perhaps because I thought it better not to inquire too closely.

The Metropolis was a dingy, friendly place. Its walls, from which the plaster was peeling, were festooned with the dusty net-work of electric wires, like the web of an immense spider, which are a familiar sight in all the older houses in Zanzibar. There were advertisements for brands of beer all round the room and, in one corner, there was a piano which made odd noises when its notes were struck. There were round metal tables with metal chairs dotted about. As one stood or perched at the bar, which was defended by a formidable cage of wire, small boys and aged crones peeped and gesticulated at one through the door and through the inadequately curtained windows. They pointed at their open mouths, a gesture implying a demand for alms, and made other movements with other and more dubious implications. A radio or gramophone, and sometimes both at once, made a din against which it was necessary to shout to make oneself heard, proclaiming the gaiety and glamour of the Metropolis all down the street as far as 'Curiousities' and farther.

The Metropolis, like the other pubs of Zanzibar, was kept by a Goanese family. Each establishment had its own particular clientele, though it was the thing to do to stroll, or totter or crawl, from one to the other. One was frequented mostly by the wealthier Hindus who sat about talking rapidly in what sounded like Welsh, but was, in fact, Gujerati. Another was the rendezvous mainly of Goanese, equally wealthy and equally absorbed in what appeared to be earnest and profound debate. The conversation in both these establishments always appeared to be of deep and absorbing interest and it obviously was, for it was almost exclusively concerned with money. Another was patronized by the better educated Africans, often school teachers, customs officials and clerks. Here the talk was often conducted, especially if a European were present, in mellifluous and slightly old-fashioned English, spoken with beautiful deep, bell-like voices. The speakers wore hacking jackets or blue blazers with brass buttons and a crest on the breast pocket, grey flannels and suede shoes. Only they, of course, could possibly do so in such a climate. They had handkerchiefs projecting in an elegant manner from their cuffs. They parted their woolly hair and often wore glasses, for education seems to have an odd effect on the eyesight of Africans. The more educated they become the larger and thicker their spectacles. In this rendezvous the conversation was extremely intelligent and was apt to become so involved as to be difficult to keep pace with at all. I believe that the African's brain, when properly educated and trained, can be fully equal to that of the European but what is as yet lacking, I was told, is integrity. An African doctor I knew had a knowledge and skill equal to those of any of his European colleagues. Yet if he had a woman dying in childbirth and a party on the same night he would choose the latter without a moment's hesitation. The Hippocratic oath meant nothing. Similarly, in positions of trust involving the care of money, the hand still has a tendency to find its way into the till. Temptations to nepotism and corruption are often too strong, and as for the abuse of power— well, what is power for after all?

But the Metropolis was frequented mainly by young Arabs. It had a club-like and *gemütlich* air. The clientele used to sit at the metal tables with glasses of beer in front of them and hold forth for hours in Swahili, or in English if strangers like myself were present. There were some who were always there and treated the place, indeed, as though it were a club, running an account at the bar and always occupying the same table, like the *stammtisch* in a German café.

The Goanese family who owned and ran the Metropolis acted as hosts to all the patrons, watched them carefully from behind the wire cage, welcomed them in and shepherded them out. Other Goanese families similarly owned and ran the four other pubs in the town, and it is true to say that the Goanese owned and ran, or ran if they did not actually own, a very great deal, not only in Zanzibar but in East Africa generally. By means of industry, a remarkable aptitude for detail and, I suppose, the extraordinary blotting-paper memory which they seem to possess, these immigrants from Goa, the Portuguese colony on the west coast of India, have made themselves indispensable in many places in the new country where they have only recently arrived. They have, in many instances, also made themselves very wealthy. Your head clerk, your chief cashier, your foreman is nearly always a Goan. His knowledge of his own particular line seems to be encyclopaedic, his memory for the smallest detail rivalled only by that of the elephant. He is always there when wanted, at the strike of a bell, with the very file, the very letter, the very list of figures that is needed. Does he do it by listening at the key-hole? Or does he see into your brain and, beholding a horrible, windy, empty space there, proceed to occupy it? At any rate it is fairly safe to say that if, on any matter of business, you go into any office in Zanzibar, or Dar-es-Salaam, or Mombasa, or Nairobi for all I know, whether it be a Government office or that of a private firm, you will find behind a desk, with white blotting paper and telephones, a courteous European, usually an Englishman. He wears a white shirt, collar and tie and motions you to a comfortable chair.

'Good morning. Do sit down. What can I do for you?'

'Good morning. I came to inquire about—,' say, '—that consignment of bicycles expected on the *Kenya Castle*, or your outstanding account for Shs 5,000.00, or the new home for maladjusted young African ladies, or the town planning scheme for Nachingwea, or my new refrigerator'—or any other matter under the sun you like to mention.

'Oh yes. Yes. Now let me see. I'm so sorry—do have a cigarette.'

'Thanks.'

'Yes, well. I'm not quite in the picture, I'm afraid.'

He strikes a bell on his desk. A Swahili messenger appears.

'Ask Mr. Fernandez (or Mr. Gomez or Mr. Pereira or Mr. Costa) to come in.'

Almost before the messenger is out of the room a little man with a yellowish-brown face has materialized beside the desk, with a file or a letter or a sheet of figures in his hand.

'Oh, Mr. Fernandez (Gomez, Pereira or Costa), do you remember what happened about that consignment of bicycles expected on the *Kenya Castle* (or our outstanding account with

So-and-so's, or the home for maladjusted young African ladies, or the town planning scheme for Nachingwea, or this gentleman's new refrigerator or anything else)?'

Of course Mr. Fernandez does. 'Yes sir, here is the file, the correspondence or the figures.' He waits for a moment.

'No, sir. Not that letter. This one. These are the correct figures, sir. Those are last year's that you're looking at.'

'Oh yes, of course. Thank you, Mr. Fernandez (Gomez, Pereira or Costa).'

And he effaces himself, vanishing as swiftly and silently as he came. Nevertheless you realize that but for him the interview would have been, no doubt, a pleasant social occasion, possibly ending with a drink or even lunch at the club, but otherwise a waste of time.

Many of the Goans of East Africa are so recently arrived from their home on the other side of the Indian Ocean that they are still Portuguese subjects and speak Portuguese among themselves. Although they are largely of Indian descent there is a very large element of Portuguese blood in all of them. They feel Portuguese and, indeed, look it, being paler, more olive-skinned and European in appearance than their Indian forebears. Nothing makes a Goan angrier than to be mistaken for an Indian. Many of the Goans whom I met in Zanzibar had relatives in Goa. Some, indeed, still had their wives and families there and many firms in East Africa who have Goanese employees make special arrangements for them to take periodic leave in their native city.

The Goanese in East Africa, as in Goa itself, are devoutly and fervently Roman Catholic, a state of affairs which they owe to the Jesuits and to the missionary journey of St. Francis Xavier of 1542. In Zanzibar they attend the Roman Catholic Cathedral of St. Joseph and make up the large majority of the congregation which packs the great romanesque church to the doors at every mass.

The convent school of the Sacred Heart, a big building overlooking the sea, educates young Goans in the way they should go and it is a very good way. The little boys and girls, who can be seen coming out of school at midday and in the late afternoon, trotting along in busy groups with their satchels, are creditable imitations of those who can be seen emerging from

similar institutions all over the world. The little girls wear
gym tunics and chatter about their prep. Perhaps they have
crushes on the convent sisters. The boys are clean-limbed
and sprightly and keep themselves aloof from the soppy girls.
Only their complexions and their hair are different from their
small cousins far away in Europe. Watching them skipping
along in the hot sun I used to think how standardized and uniform the human race will be in generations to come. For there
only seems to be one kind of education and the young are
moving forward on a vast assembly belt. Yet, I suppose and
hope, occasionally some careless worker will put in a screw
wrong here or give a turn too much there and an oddity will
result who will like the wrong things, think the wrong thoughts,
like going to the wrong places and be really, I am afraid, not
quite up to sample.

Young Goanese are very up-to-date and westernized nowadays, but it is not long since the young Goanese women in
Zanzibar went about demurely and frumpishly in straight
plain frocks, flat heels and unalluring pig-tails. It was as the
Mother Church commanded. But since the cinemas have
burst into flower here and there about the town, the Goanese
girls have quite changed their ideas. Nowadays they do not do
so badly, except for a tendency to look as though they had
dipped their olive and often piquant faces into the flour tub.

The Costa family, who ran the Metropolis, consisted of
father and son and son-in-law. I never met the daughter, but
then one does not meet Portuguese ladies. They maintain a
near purdah system and are content to spend their lives having
large numbers of babies upstairs. It was the son-in-law,
Fernaldo, and the son, Scolastico, whom I knew since it was
they who presided behind the bar and made incomprehensible
but infallible signs in a very dog-eared account book. The
usage in bars and places where they sing in Zanzibar was quite
different from that which prevails in England. You did not
pay for your drinks as you bought them, but gave your order
with a wave of the hand and forgot all about it. You nodded to
Fernaldo or Scolastico when you wanted more. When at
midnight they closed the wire cage that fenced off the bar,
they referred to the book. What they had written there was
often rather shocking but it was law. There was no appeal.

On the other hand credit was freely given and some of our friends among the Costas' clientele owed quite large sums of money, which they were always going to pay quite soon. But not to-night.

Both Fernaldo and his brother-in-law, Scolastico, looked more Portuguese than Indian and spoke Portuguese to each other. Both were charming people in their own way. Fernaldo was very jolly and friendly and often sat with his customers at their tables, stood them drinks and was stood drinks by them. Towards midnight he often became very convivial. Once or twice he brought down to show us a little sleepy, sloe-eyed girl perched in the crook of his arm, with two white bows on either side of her forehead. She rubbed her eyes with her knuckles, yawned and buried her face in her father's shoulder. This was Senhorina Maria Francesca and she was bored with the whole affair. On some evenings Fernaldo passed through the bar resplendent in white shark-skin dinner jacket, black tie and black pocket handkerchief, leaving a lovable fragrance behind him as he went. There was a dance, one understood, at the Goan Club. But Scolastico seldom went out, did not drink and never sat at the metal tables with the customers. He spoke little, but brooded over his account book with a mild yet watchful expression, smiled and wrote things down. Two or three times a week he went to the cinema and was very knowledgable about the gods and goddesses of the screen. Shortly before midnight, when the bar closed, Costa Senior appeared in the background, a thin, white-haired old gentleman who smiled perpetually and with meaning. The meaning seemed to be quite clear, without the aid of any words. It was—'Will you now please all go home and let me get back to bed?' To add point to this interpretation he was never seen in anything but a rather unattractive pair of blue striped pyjamas. One gathered that he went to bed early and then roused himself at midnight in order to see his customers off the premises and the place duly locked up in accordance with the law. His manner conveyed that he really disapproved of all this drinking and that it was only by a curious twist of fortune that he found himself running an establishment that actually, in the line of business, encouraged that sort of thing.

But from the first day of the holy month of Ramadhan, when

the Sultan first sees the new moon and the guns are fired on the
Maidan, until he again sees it and the guns are fired at the
beginning of the tenth month, Costa Senior can sleep in peace.
He does not have to get up at midnight for the Metropolis
closes at nine. There is no point in keeping open any longer
for there are no customers. The tables are vacant and Victor
and I stay away, for no one would allow himself to be seen in a
bar during the holy month. About the middle of the month I
met handsome Salim in the street. Gone were the London-
made hacking jacket, the Sulka tie, the suede shoes. He wore the
long white kanzu and embroidered cap. His face had a fortnight's beard. He bowed gravely as he passed, with both
hands on his breast, and passed on with downcast eyes. Guide
No. 1 is not to be seen around the landing stage when passengers
come ashore and you need not fear that your female relatives
will overhear anything they should not.

3

The first ten days of the first month of the Mohammedan
year, the month of Mohurram, are sacred to all Moslems. For
the Sunnis this is the time of thanksgiving for the Creation, but
for the Shiites it is a time of mourning and penance. They
mourn for al-Hussein, second son of Ali, the fourth Caliph, and
of Fatimah, daughter of the Prophet.

Ali and Fatimah had two sons, al-Hassan and al-Hussein.
They were very different in character, for while Hassan was a
wild, extravagant and sensual young man, Hussein was retiring,
shy and irresolute. Their father said of them: 'Hassan is a
spendthrift, thinking of nothing but the pleasures of the table
and of entertaining. As to Hussein, he is mine and I am his.'

Hussein was born in the fourth or fifth year A.H. and lived
quietly at Medina until the accession of Yazid, the seventh
Sunni Caliph, at Damascus. Yazid was a tyrant who resolved
to put an end to all schisms is Islam. He issued orders to all the
Governors under him to extract an oath of obedience from their
subjects and to kill all who hesitated or refused. For some time
before his accession the people of the Shia faith in the now

vanished city of Kufa, 60 miles south-west of Baghdad, had been intriguing to get Hussein to come to their city and lead them in revolt as the true leader of the Faithful. Until the accession of Yazid he had turned a deaf ear to their entreaties, but when presented with the oath of allegiance to the new Caliph he refused to swear and took refuge in Mecca. He also wrote to a cousin of his, Muslim-bin-Akir, in Kufa to sound the situation there. Muslim replied advising him to come to Kufa and, accordingly, Hussein set out, intending to place himself at the head of an army of the Faithful. Caliph Yazid, however, got wind of the affair and replaced the easy-going Governor of Baghdad by another, the ruthless Governor of Basrah, Ubaid Allah-bin-Zayid. The new Governor drove the conspirators into premature revolt, captured Hussein's cousin, Muslim, and sent his head to the Caliph as a present. He stationed outposts and cavalry patrols on all the roads leading to Kufa from the west in order to intercept Hussein should he attempt the journey. One of these detachments met Hussein, with his escort of relatives and followers, at a place called Kerbala on the River Euphrates and called upon him to surrender. 'We are commanded as soon as we meet you,' the Captain of the Cavalry said, 'to bring you to Kufa, to the presence of Ubaid Allah-bin-Zayid.' But Hussein replied that he would sooner die and ordered his escort to ride on. The cavalry then made a movement to cut him and his followers off from the river, hoping to reduce them by thirst. 'I have no commision to fight with you,' said the Captain of Cavalry, 'but I am commanded not to part with you until I have conducted you to Kufa.' From this Hussein was led to believe that, as the son of Caliph Ali, son-in-law of the Prophet, his person was held inviolate by his enemies and that there must be sympathizers among the opposing cavalry force who would not harm him. However, at this moment there appeared on the scene one Omar-bin-Said at the head of 4,000 horsemen on the march to Dhaila. If there were any hesitants among Ubaid Allah's men, there was none among Omar's. He summoned Hussein for the last time to surrender and, when he refused, fell upon him and his followers and slew them to the last man. When Hussein saw the horsemen bearing down upon him, he clasped his small son to his arms and cried out, 'There is nothing save these horsemen between us and the black-eyed girls of paradise.' And he fell wounded in many places.

This tragic event took place on the 10th day of Mohurram, in the year 61 A.H. (10th October, A.D. 680). In memory of it all the people of the Shia faith all over the world to this day mourn and do penance for the first ten days of the month of Mohurram every year. On the tenth day in Zanzibar the Ithna'ashariyah or 'Twelvers' do public penance through the streets and mortify the flesh.

The mosque of the Ithna'ashariyah is a gaunt and shabby building in a narrow street, smelling of spices. The tall houses on either side seem to lean towards one another so that only shafts of sunlight pierce the mote-laden air between them. There is a shrine outside the mosque with the effigy of a white horse, under which is written in fading letters, 'In Memory of the Tragedy of Kerbala'. The white horse is the horse of Hussein which he was riding on the way to Kufa and the monument is as touching and pious, for all its crudity and shabbiness, as any of the Christian shrines that adorn the roadsides of Roman Catholic countries. During the first ten days of Mohurram, which I think fell in October in 1951, the mosque, the shrine and many of the humble houses round about were heavily draped in black. The people who lived in that part of the town went about wearing black clothes, in mourning for Hussein, the women draped in black and veiled, the men in black shirts and black trousers or shorts.

After dark on the tenth evening, which was a lovely starry night, the mosque was the centre of a great chattering crowd which thronged all the streets around it, especially that leading to the bridge over the creek. For this would be the route of the Ithnasheri penitents who would walk through the streets and chastise themselves in public. The Europeans said it was a revolting sight and that it was extraordinary that such things should be allowed in these days, but if I hadn't seen it I certainly shouldn't miss it.

'My dear, the blood!' said a lady in the hotel over her morning coffee. 'All over the spectators and all up the sides of the houses! I've seen it once, but I really couldn't bear to see it again. Of course, if you've never seen it . . .'

Religious occasions in the east are usually rather a muddle, rather badly organized, very friendly and jolly, even on grue-some occasions like fire-walking, and very smelly. There is a general air of vague disorder, with people milling about in an unregulated manner and very important people hurrying to and fro looking agitated but not, so far as one can see, achieving anything much. This is largely due, I think, to a lack of the flair for organizing these things on the part of those responsible for the arrangements. The organizers are almost certainly not being paid much, if at all, for their services, but since it may be taken as an axiom in the east that nobody ever does anything for absolutely nothing, one must suppose that their services are given for rewards of an intangible nature, a place in paradise, perhaps, for prestige, for 'face'. In any case the organization is apt to take on the character of a competition, the organizers not pulling together but each trying to outrival the other. Thus it may happen that there are too many people giving orders and not enough obeying them. A friendly sort of jostling chaos is the result. The amiability with which strangers are received into the midst of it all is delightful. My companion and I, arriving on the scene, were greeted with nods and smiles as we wove and pushed through the crowd, which smilingly made way for us, handing and pushing us to the front. We had emerged from the Metropolis and so were not, I am afraid, in a penitential mood such as befitted the occasion, but neither did the crowd seem to be. A man was weaving in and out among the people carrying a sheaf of papers in his arms. He was uttering cries which in English might have been interpreted as 'Read all abaht it!' When he saw us his face brightened and he eagerly thrust several of his leaflets upon us. 'The Night of Martyrdom,' I read upon a black-bordered sheet.

'In Hussein's bosom was smouldering the dormant volcano of the feelings of Islam. If he swore fealty to Yazid that would have meant selling himself, Islam, the rights of the Muslims, and the assets of the nation to the pleasure of Yazid who obeyed Islam more in the breach than obedience. He preferred to die an honourable death to a dishonourable living. So widespread was the baneful influence of irreligion that Islam appeared bordering extinction. The degradation of life and the spiritual stagnation was the order of the day. Human right and human soul was a plaything. Gambling and drinking was the pastime and all sorts of indignities were heaped upon the public by the Tyrant of Damascus, who assumed the mantile of the Prophet.'

But alas! 'Who cares a damn who died at Salamis?' In Zanzibar they still gamble and drink for all the blood spilt upon the desert sand by Hussein and his noble army of martyrs.

'On the 2nd Mohurram', I read, 'Hussein with his family and helpers was halted at Kerbala by an enemy detachment. Hussein took up the position on a mound and formed a triangle of his small army. From the 2nd to the 10th the enemies were pouring down the plains like swarms of locusts. . . . Some twelve thousand strong guarded the Euphrates to ban the water on Hussein. From the 7th the supply of water in the tents of Hussein was exhausted. . . . A terrible thirst, unequalled in history, followed. The women screamed for water and the children swooned in the tents. The heat of the day aggravated the pangs of thirst and hunger so much that the flower of the youth of Hussein appeared weltering for want of moisture. . . . Never was so few overwhelmed by so many and never was so much achieved in so short hours by so few.'

I seemed to have heard something of the same sort before somewhere.

Someone came forward and smilingly begged us to stay and watch the procession from the wide entrance of his shop. He placed chairs for us and motioned to us to be seated, so we sat down among his sacks of maize and mealies, and suffered ourselves to have whisky and water pressed upon us in such proportions that I began to wonder before long whether I should see several processions or none at all. However, I was saved from this predicament because some ten minutes before the procession was due to pass our host calmly but firmly relieved us of our glasses. He explained that it was not seemly for anyone, even an unbeliever, to be seen taking alcohol upon such an occasion.

First there came a mock procession staged by young Sunnis, the rival sect, the followers of the True Path. It was intended to ridicule the heretic Ithnasheri procession which was to follow. But it was a sad little joke. In times past such an insult, perhaps, if this company of mild young Indians could be called such, might have touched off a riot, knives might have been drawn and blood have flowed. The police and presently troops might have been involved. But these slowly moving groups of shy and self-important young men could not arouse any emotion. They were so frequently held up by their inattentive audience, which kept milling and jostling around them, that they could not keep the form of a procession and, indeed, could scarcely make their way along the street, but were often brought to a halt and stood with the lights from the open shop fronts shining on their dark skins and blue-black hair. They carried arrangements of cardboard, tinsel and artificial flowers which were supposed to imitate the much more beautiful ones we were to see when the true procession passed. But the crowd paid little attention and hardly saw them. It was listening.

We could hear a distant threefold rhythm and the sound of indistinct chanting coming from the direction of the Ithnasheri mosque. As the sound grew louder it became like that of a heart beating a triple pulse inside a suit of chain mail, while the chant took shape and filled the lighted street and the dark sky that brooded above it. It had something sinister in it, like the echo of that terrible and bloody deed done long ago in the desert. It was an agonized refrain, holding a note of hysteria and threaded through with the oft-repeated cry, growing every second more distinct, 'Hussein! Hussein! O! Husseini!' And the cry was followed every time by the dull triple beat of chain mail, striking with a sombre pulse, one, two, three, 'Hussein! O! Husseini!'

They were visible at first as a confusion of moving lights down the length of the narrow street. Presently we could see that these were lights carried by small African boys who ran before the procession with hurricane lamps on their heads. They wore broad grins of pride and pleasure, delighted with the important role they were playing on this public occasion, though Hussein, one felt, meant even less to them than he did to us. They were enjoying the fun. The van of the true procession consisted of young Indians carrying the white hand of Hussein, fashioned in cardboard, mounted on the top of poles draped with white cloth. Then came others carrying, by means of supports made of poles, with two handles at each end, the weird and lovely symbols that once a year, on this occasion only, are brought out of the temple and carried round the town, like the effigies and relics in Roman Catholic towns. For the rest of the year they were kept in the Ithnasheri mosque and no doubt looked dim enough there, dingy with dust and catching no bright lights. But seen now, as they were borne along under the lights from the naked bulbs in the shop fronts and the hurricane lamps, they were unbelievably beautiful, fantastic and gay and seemed to tower aloft, above the heads of those who carried them, into the shadows. No doubt each one meant something, but I have no idea what it was. They were like miniature temples, with domes and minarets, decorated with tinsel, artificial flowers, little bits of coloured glass and tiny electric bulbs. If you looked closely, which you should never do, you saw that they were rather worn and shabby, as though they had taken part in many such processions and were themselves a little tired of all this devotion. They must have been built a long time ago and never repaired very much, for Indians hardly ever repair anything. The dust of twelve months' dark repose in the mosque was still upon them. Some of the little coloured lights strung about them were out. Some of the artificial flowers had come off and had not been replaced. Some of the domes and minarets were in poor shape, broken and cracked. But at a slight distance, seen in this kind and shifting light, they seemed like apparitions in a dream. So did their bearers, who walked with slow steps and downcast eyes as though in a trance.

Behind them, rather an anti-climax, came a life-size effigy of Hussein's white horse, borne along on a rickety four-wheeled trolley. This was a great pity because the horse was really supposed to be the centre-piece of the show. Only a year ago the part of this valiant steed had been taken by a real live white horse. He was, in fact, the only horse on the island and led an idyllic existence all the other days of the year, flicking flies and cropping grass under the coconut trees outside the town. His public appearance in the Ithnasheri procession was all the work he did during the year. But in the year before this procession, that of 1951, he incontinently died, presumably of a surfeit of pleasure and idleness, and now his place had to be taken by this rather regrettable and undistinguished effigy.

The street was narrow where we were standing but it widened out to our right in the direction of the mosque, and to our left ran into a small square before it came to the bridge over the creek leading to Ngambo. As the rhythmic chanting sound approached we saw the repeated rise and fall of many arms above the heads of the people. 'Hussein! O! Husseini!' the voices shouted in a wild uncanny lamentation.

Suddenly the street was filled with half-naked figures. They carried lengths of fine chain in each hand, raised them aloft and brought them down again and again upon their breasts. Their skins shone with sweat, which stood upon their brows, and from their breasts trickles of blood ran down to their navels in dark stripes. Where the street opened out to the left to form a small square they drew up in two rows facing each other. '*Hussein! Hussein! O! Husseini!*' they cried again with a wild abandon and, raising their arms, brought them down with a dull thump once, twice, three times upon their chests.

There were several groups of flagellants and, as each group passed the open-fronted shop where we stood, I could see some in whose eyes there seemed to shine a glare of madness such as grips the devotee and the fanatic. Some, indeed, were in the state of trance and semi-collapse that one sees in the religious ceremonies of the Hindus, those fire-walking, cheek-skewering exhibitions so incomprehensible to us Christians and nominal members of the C. of E. The breasts of these, more holy than their fellows, were raw from self-infliction and the blood trickled down to their waists. They made their flesh suffer in truth. But others, I noticed, made a feint of their self-chastisement and were content with one stroke that drew a bead of scarlet among many that were less effective. It was only when one saw these that one noticed that the chains they carried were lengths of lavatory chain.

We left the shop, after thanking the proprietor for his hospitality, and pushed through the crowd to the little square. As the last group of penitents formed up, raised their arms and brought their chains down with a thud upon their chests, crying '*Hussein! O! Husseini!*' I caught the eye of one of them, a boy of about fifteen. There was an elderly man next to him in the row in an advanced stage of religious ecstasy. The boy, seeing my eye upon him, threw out his chest for the next blow and glanced down with pride at the thin pencil line of blood he had produced among the few sparse hairs which grew there.

4

Mohammedans do not believe in the divinity of Christ. Though they revere His teaching they hold that He was but one of a long line of prophets of whom Mohammed was the last and the greatest and the true Prophet. What Christians of all races, colours and languages in Zanzibar believe they affirm in the two great Christian churches whose pointed towers overtop the mountainous landscape of corrugated iron which is Zanzibar seen from above, in angel's-eye view.

When David Livingstone returned from Africa in the fifties of the nineteenth century his stories of the cruelties inflicted upon Africans by the Arab slave traders roused the public conscience at home and, as a result of his appeal to the universities of Oxford and Cambridge, there came into being in 1856 the Universities' Mission to Central Africa. It started work in the Shire district of Nyasaland, but in those days the climate of that part of Africa was deadly and during the first year the leader of the mission, Bishop Mackenzie, and most of his helpers died. The mission therefore moved to the coast and chose Zanzibar as its base and jumping-off point because of its central position. The mission began work in 1864 with five little boys from an Arab dhow, a present from Sultan Majid. But presently other boys joined them and at length there came into being a college, St. Andrew's, outside Zanzibar where African boys were trained for the ministry. It exists and flourishes to-day. When the slave market was finally closed down in 1873 the Universities' Mission, then led by Bishop Steere, writer of the first grammar and compiler of the first dictionary of the Kiswahili language, bought part of the site. The rest was given to the mission by a rich Hindu. Here, then, under the Bishop's personal direction, arose the Cathedral Church of Christ with its altar on the spot where once stood the whipping post of the slave market. It is said that the Bishop designed the building himself, attending to every detail of its construction, and trained the masons and craftsmen who worked on it. It was a labour of love and to-day it draws large congregations from among all the races in the town, and the devoted and scholarly Bishop lies buried behind the High Altar. No one, however, could say that it is a particularly beautiful church for the style is a curious sort of Arabic-Gothic the like of which never was on land or sea. And the acoustics are such that, before the invention of microphones and loud-speakers, anyone unfamiliar with the Anglican ritual, who might have chanced to wander into it, would have gathered very little idea of what was going on beyond the chancel arch.

The Roman Catholic Cathedral of St. Joseph was built by the Fathers of the Society of the Holy Ghost at about the same time as the Anglican Cathedral.

The Roman Catholic ritual gives to the Oriental and to the African all that he craves for in the way of mystery, awe and adoration. It is gaining ground in Zanzibar, no less than elsewhere in Africa and the East. On the festivals of the Church, but especially on Easter and Christmas Day, great crowds of people of every race, colour and tongue pack the Cathedral to the doors. Unless you have a ticket you cannot get in by the west door where a dense throng collects for hours before Mass begins. But you can go in by the side door through the Sacristy, and you come suddenly from that cool, twilight, stone-smelling place into the presence of a kneeling and murmurous multitude. The candles they hold in their hands are like stars reflected in troubled water. They shift and wink continually and shine fitfully on dark faces. You might so easily, but for these dusky faces catching the light, be in some great church in France or Italy. The Romanesque arches soar up out of reach of the constellations of lights to the flaking cherubs and the mildewed paintings of saints. Goanese acolytes with rapt demeanour swing the censers and rows of little choristers in red cassocks wink and giggle and fidget. The people stir and murmur in the gloom of the nave, and children cough and wail in the side aisles. When the moment comes the whole great company, black, brown and white, moves forward in a long slow procession to line the altar rail, the British Government servant and his wife, the Indian merchant, the trim well-dressed Goanese, the African in his 'kikoi' and singlet, the woman with her sleeping infant nodding on her back. They all stand and wait their turn while the Irish father moves along the kneeling line.

On Christmas Eve, after my Swahili lesson, I dropped Abdulla as usual at the little mosque just as the people were going in to pray.

'To-morrow,' he said, 'will be your *Siku Kuu*, your great day. Will you not pray on your *Siku Kuu*?'

'Perhaps I will,' I said.

Chapter Seven

PEMBA

I

I<small>N</small> the Colonial Service all 'expatriate' officers, as those not native to the colony are always now, somewhat disparagingly, called, are allowed to take annually a certain amount of what is known as 'local' leave. This is additional to the 'vacation' leave which, once in a tour of two, three or four years, allows the exile to go home to his native land in order to refresh his body in a cool climate, his eyes with the sight of green fields and his spirit with familiar scenes and faces. Local leave must be taken in the colony where the officer is serving, or sufficiently near it for him to be speedily recalled within a stipulated time should his presence become suddenly necessary. The amount of local leave allowed varies from colony to colony, as does the amount of vacation leave and the length of the tour of duty. So also do the rules which govern the distance from the colony it is permissible to go for local leave. In Zanzibar, as in most colonies and protectorates, one was allowed to take a fortnight's local leave a year and one could spend it at any place within a day or so by air or sea.

In most, if not all, colonies the Government owns and maintains a number of holiday bungalows where officials and their families can spend their local leave. The amenities, convenience and desirability of these rest-houses, as places in which to relax for a fortnight, are graded according to the rank of the officials using them. Highly paid senior secretaries spend their holidays in rather pleasanter, more commodious and more convenient rest-houses than do lower paid, less senior secretaries, who, in their turn, have rather more comfortable holidays than still lower paid junior officers. There is usually rather a rush for these rest-houses and you have to apply well in advance for a fortnight in one suitable to your rank. You will, in due course, be notified when the bungalow will be available. On the given date you transport yourself, your wife, your children, your servants, your bedding, linen and crockery to the place where you will enjoy your fortnight of relaxation. You yourself may enjoy it, but it is doubtful if your wife will. All the family housekeeping has to go on just the same, whether this is a holiday or not, except that the cook or the ayah or both have decided not to come. They hate to be uprooted and so someone in their family, usually the inevitable mother, is sick and has to be nursed. Shops are miles away and the nearest Indian store has only the barest necessities. The lighting is entirely by paraffin lamp and so is the cooking if you have not brought your cookboy with you. All the water has to be carried from a well and drinking water must be boiled. The children, who are deliriously happy for the first few days, get bitten by insects, develop heat rash, hurt themselves on the coral rocks, get overtired in the sun and finish up every day with screams and yells. But you yourself may enjoy it all quite well—at first at any rate. For the first few days you bathe before breakfast. The early morning is the best time of day out here, you always say. You bathe again after breakfast, at which there were no eggs because something has gone wrong with the primus stove.

'Tea tastes rather funny, doesn't it, dear?'

'I daresay, dear. It's the tinned milk. Don't fuss.'

When you have your second bathe you go goggling with a mask and breathing tube. Great fun—you could do it for hours.

'Really wonderful what you can see on that reef, dear. You really ought to come and have a try.'

'Don't be silly, darling. What time have I got for that sort of thing? I've got the lunch to think of.'

Anything you like doing is always called 'that sort of thing', you notice.

After lunch you rest. Wonderful to be able to. After all, that is what you have come for. 'Oh, for goodness sake! What's the matter now?'

'Tony took my bucket away and pushed me so's I nearly fell down on a sharp rock and cut myself.'

'Well, never mind. So long as you didn't quite cut yourself. Now run along, because Daddy's resting.'

'But Tony's took my bucket.'

'Tony! Give June her bucket—at once, do you hear?'

'Well, she took my starfish and put it in her bucket and I can't use my bucket because it's part of the entrance to the dry dock and I can't take it away because I've got a big aircraft carrier in there having some new plates put on. I do think it's beastly of June, she never plays properly.'

After tea, which is rather late, you read until the sun is below the yard-arm.

'What about a little something, darling?'

'What, dear? Oh, all right. I'll join you as soon as I can, only I must put the children to bed first.'

'I say, darling! Don't make so much noise, you children. I can't hear myself think. Where's Mummy? I say, darling!'

'Yes, dear. What is it?'

'I can't find the gin.'

'Oh God! Don't say we've forgotten it! I knew there was something.'

After dinner ('I'm afraid we'll have to have a cold meal to-night. The *duka* doesn't keep primus prickers. I'll simply have to run into town to-morrow and get some at Haji Abdulla's.') you read some more. But hurricane lamps are not very satisfactory. All the insects in the world come and gyrate round them. If you sit near the lamp it is too hot and the insects drive you crazy, fly into your face, tickle your neck and fall on to your book. If you push the lamp away you cannot see. When the darkness falls the silver moonlight is loud with the din of crickets and very soon the mosquitoes drive you under the mosquito net and to bed. What a pity the Government provides such hard beds!

In about a week you begin to feel a little restless.

'Did you say you were going into town this morning, dear?'

'No, I don't think so. I don't think I need to to-day. Why?'

'Oh, nothing. I just wondered, that's all.'

In two more days you have finished that amusing travel book. There is always goggling, of course, but you have got rather sunburnt on the back and you don't think you'll do that to-day.

'If you're going into town to-day, dear, I think I'll come with you. I want to go to the club library and get something to read.'

'I shouldn't bother. I can take your list in and get something from it. I've got to go to the club anyway. You stay here and have a nice swim.'

'Well now, really! You know perfectly well—at least, if you don't you ought to because I've said it often enough—that if there's one thing I dislike more than another it is somebody else choosing my books for me. My list isn't complete at all and something may have come in that I might like which is not on the list, and if you go there with just that list you might miss it altogether and it'll be weeks and weeks before I get a chance to read it. Even now you don't know what I like and what I don't like. The last time you chose a book for me that was not on my list I couldn't read the beastly thing. Some tommy rot all about sex. . . .'

'All right, dear. I was only suggesting. Don't fuss!'

Many people, however, are more gregarious and many in Zanzibar preferred to go up country on the mainland to a place where they could sit by a fire in the evening, get their thick clothes out of moth balls and sleep under a blanket at night. For a single man, anyhow, rest-houses were not to be thought of. Unless one was passionately devoted, as some undoubtedly were but I was not, to the sport of underwater fishing and could organize a large party of congenial companions, which I could not, a rest-house holiday merely meant an elaborate form of solitary confinement.

Civil servants are quite ruthless about their leave. If it is due to them, and the time for it has arrived, they will take it even if earth's foundations are trembling. Let them tremble. It was, therefore, expected that every year one would duly take one's fortnight of local leave without question. Consternation was caused if one said one did not think one particularly wanted to take it.

'Oh, but you must take it, you know.'

'Must I? Why?'

'Well, it's due to you.'

'I haven't got to take it simply because it's due to me, have I?'

This was obviously a novel and quite heretical attitude of mind.

'We encourage officers to take their leave as it falls due, you know.'

By 'encouraging' someone to do something is meant inferring that it is really rather disgraceful and letting down the side not to do it.

'But I've nowhere to go.'

'Why not go up to M——?' This was a place some two hundred miles inland from the coast of Tanganyika. I have forgotten the name of it. People frequently went there on local leave from Zanzibar and stayed in a large guest-house there, frequented by the gregarious and the convivial. It was not on the railway and you flew to Tabora or somewhere by East African Airways and were then driven in the hotel car for the remaining sixty or seventy miles. It was a lovely place among the hills, everyone said, with a cool dry climate, English flowers growing in the large hotel garden, log fires in the evening and blankets at night.

'Yes, but what should I do there?'

'Do? My dear fellow, plenty to do. There's a very good eighteen-hole golf-course.'

'But I don't play golf.'

'Very good tennis courts, too, and there's riding.'

'Yes, I see. But there are very good tennis courts here so I don't have to go 250 miles up country to do that. And I'm frightened of horses.'

It was at this point that Keith and Marie Young came to my rescue.

'We're going to Pemba for some months. I'm going to do a survey. Why not come and spend a fortnight with us, if you've never seen our other island? You could even help me with my survey.'

Keith was, and still is, a doctor in the Colonial Medical Service and his wife, Marie, had been a nurse. They had been great friends of mine since I first arrived in Zanzibar and laughed at the things I laughed at. Our conversation was always that distillation of sense and nonsense that makes talk enjoyable. They had a flat at the top of a fine old Arab house near the Law Courts and, in spite of the fact that the large, handsome rooms with their heavy arches and pillars had been carved up in such a way as to destroy their architectural beauty altogether, Marie had made the place charming. I used to arrive early and stay late. I talked far too much and drove chortling back to Mazzizini early in the morning.

I always enjoy the society of doctors. Their shop talk is more interesting to me than most and they are usually what the French call '*sympathique*'. There is no English word for this. 'Sympathetic' does not quite convey the same sense, which embraces tolerance, understanding, breadth of mind, gentleness, humour. All these things come from contact with suffering humanity, from seeing life with the lid off and from the knowledge, born of these experiences, that scarcely any one is evil but that almost everyone is frail. And that life in this sad world is altogether too difficult for many.

Keith specializes in tuberculosis of the lungs and had already carried out a survey of this disease, designed to provide an estimate of its incidence among all sections of the population, among the inhabitants of Zanzibar Island. He was going to Pemba for some months to carry out a similar survey there. It was simple, though tedious, work. He took as large a sample of the population as possible. On the skin of each individual, usually just below the nape of the neck between the shoulder blades, he placed, in the shape of a V, a light smear of jelly containing an extract of tubercle bacilli, and covered it with plaster. Seventy-two hours later he re-examined these individuals, or those of them who consented to present themselves for re-examination. Some showed a slight skin reaction under the plaster, while others showed none at all. A reaction indicated that the person had already been sensitized to the tubercle bacillus either by a very slight infection or by an actual attack of the disease. Those who showed no reaction had never been infected by the bacillus at all. The difficulty was to obtain a large enough sample of the population. The number of those on whose brown or black nape he placed a dressing had to be several times larger than the number required to give a representative sample of the population because only a proportion of those who turned up for the first operation, the application of the dressing, would bother to turn up for the second one, its removal. As is usual, the poor and uneducated thought the doctor was a magician about to work a miracle. When no miracle occurred they lost interest. In addition to this difficulty was the fact that the people in

Zanzibar were suffering from a surfeit of surveys. It was the
latest craze. The Medical Department conducted surveys of the
incidence of various diseases, the Health Department worried
about mosquitoes, drinking water and sanitary arrangements,
the Education Department were concerned about intelligence
quotas and school attendance. Not unnaturally a feeling was
developing in the villages that all this was rather a bore and an
impertinence to boot. It remained to be seen whether the
people of Pemba had been less or more surveyed than the people
of Zanzibar.

2

The steamship *Al-Said*, which made the passage from Zanzibar to Wete, in Pemba, once a week, was a ship rather after my
own heart. Her slim, elegant lines, tall thin funnel and raked
masts showed that she belonged to the English Augustan age of
Edward VII. She was of the same vintage as the old *Mauretania*,
the *Lusitania* and the *Titanic*. The brass-work in her cabins was
worn paper thin with years of polishing and in her dining saloon
was a portrait of His Highness the Sultan looking very young
with a full black beard. As she lay at the jetty things whined
softly in her entrails. She was a coal-burner and every so often
moved majestically from her anchorage in the roads to the
quayside and lay there getting grubbier and grubbier, while
endless chains of labourers, covered from head to foot in coal
dust, trooped up one gangway with baskets of coal on their
heads and down another with the baskets empty, chanting
incessantly and enveloping the ship in black gritty clouds.
   The departure of the *Al-Said* every Thursday evening for
Pemba was something of a function in Zanzibar. Crowds of
people of all races assembled on the quay to bid good-bye to
their friends. It is about fourteen hours' passage and, since as
yet there is no air route, it is, in this modern age, quite a
journey. The *Al-Said* always left the harbour packed to the
rails with deck passengers, for most of the Arabs and Africans
made the overnight journey under the stars with their families
and all their possessions around them. The foredeck and the

alleyways were thronged with a black and brown multitude, the men mostly white-robed, the women in brightly coloured kangas or in black bui-bui. They came on board with all their voluminous luggage, making a cheerful hubbub and a great deal of cackling laughter. They spread their mats on every available inch of the deck and gradually settled themselves down in family groups, surrounded by their friends who were bidding them farewell. After the ship had left the harbour the noise of their chatter died down and you heard only the swish of the bow wave, the pulse of the engines and the fretful cries of children. The families composed themselves for sleep, having first said their prayers facing the bows in the direction of Mecca. The women, before they slept, pulled their kangas over their heads and drew their children to their breasts. But when, towards midnight, the ship ran out of the lee of Zanzibar Island, the swell from the North-East Monsoon was enough to upset these comfortable arrangements and send many of these poor people, just settling into their first sleep, scrambling to the rail. Others, who had evidently made the journey before, had provided themselves with receptacles of various sorts for which they languidly reached and used as though in a trance.

On the first-class deck space, which was occupied by the Europeans, mostly Government officials, and a few of the richer Indians and Arabs, the farewell party became extremely convivial before the ship sailed, and you might have imagined that evening that I was going on a honeymoon. When it was over and the ship, silently and with dignity, drew away from the quay I went below to my cabin which I shared with an Irish padre. Later in the night the heat in the cabin became stifling because we were on the lee side of the ship and the fan could only blow its blasts of vitiated air on to the upper bunk, where the padre was lying, and missed the lower one where I was lying. I got up very early, therefore, before dawn, dressed quietly in the dark and went on deck. The first-class deck space was empty and I sat in a deck-chair and watched the morning come.

On this deck there was a luxurious suite consisting of a stateroom and a bedroom with its own lavatory. It was panelled in dark mahogany and had a bed with brass knobs. It was used by the Sultan and the Sultana on the occasions when they travelled by the *Al-Said* to visit Pemba or, more rarely, Mombasa, and by the British Resident likewise, when he travelled. At other times, that is to say during most of the year, it was assigned to the most senior Government official taking passage and his wife and family. If no one sufficiently grand to merit the royal suite were travelling it was kept locked, but this was seldom for there was nearly always someone on board who considered that he qualified to occupy the royal state room. Inevitably skirmishes broke out over this matter, for the suite was far more comfortable than any other accommodation on board, and it was an affair of precedence and honour. One of these minor engagements occurred on the night I travelled and I listened with ghoulish glee from a distance.

'Oh dear, oh dear! How very tiresome! Really most difficult! I was given to understand quite definitely that I could have the suite on the return journey as well. My wife isn't at all a good sailor and she finds the heat so trying. . . .'

'Well, I'm awfully sorry, but I'm afraid I shall really have to insist. I have my wife and daughter with me and my wife's rheumatism . . . Of course, I wouldn't mind a bit if I were alone.'

'Oh no, of course. I quite understand. It's all the fault of those wretched clerks at the shipping office. Really, it's too bad! I wouldn't be at all surprised if my wife had a relapse.'

And as I sat watching the day increase over the green and feathery shore of the island, inhaling the sweet scents of the newly awakened earth, I heard from the royal suite the triumphant snores of the victors.

The passengers were stirring down on the well-deck. Some were spreading out their mats for prayer, others were fetching water to wash themselves while others were rinsing their arms and hands and feet, or cleaning their teeth with sticks frayed at the ends as is the native habit. Four or five old gentlemen, unable to find enough space among the crowd below, came diffidently up the companion ladder to the empty first-class deck, carrying their prayer mats. Just as they were about to lay them down they saw me in the half-light sitting in my deckchair. Confused and embarrassed, they began to retreat down the companion ladder.

'*Karibuni, mabwana!*—Welcome, gentlemen!' I called to

them and, rising, walked away down the deck and continued
watching the dawn from a place near the funnel. The elders
smiled, bowed, laid down their mats and bowed themselves
down before Allah as each had done every morning for over
seventy years. The Irish padre came on deck at that moment
with his rosary and his prayer book. All the world was already
at prayer below him on the foredeck, as were the elders on the
first-class deck and so, in a way, was I. The sun was above the
tree-tops of Pemba Island before the passengers and the padre
had finished.

''Tis extraordinary the hold their religion has on these
people!' mused the padre, with satisfaction, leaning over the
rail by my side with his rosary in his hands.

The anchorage at Wete lies on the west coast of the island
about a third of the total length of the coast from the northern-
most point. To reach it the ship steams down the great open
lagoon that flanks the western seaboard of the island. On her
port side are the low flat islets of black coral rock, undercut
and overhanging, that are a feature of the fringes of the East
African coast and of many islands of the Western Indian
Ocean. A tough scrub grows along their flat tops and terns
were fluttering above them. On the ship's starboard side the
green, plumed shores of the island came down to the lagoon,
the coconut palms giving place at the water's edge to mangroves
which seemed to be wading out into the lagoon with a million
spidery legs. The lagoon itself, pale pastel in the morning light,
lay smooth as polished glass around us and we drew a widening
arrow across it. Long arms of the lagoon ran into the land and
lost themselves among the greenness. Here and there upon the
mirror-like surface a ring appeared and faded where a fish
jumped or a tern touched the water with its sharp beak. Fishermen sat motionless in their canoes and watched us pass,
remotely and without apparent interest. Wete itself lies at
the end of one of the long arms of the lagoon on a considerable
rise where the lagoon peters out into a river mouth with mangroves. The ship cannot get very close to the shore but anchors
a long way out and motor-boats ply to and fro taking off the
passengers, while lighters arrive in strings for the cargo. Keith
came out in a motor-boat and met me. I was having one of
those moments, that are apt to occur on any journey, when one

wonders rather anxiously about one's luggage, but does not quite like to fuss too much. My bag had been whisked ashore in another boat and I was thinking of performing the operation known as 'getting hold of someone'.

'Look here! I'm a little worried about my . . . I suppose it will be all right, will it? . . . Oh, I see. Yes, thank you. . . . I just wondered. . . . Oh, yes, there it is.'

And it was, sitting on the jetty waiting for me all alone when we came alongside. No one in the gay and chattering crowd of Arabs and Africans, small boys and lazybones, who thronged the jetty to see the motor-boats arrive, had bothered about it.

Wete is a long, shabby, shambling ribbon development of shanty shops and unprepossessing temporary-looking erections that trickles along the roads leading out of the town for miles. There is a fruit and vegetable market under some trees where the lazybones lounge about and chatter and laugh and the coffee sellers wander to and fro clinking their porcelain cups. Many of the shops have a gala appearance by reason of the festoons of brilliantly coloured kangas that hang outside. All are full of the usual trash that pours in a flood over Africa. Radios, wrist-watches, motor-car gadgets and trinkets are very much in evidence to catch the money which resulted from the clove boom in 1950. When darkness falls on the long, rambling, ramshackle street a million hurricane lamps lend it a hard brilliance, some hoisted into position on posts constructed for their reception, others in the open shops. Everyone stared very hard at me because visitors are rare in Pemba and all the possible varieties of European countenance that might be seen in the street were already known and numbered. Mine was a new one and had a charm for that reason, if for no other. Some new Bwana Doktari come to find out about something, one presumed.

The District Commissioner lives in a pleasant house with a garden and large trees around it. Other Europeans live in two blocks, each containing two flats, and the suburban illusion is well maintained. Keith and Marie had been assigned a flat on the upper floor of one of these blocks, a gaunt, empty place, furnished only with government furniture and bearing the marks of many previous transitory occupants. No one, it was evident, had ever made a home there. The walls were blank

HOMALI CART

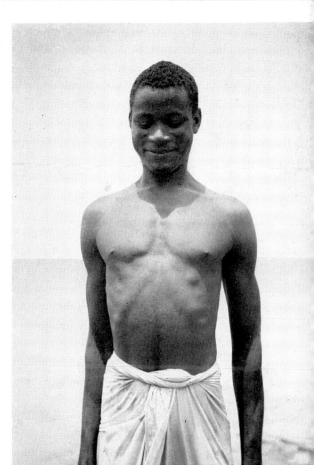

FISHERMAN

*SOKOMAHOGO
STREET*

*WATOTO WAWILI
WAZURI*
(Two good boys)

and washed with the inevitable sickly cream which is the
standard colour for all government quarters. There was no
indication of the identity of previous occupants. It seemed to
be eloquent of the nomadic life of colonial servants, never
making a home anywhere but always up and off somewhere
else, leaving no trace but a mark on a wall, a scratch on a table,
a spring broken in a sofa. 'The people who were here before.'

In the flat below, however, lived an elderly couple who seemed
to have dug themselves in fairly well. They solaced themselves by playing the radio all day long, as loud as it could be
played, from early morning until late evening. It was February
1952 and King George VI had just died. Nothing was spared
us in the flat above. The old lady kept chickens and, though
they were scruffy and bare-bottomed as chickens always are in
the tropics, she was devoted to them and they obviously filled
a gap in her life. 'Now, Trixie, that's naughty. I believe you've
laid an egg where Granny can't find it. Show Granny where it
is at once. Now come along.'

If one lived in Pemba for any length of time one would
certainly need something like chickens to fill the gaps that would
appear in one's life, for there is nothing whatever to 'do'. There
is no golf course. There is a hard tennis court, but when I was
there it looked as though it had not been used for a very long
time. There is no club and no hotel. I do not think there is
even a cinema. In order to bathe or fish, a journey of about
two hours must be made by motor-boat to one of the coral
islands. For European society there is the District Commissioner, when he is there, and his family, if any. When I was
there, I seem to remember, the Commissioner was a bachelor
and was away on safari. There are also the other three families
occupying the other three flats. The equipment necessary,
therefore, for life in Pemba consists in a contented mind and
a capacity to be happy with small pleasures. 'I simply don't
know what I'd do without my wireless,' said the old lady
down below, placidly knitting to the accompaniment of the
'Dead March' in *Saul*. Funeral dirges, orations and slow
music had been going on gloomily since breakfast. 'I really
think I'd go mad,' she said.

The only other town of any size in the island is Chake-
Chake, the old capital. It stands, like Wete, on a rise, crowned

H

by the old Portuguese fort, at the end of another long arm o.
the lagoon, which winds in among the mangroves on the west
coast about two-thirds of the total distance from the northern-
most tip. The town is like a small Zanzibar, perched on the
top of a hill, with the same kind of huge old Arab houses and an
air of happy-go-lucky decay. The old fort is a tremendous
square block of masonry overlooking the mangrove creek
and is now used as a police station. All the sweet sad air of decay
and of the past that hangs over the town is concentrated here,
or perhaps it is just the decadent fragrance of the frangipanis,
dropping their waxen trumpets on the grass, that gives that
impression of agreeable melancholy.

One of the most noteworthy, and certainly one of the most
notorious, inhabitants of Chake-Chake is perhaps the sacred
fish who lives in a dark and spooky fresh-water pool, all overgrown with bushes, below the town. No one, I was told, knows
what sort of fish he is. He is believed to be of immense age and
even the oldest inhabitant of Chake-Chake cannot remember
the day when he was not in his pool. He is greatly venerated
by the natives who attribute all sorts of occult powers to him,
offer him prayers and propitiate him with food. The result is
that he always expects to be propitiated, even by those, such
as I, who want no part of him at all. His preference is for eggs,
rather hard boiled and with the shells removed, if you please.
He is said to get very angry if he finds that nothing is forthcoming when visitors come to see him and once a visitor, who
tried to play a trick on him, got bitten in the hand. We had
some difficulty in finding the creature's pool, but a kind stranger
led us there and I must say I thought it an uninviting residence,
heavily overshadowed by dark rocks and thick bushes. In the
inky depths something glimmered up towards us, a lugubrious
gaping mouth in a flat head. There seemed to be a dark sin-
uous body behind it. But the Youngs' little boys had no respect
for him and, while one waved a stick, the other threw a stone.
The monster rippled backwards into the pool and vanished, to
reappear soon afterwards glaring balefully. Whenever he saw
a movement on the bank he rippled backwards into the darkness, never disturbing the surface.

'It's an eel,' I pronounced. I said this purely as a guess
because I believe that eels are the only fish that can swim in

reverse with the same undulating motion as that which propels them forward. There are large fresh-water eels on the mainland and Professor J. L. B. Smith, who visited Zanzibar after I left and subsequently acquired the second Coelacanth in the Comores, found large fresh-water eels in the reservoirs on Zanzibar Island.

The veneration in which the inhabitants of Chake-Chake, indeed of the whole island, hold this unattractive animal is an example of the widespread belief in fetishism and magic which still exists in Pemba. The island, cut off for centuries from European influence and even to-day seldom visited, remains largely under the spell of witch doctors and magic guilds. The swearing of fearful oaths and the performance of repulsive ceremonies are said to be still common in the remoter villages. Tribes on the mainland are said to send novices to Pemba to graduate in the subtle science of witch doctoring.

The road from Wete to Chake-Chake dips down into a green valley and then climbs up and winds along a ridge which forms the central backbone of the island. Pemba is hillier than Zanzibar and from the road we looked over a wide, wooded landscape, dark green, with aisles and avenues of clove trees. Everywhere silver lances of the lagoon ran in among them. The main road was narrow and asphalted only on the crown. There was a sandy strip, to allow for 'errors and omissions', on each side of the tarmac, which was crumbling and distintegrating at the edges like a coastline which is being eroded. As we drove along this tortuous highway we were frequently obliged to slide off the tarmac into the sandy strip, often with a sudden application of the brakes. There would be angry looks, and sometimes imprecations, all equally useless. For in 1950 there had been a bumper clove crop in Pemba, and everyone, from the Arab plantation owner to the African labourer, became suddenly rich. Richer still became the Indians into whose hands the money eventually found its way. They imported the trash and the gew-gaws for the Arabs and Africans to buy with their newly won wealth. Expensive motor-cars were among the gew-gaws they bought. But so much damage was done to the clove trees in gathering the bumper crop of 1950 that during 1951 and 1952 the trees were recovering from their maltreatment and the bumper crop was not repeated.

So the boom was followed by a slump. In 1952 one could buy
a second-hand motor-car of globular design quite cheaply in
Wete. One could, but one was well advised not to, for they had
all been through the mill since they were new. In a garage
showroom in Zanzibar I remember admiring for months a low-
slung, aluminium saloon of an expensive and highly specialized
continental make. An Arab clove grower in Pemba bought it
and it became what I believe is known in the trade as 'a complete write off' in a month. In 1950, the year of the boom, you
drove along the narrow winding roads of Pemba at your peril,
for very few of the new owners of high-powered vehicles knew
how to drive them. They careered along at high speed cease-
lessly blowing the horn. In 1951 motoring was still risky in
Pemba, though many of the motor-cars bought the year before
were no longer on the road. In 1952 things were better still,
for two indifferent clove crops had made the roads fairly safe
again.

I travelled about the island with Keith and his attendant
and helped him to apply small rectangular dressings to the napes
of several hundred necks varying in colour from ebony to light
cream. It was a pity that this was unfinished business, so far
as I was concerned, because although I saw the dressings
applied, I never saw them removed or knew the outcome of the
work in which I had, though in only a small degree, assisted.
Nevertheless it was interesting and amusing and sometimes
touching. It was touching to see the eagerness with which
the people came forward in droves and brought their children,
not knowing what it was all about, but convinced there must be
some good in it for them somewhere and somehow. It was
mainly men, boys and small children who seemed to get surveyed for the women were rather more difficult. Indian women
would loosen and lower their saris a little way below their
plump brown necks so that one could apply the little dressing
a trifle higher up than one applied it to the men. But for the
Arab and African women decency forbade, and I do not remember that they came forward in any village. However, we made
up for this gap in the records by putting the pupils in the girls'
schools through it. Schools were fair game and in one we stuck
dressings on the napes of some two hundred gigglers, and then
did the same to the mistresses.

A school in Pemba, as in Zanzibar also, was often merely a roof on concrete pillars with rows of desks and a blackboard underneath it. When Keith and his attendant and I arrived the rows of black and brown heads were bent over exercise books or over slates. We were a most welcome distraction from the boredom of multiplication, both for the pupils and for the teachers, I suspected, and every head was raised at once as we approached. The first school we visited was a very isolated one in a remote village at the end of a long, hot, sandy cart track. We had to leave the car and walk the last mile and a half and arrived sweaty and thirsty. The children, who were playing outside their open-sided school building, saw us approaching a long way off and fled into the surrounding bush. When we at last arrived at the school building, hot and dusty and streaming with sweat, there was only the young Arab schoolmaster who laughed and apologized. 'They are not used to strangers,' he said. One tiny black boy, however, with a large red tarboosh on his head, did not run away but came towards us with a shy smile and held out his hand, which we bent down and gravely took. This was a sign for the others to emerge one by one from their hiding places among the bushes and to come forward, each with his hand out, until finally we were shaking hands like royalty, surrounded waist deep in a sea of woolly heads, black faces upraised and lit by white smiles, and tiny fluttering hands.

In every school the boys lined up in ranks with their shirts off and we walked down the rows of backs of various colours and shapes. It was sad to see the amount of scabies and other skin complaints among the children. Some of the little bodies were covered with open sores, but they did not seem to worry about it much and seemed to be immune from the agonizing irritation of this disease, which is due to the burrowing activities of a small mite under the skin. It would have been useless to treat them, Keith said, even if there were time, because they would immediately become re-infected in their homes. There were also the signs of undernourishment and vitamin deficiency, pot bellies, crooked rickety legs, patchy discolorations of the skin. But the shy smile and the soft confiding look were always the same. Nearly always there was the alert boy, and the funny boy who showed off, and the stupid boy who was the butt of his fellows. And I thought that school is always school the world over, even in Pemba. In many of them the sizes of the classes were enormous, sixty or seventy children all in the charge of one young schoolmaster. I wondered how on earth they could possibly learn anything, and came to the obvious conclusion that very few of them did learn anything and that education is a farce.

We visited the leper settlement and applied the dressings to the backs of the male patients there. Leprosy, which is spread by contact and flourishes in dirty and insanitary housing conditions, is still a fairly common disease in Africa and the East, as it was in the Middle Ages in Europe. It is due to a bacillus related to the tubercle bacillus which causes the death of the tissues. In advanced cases the extremities may be lost altogether, but in less advanced cases all that one sees is a tuberosity of the organs. In Pemba we saw both. We saw noses, ears and toes swollen up into shapeless, bulbous lumps and sometimes missing altogether. Lepers are always segregated into encampments as far away as possible from the rest of the community. In British Colonies and Protectorates the encampments are run either by the Government Medical Department or by the Church missions, often by the Roman Catholics. Outside the city of Zanzibar itself the settlement was run by the Roman Catholic Mission, but the settlement we visited outside Wete was run by the Government Medical Authorities.

This segregation of lepers from their fellow men is a curious example of popular superstition lagging behind medical knowledge. Until comparatively recently leprosy was regarded as an extremely contagious and fatal disease, quite incurable. In the Middle Ages in Europe lepers were pronounced unclean by the Church and driven out of the community. They had to cry 'Unclean! Unclean!' as they walked along and people avoided them. In the reign of Edward III they were buried alive with all their possessions. But as a matter of fact, it is now known, leprosy is one of the most difficult diseases of all to catch and is much rarer than was formerly thought. Many of the lepers who in the Middle Ages were pronounced unclean, driven out with bell and book and even buried alive, were probably only suffering from scabies like the little boys in

Pemba. However, during the last 2,000 years the disease seems to have changed its character. The relationship between the host, man, and the parasite, the bacillus, seems to have altered, the host gaining in vigour while the bacillus has lost in virulence. It is, in fact, not even certain that what we now know as leprosy is the same disease as the contagion so desperately feared in the Middle Ages. So it may be they were right to bury their lepers alive. Leprosy is conveyed under insanitary conditions by prolonged close contact, and one would have to live constantly with a leper for years in order to become infected. There are drugs nowadays that can check the disease and, if taken in the early stages, can cure it. Nevertheless, the superstitious horror with which the community regards the leper within its gates still dictates that he be driven out and isolated. The medical authorities, however, prefer that this should be so in order that cases can be kept under observation and treated. For the drug must be taken continuously to be effective and is slow in action, and native peoples soon get bored with treatments that are not immediately and miraculously effective and usually do not persist with them. But isolation implies a social stigma, and since the disease is by no means always confined to the poor and humble, it is difficult to deal with when it occurs in the upper strata of society.

Some of the patients at Wete were in advanced stages of the disease and little could be done for them, the attendant said, except to make life easy for them. Many of them had their wives with them, from whom they would not be parted and who would not part from them. They all seemed cheerful and happy enough and some even rather proud of their affliction, as though it gave them an importance they would not have had without it. Some of the young patients attended school within the settlement and some were learning handicrafts. Some were on the way to recovery and were soon to be discharged. One could feel in the leper settlement something of that encouraging air of hope and selfless devotion which makes a great hospital an inspiring place to visit and makes one feel less depressed about the twentieth century.

With the help of the heads of the various communities in the island, both religious and secular, Keith was able to collect samples from various levels of the population. In Chake-Chake we dealt with a hundred or so taxi drivers and labourers in an open shed. They thought it an enormous joke and came running from all directions, sweaty and roaring with laughter. After them came a company of Indian ladies in saris, bringing their babies whose luminous eyes were shaded with kohl. Scores more people lined up in the public reading-room, and the public itself kept dropping in by twos and threes in order to be in on what might (one never knew) turn out to be a good thing. A few dozen more were waiting for us in a mosque and we took off our shoes to deal with them. Everywhere it developed into a jolly sort of party. The men laughed, the women tittered and wriggled, and the small children yelled with terror at the sight of the doctor with his paraphernalia. But when the expected jab, tweak or sting of pain did not materialize, the yells gave place to disbelieving suspicious silence, and then to cooings of pleasure, the showers over, the sorrow all forgotten. Afterwards Keith told me that over 80 per cent of all these people turned up for the removal of the dressing. And Keith moved among the people with that sure touch, gentle, firm and patient, which makes the poor believe that doctors are infallible and even such as I believe that some of them are wiser than other men.

In the main street of Chake-Chake, having thumbed a dressing on to the last brown back for the day and hoping never to see another torso, we ran into the suave young Indian who kept the millinery shop in Zanzibar. He had come to see what the prospects were in Pemba. He did a very good business in Zanzibar and his shop was always full of Arab ladies, heavily perfumed, with black bui-bui over their bright frocks. They were buying dress lengths to make more bright frocks to wear under their bui-bui. He stopped us in the narrow street. He did not think much of the prospects for millinery now in Chake-Chake, he said, because the boom was over. There was not the money about there used to be. He thought he might start in a small way in Wete. What were the prospects for our business? Were we having a profitable time? On the whole, we said, we thought we were.

Chapter Eight

ON THE REEFS

I

I BELONG to the age of steam. I am out of tune with the internal-combustion engine. Petrol, oil and the paraffin jet belong to an alien world into which I have somehow or other survived. I am deeply suspicious of electricity. When I drive a motor-car at a speed of over fifty miles an hour I have a feeling that the engine may blow up or fly apart. This becomes a conviction when I am driven at any speed at all by someone else. When I travel by air there is a tiny seed of apprehension at the back of my mind which makes it difficult for me either to read or sleep in peace. But in a steam train I am perfectly at ease, and my memories of childhood are filled with railway joys, of admiring the engine at the start of a long journey, of halts on country single lines with the sound of the engine softly hissing and the air full of bird song and the smell of meadow-sweet, of panting asthmatically through bluebell woods and cuttings deep in primroses. By ties that can never be dissolved I am deeply attached to steam engines, but at sea this attachment has a practical as well as a sentimental side. For the steam engine, as a means of propelling a ship through the water, remains unmatched for flexibility and ease of handling. With no gears or other expensive and complicated mechanisms your smooth, elastic steam engine can go from stationary to full speed ahead or astern with a simple turn of a throttle valve in one direction or another. Furthermore steam can be led from the engine by means of pipes all about the deck to winches and donkey engines which, again, can be controlled by the simple movement of a screw throttle. Yet in spite of all this, and in spite of the beauty of their great smoothly turning shafts, steam engines have a disadvantage that nowadays overrides everything else. They are hopelessly expensive to run because of the high cost of fuel oil. They are also of relatively enormous size and take up a disproportionate amount of room in a ship. They have to be housed in an engine-room which occupies a very large amount of the space available. For these reasons, and doubtless many others which I know nothing about because I am not an engineer, they are being more and more replaced by other types of engine at sea, especially by diesels, which are far less flexible and less simple, will only turn in one direction and have to be coupled to elaborate and expensive gearing, but yet are far more compact and much cheaper to run.

This state of affairs is producing a human problem which time may perhaps solve in due course, but certainly has not done so yet. The problem is that there are not nearly enough qualified diesel engineers to go round among the diesel engines. It is exceedingly difficult to induce engineers to go to sea in small ships because of the demand for their services in large ones or, better still for them, in comfortable jobs ashore. For the development of the diesel engine has been as rapid ashore as at sea and the clamour for engineers almost as insistent. So the qualified diesel engineer is a privileged person at present. He can pick and choose. No one can blame him for not choosing a small, dirty, smelly ship in a rough sea. Fishing companies who run fleets of small diesel-driven craft have solved the problem, partially at any rate, by employing consulting diesel engineers, or a single qualified man among a fleet of ships. The craft go to sea in charge of a driver, who is only competent to turn a throttle handle, to start and to stop. When the craft comes into port the maintenance and repairs are done by the consultant or by the engineer in charge who turns up grandly in his motor-car at a gentlemanly hour.

In the tropics the situation is practically hopeless. Nearly all the small craft powered by diesel engines have been built in Great Britain and subsequently brought out to tropical waters. The design of their engine-rooms has no relation to the climate, for ship-builders in Great Britain never seen to envisage that the ships they build may have to work in waters other than the chilly ones around their own islands. So that even if the qualified engineers were available, they would be unable to work efficiently in the suffocating cabins in which their machines are housed.

The *Cumulus*, with which we had explored the banks between Mauritius and the Seychelles and which we were now to use off the East African coast, was a diesel-driven craft and her engine-room was as horrifying as any, for she had been built in Scotland for the herring fishing. In those islands the engineer problem had been extremely serious. Competent men were non-existent, but there had been plenty of drivers and we had employed a succession of them. They were all very amiable, cheerful, willing and self-confident. But they all had one characteristic in common. They knew nothing about diesel engines, nor about how to run or maintain them. They were Creoles and had that curious lack of sympathy and feeling for the machine under their charge which is shown by Africans and many Indians. So long as the wheels were revolving they were content and sat on their hams, rolled cigarettes, chattered, played cards or slept, until the wheels for one reason or another ceased to revolve. It made no difference what strange noises or other symptoms of distress the engine might be giving out. In the *Cumulus* these sometimes became so obvious that even I could tell that something was not quite right. But the driver continued to squat near the lifeboat contentedly smoking or chattering to his shipmates. If his attention were called to the strange noises coming from his engine, he would cock his ear to listen for a second, shrug and pronounce everything to be quite in order. The noise you heard was not what you thought it was, or it was your imagination. Such a thing as a feeling for the engine was foreign to them all, as was any idea of a maintenance routine. The constant oiling, checking and recording, which is part of the job of an engineer in a ship, was entirely beyond them.

The result of being forced to employ these pleasant but incompetent young men was that our beautiful 170 h.p. diesel, built to run under reasonable conditions like a sewing machine, staggered from breakdown to breakdown. These breakdowns were often embarrassing and might have been fatal. When they occurred in port they held up the ship, keeping her tied firmly to the jetty for days, sometimes weeks, at a time. People made rude jokes. But when they occurred at sea they were alarming, for the *Cumulus* was too heavily built to make any way under sail with her small jib-sail and spanker. She had no adequate radio. On more than one occasion we drifted helplessly for several days across the Indian Ocean with the ship's entrails spread out on the deck. The amiable Creole driver, suddenly galvanized into activity, covered in oil from head to foot, strove to get the wheels going again in order to get back to his poker game. But he obviously had no idea what he was doing. Only the energy, self-taught knowledge and resource of our Welsh skipper, who worked below in the heat and oil directing the driver and his greasers for hours on end, saved us from something exceedingly unpleasant. What that was we only thought about when we were certainly and safely under way again. Then we joked about it. In the South-East Monsoon, from the position in which these mishaps commonly occurred, we should have drifted slowly, at a speed of about five miles a day, westwards in the North Equatorial current and northwards on the fringe of the Somali Current into the Arabian Sea. In the North-West Monsoon we should have been borne eastwards in the Equatorial Counter Current far out into the empty spaces of the Indian Ocean. In neither case should we have come within hundreds of miles of any land. In that vast expanse of ocean, several times larger than the Sahara on the one hand or than Australia on the other, miles off any shipping route, we should have been lost beyond all hope of help or call, circling slowly until first our water and then our food ran out.

On the east coast of Africa the shortage of engineers was as acute as it was in Mauritius and the Seychelles, but it was not quite true to say that engineers were non-existent on the coast. There were, however, more shore jobs to attract them. There was a number of highly competent Italians, who had come south after the war from what used to be, and is now again, Italian Somaliland, and from Eritrea. But they, not surprisingly, preferred to work ashore for a high salary rather than in the hot bowels of a tiny ship for the low salary the Government was prepared to pay. So they were not for us, these Italians, with their dark intelligent faces and expressive hands. But on the coast of East Africa the problem was complicated by another difficulty, for there was also a shortage of drivers.

Anybody who has any special knowledge and applies it with

his hands, a carpenter, a joiner, a mason, a driver, is known on the coast as a '*fundi*', an expert. Such specialized knowledge often confers great social prestige and leads to the adoption of stockings and shoes, and to the parting of woolly hair on one side or other of the round head. On the coast, and in Zanzibar especially, most of the driver '*fundis*' parted their hair and wore shoes on the slenderest of pretexts, for their qualifications to do so, the knowledge on which they based their implied claim to a rise in the social scale, were very slight indeed.

Africans do not really like or understand machines. They mostly lack the reasoning power, through lack of training but not through lack of ability, to deduce causes from effects. There is also a lack of the power of concentration, also due to lack of training, so that they are apt before long to get bored with the beastly thing. And who can blame them?

These difficulties had a special significance for us in Zanzibar. They greatly increased the risks and hazards of the new task which the *Cumulus* had to undertake along that coast. For it was not only in the type of fishing we should have to do that conditions on the coast would differ from anything we had met with around Mauritius or the Seychelles. During half the year the South-East Trades blow across the Indian Ocean straight on to the coral reef that fringes the whole coast. Only in the lee of Zanzibar and Pemba Islands is there shelter from them. During the rest of the year the North-East Monsoon blows in the other direction, also on to the reef. At times these winds blow strongly and huge rollers race inshore to break on the reef. In December and January the North-East Monsoon is at its strongest and in June the South-East Trades come in hard after the rains. We had reason to believe, and it proved to be the case, that the surface-living predatory fishes we should be trolling for were to be found close in along the fringing reef, for it is there they seek their food. All the year round, therefore, we should be fishing close in to a dangerous lee shore. If our engine were to break down there would be no time for the driver to cover himself with oil, spread the engine on the deck, grin and say he thought he knew what was the matter. We should be on to the reef and under the curl of the breakers in a matter of minutes.

Steve, our new skipper, was fully alive to this. He was a man in late middle age who had begun life at sea many years ago in sail, but had for some years been captain of a ferry on Lake Victoria. He was delighted to take a ship on the real sea again, though he said that the weather could often be rough and disagreeable on the lake. When squalls blew down from the mountains the lake gave a lively, if short-lived, imitation of the real thing. But Steve never felt it was really worthy of his mettle. Chicken feed, he said. He felt a kind of sailor's claustrophobia on his paltry pond. But he was a fine sailor and seaman and knew the dangers of fishing on a lee coral reef.

Steve looked very much the old salt. He had iron-grey hair and fierce blue eyes, and a pipe, in which he smoked innumerable dottles and matches, was fixed permanently in place. He lit the first dottle when he rose at dawn and extinguished the last one when he lay down at midnight. When he ate, his pipe lay nearby in case some sudden emergency should call for thought, and thought always required a dottle to help it along. Since he was a born sailor he was also a keen yachtsman. Directly he arrived in Zanzibar he bought a small cutter and spent all his leisure time sailing it, or doing things to it or making things for it as is the way of yachtsmen. He saw immediately that if the *Cumulus* had to troll up and down the coral reef along the coast he must, if possible, make her independent of her engine. She must have enough sail at least to keep her off the reef if the engine suddenly died. But the question remained, was this possible?

The *Cumulus* was a strange sight when Steve took her over in Dar-es-Salaam, for she had been fitted out in our absence with what were supposed to be 'tangons' for multiple trolling. But no one in East Africa knew what tangons were really like nor how they were used. Still, one had done one's best. Two heavy and immensely cumbersome booms, like telegraph poles but rectangular in cross section, stood upright on hinges at the base of the foremast and rested in iron forks below the truck. By means of pulley blocks and tackle each boom was made to be lowered into a socket on the forward rail, for it had evidently been thought that they would be used held out over the water horizontally a few feet above the surface. This, of course, would have been an impossible arrangement for the booms would have gone under each time the ship rolled and, even in flat calm, the lines would have been permanently entangled.

No one, apparently, had realized that tangons must be held out at an angle of forty-five degrees.

On the first passage from Dar-es-Salaam to Zanzibar we crept gingerly through the narrow entrance and out into the open sea with our new tangons in their vertical position. When the little ship reached the open sea the tangons in their fork-rests began to jerk horribly every time she rolled. We lowered them to an angle of forty-five degrees, which was the position in which we should use them. They swung backwards and forwards when the ship pitched, creaking and shuddering as they did so, and a jolt went through the ship with each dip and lift of her bows. No stays had been provided for carrying the tangons in that position so we were soon obliged to return them to their vertical resting position against the mast.

There is a short stretch of the passage between Dar-es-Salaam and Zanzibar, before the lee of Zanzibar Island is reached, where a ship experiences the full force of the South-East Trades, if they are blowing strongly. The *Cumulus*, making about seven knots, was thus exposed for about three-quarters of an hour, and, as I had not been to sea for some months, I did not enjoy it. It was late May, the rains had barely ceased and the South-Easter, new to its task, warm and damp, came roaring in over a dark sea streaked with white. We welcomed the lee of the long flat island and Steve swore he would not go to sea again until he had secured the tangons.

'Those damned things will have the mast out of the ship,' he said.

He stayed the tangons fore and aft to the rail so that they could no longer swing backwards and forwards when held at an oblique angle. He made new clamp rests which held them securely in position against the mast. When he was satisfied that they were no longer a danger, he took the ship to sea again.

'I hate those blasted things,' he said. 'Now to make her a decent suit of sails.'

He made an enormous three-cornered jib-sail, twice the size of the one we had before. One corner of it was made fast with a line rove through the haws'le. The other he took far aft to the quarter and made it fast round one of the frames below the rail with a purchase to heave it tight. He lengthened the after boom on the mainmast so as to take a larger spanker. He made these two great sails with his own hands, sitting with our little Arab bos'n beside what looked like an ocean of canvas, busy with needle and palm. His pipe was in place and he was perfectly happy, a craftsman exercising his craft, and there is no happier man. For weeks the sails grew slowly under their hands.

One day we at last went out into the strait to try them out. There was a gentle breeze blowing, but I was full of doubts which I did not express, for I am not a sailor and do not claim to know anything about it. And Steve seemed very sure.

'She'll sail all right,' he said.

But the *Cumulus* had a very heavy hull, built of oak with close-set, thick frames, and she had a big 170 h.p. diesel engine sitting in her belly.

When we were well out in the channel Steve brought her before the wind, stopped the engine and ran up his two big sails. There was silence except for the playful sound of little waves lapping against her sides.

'Now then!' said Steve, and we watched them fill.

I spat into the sea over the side and watched to see whether my spit went forward or aft. It did neither. It drifted away to port. We were making leeway on the tide.

But Steve was not convinced. He ran to the rail. 'It's falling astern,' he said, watching my contribution dissolve and vanish on the waves. 'We're moving. The wind's taking us.'

I spat again. It passed under the hull. I threw over a chip of wood. It kept us company and then, very slowly, bobbed astern. We watched it with anxiety as it became involved with a piece of sargassum weed and crept forward again to bob once more roughly where I had first thrown it.

'Keep her before the wind, damn it!' shouted Steve to the African boy at the wheel. The African boy thought it all immense fun. He loved to see Europeans getting excited, though he never knew quite what they got so excited about. He grinned and turned the wheel a point or two.

'Keep her before the wind! Port *kidogo*! You've got the wind on her quarter!'

Steve was clever with Africans. They loved him for he made them laugh, jollying them along and cracking jokes in a way that they understood. When there was a hard job to do he would shout, 'Come along now! *Kazi nyingi, shillingi kidogo!* Much work, small pay!' And they would roar with laughter, that high laugh ending in a squeak—'*Ee-hee!*'—which the negro laughs when he is really tickled. '*Kazi nyingi, shillingi kidogo! Ee-hee, ee-hee!*' they would all cackle, double up with laughter at this splendid example of European wit, and go to it with renewed vigour. The result was that Steve had a happy ship, though the crew changed frequently because of the African's disinclination to stay in anything very long. Some got drunk and missed the ship. Some felt they could do better elsewhere. Others wanted to go clove picking, or back to their villages. But they worked willingly enough as long as they stayed with us.

The crew thought it was a great joke to see Steve gazing anxiously at his sails, shouting helm orders so as to trim the ship to the least change in the wind and telling them to haul on a sheet here or let go a little there. Still funnier to see me spitting earnestly over the side. They spat too and soon there was a row of us at the ship's rail spitting into the water. I was the only one who knew why. The others just did it because it seemed to be the thing to do that afternoon. It was impossible to understand what Europeans did anyway.

'She's moving!' shouted Steve from the wheelhouse. 'I swear there's some way on her!'

On our starboard bow there reared up out of the water a triangular hulk, the bows of a wrecked ship pointing heavenwards. This had been a cable ship belonging to the Eastern Telegraph Company. On Christmas Eve, 1903, she was coming into Zanzibar after repairing a cable and there was to be a party in the Eastern Telegraph Company's mess. As he was a little late the captain took a short cut and never got to the party at all. His ship ran bows up on a coral reef and has been there ever since. Above the water line the shell of her hull remains more or less intact. Indeed some of her white paint is still left on her bows and elderly residents do not fail to point to the white streak of paint, visible four miles away from the verandah of the club, as evidence that things are not what they used to be. 'You don't get paint like that nowadays.' But below the water line a great mass of coral has grown out around and upon her, the growth of fifty years, cups, antlers, plates and convolutions, among which, in a blue translucence, fishes glimmer and flash, waver and disappear.

I kept my eyes on this wreck. It was moving slowly in relation to the distant line of houses of the town behind it. We were moving towards it slowly but surely on the tide.

'We're not going ahead, skipper,' I said. 'We're drifting towards the wreck.'

He started the engine. It was a sad disappointment. All that work for nothing. Steve looked up at his sails and shook his head.

'And yet she did move!' he said, like Galileo.

2

Lathom Island is without doubt the least known and the smallest of the Sultan's dominions. But it is by no means the least important. It lies about a hundred miles due south of Zanzibar town and perhaps fifty miles south of the southernmost tip of Zanzibar Island itself. It is exceedingly difficult to find and the first time we tried to go there we missed it altogether. It is about fourteen hours' steaming from Zanzibar for a ship doing seven knots, so by leaving about six in the evening you may get there about eight o'clock in the morning. But when the morning comes you are apt to see nothing but a waste of sea and no sign of the island at all. For Lathom Island is totally invisible unless you are right on top of it, and is therefore almost impossible to find by laying a course on a chart and trusting to dead reckoning. There is a strong easterly set round the southern end of Zanzibar Island and we found, on the first occasion, that we had been carried some ten miles to the east of our island.

Lathom Island shows nothing above the water line but a bald pate of sand, roughly circular in shape and a few hundred yards in diameter, rising some twenty feet above sea-level. Nothing of any kind grows on it, though attempts have been made to induce a few casuarinas to grow there to stop the sand from shifting. But even for them the place was too bleak and exposed. A few terns flutter above it, but they are only visitors and nest elsewhere. Beneath the water line, however, the island spreads out to form a shelf of coral many times larger in area than the central knob of sand, so that it is in fact shaped rather like a mushroom with only the crown of its cap exposed. The coral shelf is two or three square miles in area and you come upon it very suddenly, usually before you can see the sand patch which is the island itself. All around the ship the water is suddenly pale emerald green, instead of wine dark, and you can see the strange shapes of the coral apparently within touching distance of the ship's bottom. It is like riding over an enormous open tart of crinkly pastry.

Although the island itself is barren, the coral shelf around it teems with life. All the big predatory fish we were seeking can be found there, especially a miraculously beautiful big green-and-blue jackfish, which the Africans call '*koli-koli*'— a name they give to all jackfish indiscriminately. There are big barracuda here and bonito and the olive green dorado or dolphin fish. Shoals of big fish can be seen jumping through the water in all directions directly you reach the shelf, and the contrast between the abundance of life in these green waters and the emptiness of the dark deeps around the shelf is astonishing.

Perhaps it is because Lathom Island, or rather the coral shelf around it, is such an excellent fishing ground that elaborate steps are taken once every few years to maintain the Sultan's jurisdiction over it by landing a senior officer of the Zanzibar Government upon it and planting the Sultan's red flag. This is apt to be a hazardous operation, for the island gives no shelter of any kind from either monsoon and is too small and too low to make much of a lee. The tide swirls round it as though round the piers of a bridge. The water over the coral shelf is so shallow that a launch or ship cannot approach close to the island but must lie a long way off. The distinguished personage has to put off in a small pram and perhaps land through heavy surf. The more senior and distinguished the personage the more hazardous and tricky does the operation become. Does one get into the pram first and help the distinguished personage down? Or does one hand him down to the African sailor in the pram and descend oneself after him? What if he upsets the pram? 'I think, sir—if you wouldn't mind sitting a little more in the middle . . . ' What if he gets a wet behind? Does one carry him ashore on one's shoulders, or will he take off his shoes and walk the last few yards? Questions of etiquette arise, even on Lathom Island. It was usually the duty of a Port Officer to have charge of these flag-planting expeditions, and he looked forward to them with misgiving and anxiously consulted the weather beforehand. On the last occasion the British Resident, a very keen fisherman, decided that he would make the expedition himself and combine it with a fishing trip. He himself would go ashore and plant the Sultan's flag. Of course the weather did the wrong thing, as it so often does, and there was a stiff south-easterly wind blowing with a heavy surf. A swirling tide rushed round the bald dome of sand. The Resident was a great sportsman but stout and no longer in his first youth, and swimming was not one of the sports in which he excelled. Between the launch and the island a mishap occurred. The tiny pram was caught sideways on to a wave and overturned. The British Resident, the Port Officer and the African seaman were thrown into the water.

'My dear fellow,' said His Excellency, emerging gasping and spluttering on to the sand, 'if you're trying to drown me you'd better make a better job of it on the way back.'

Lathom Island was in some ways an ideal place for our purpose. For one thing it was miles from any land, either from the mainland or from the tip of Zanzibar Island, and for that reason it was a small isolated reserve of fish with its own population. Though some of the species of fish which lived there might undoubtedly migrate from elsewhere, yet the probability remained that many, the *koli-koli* for instance, and perhaps the barracuda, lived there permanently, never leaving the island. By visiting the place several times a year for several years, therefore, we would perhaps be able to build up a picture of the life cycle, breeding and feeding habits of an isolated colony of fish. But a further and more immediate, and for Steve far more important, advantage was that we could fish in what little shelter there was in the lee of the island and if, by an evil chance, our engine died we could drift away for quite a long time anyway, without worrying about running on to a reef.

Steve learnt an infallible way of pin-pointing this tiny speck of sand and arriving there dead on time in the early morning.

He ran south down the coast of the mainland so as to get the Dar-es-Salaam light on the starboard beam at midnight. There it shone, a tiny winking spark-like hope, forlorn and lonely as coast lights always seem at night. Then he turned due east and ran on for the rest of the night on that course keeping the tiny light dead astern. We still had the loom of it when the sky paled. When the sun came up we were on the coral plateau every time and there ahead, like the top of an old man's pate, was the bare sandy knoll of the island with the ring of surf around it like white hair.

I had always thought it would be too ambitious, at first at any rate, to attempt to tow eight lines aside like the Frenchmen because we had an entirely untrained crew, quite unused to this type of fishing. Further, I did not feel too expert myself and wanted to get used to it all. I foresaw terrible muddles and entanglements, and thought it better to begin modestly and perhaps advance by easy stages. Accordingly we rigged four lines a side, three from the tangons and one from the quarter rail. They were rigged pretty much as I had seen the Frenchmen rig them and on each line was a rubber stretcher, to give elasticity and play to the lines.

I made several dozen lures of various sorts which I hoped would ensnare and deceive the fish, but they were neither so gay nor so neat as the little tassels of artificial silk, like large salmon flies, that I had watched the Frenchmen making. Yet they were good enough and they worked. I bound frayed-out rope yarns round small lengths of stiff wire. These were light and skidded along the surface. After they had been used a few times the strands of yarn, which were stiff and curly to begin with, straightened out and lay together in a streamlined shape which, apparently, looked good to a barracuda. I had read that in the Pacific the American yellow-fin tuna fishermen use a lure made of white bone shaped like a small lozenge an inch or so in length with a hook bound to it by means of wire. This is called a jig. I rang up the Irish Veterinary Officer. Had he any bones? Yes, he had. How many would I like? And in a day or so he arrived in his jeep and unloaded from it about a dozen great ribs. I did not ask whose ribs they were. At that time we had only a small office in John Wheeler's house, a fine old Arab mansion overlooking the sea, in which to do everything. I laid my bones on the floor of his office and, while he wrestled with mountains of paper, with indents, with accounts and with reports, I filled the air with horrible noises and curious smells. I carved small lozenges of bone out of the flat parts of the ribs with a hacksaw. This made a deafening noise of the kind that sets the teeth on edge. It also made a smell of hot roast beef, which was one of the results of sawing through bone which I had not expected. Only occasionally did John and his wife utter a faint protest. I am not very clever at making things and, as usual, mishaps kept occurring which I always feel are reserved exclusively for me. They never happen when other people make things. The bone kept breaking and splintering. The blades of the hacksaw snapped. I sawed my own fingers. But in the end I found, rather to my surprise, that I had made several dozen white bone jigs, something like the American ones, though, again, neither so neat nor so pretty. But they deceived quite a lot of fishes and were voted a success. They, too, skidded along the surface and gleamed deceitfully, looking, one must suppose, just like a sardine, though not to me. In order to make a rather heavier affair that would run just beneath the surface and—who knows?— be more deceptive still, I bought a length of soft lead piping and cut it up with the hacksaw into small pieces about an inch long. I bound rope yarns round some of these. Round others I bound pieces of American oil cloth in the form of a skirt, cut into strips so as to form a tassel. Some of these I left white. Others I painted yellow, blue or red in order to find out whether any fish had a preference for any particular colour. It is said that tunny will often prefer yellow. However, these, though they looked very pretty when I had made them and hung them up in a row, were not very successful. After they had been towed through the water for an hour or so the American cloth disintegrated and the paint washed off. After one bite or strike they had to be renewed altogether. I cannot say from memory that the fish seemed to have any preference for any colour, though I think that yellow and white were more attractive than blue or red. We tried feathers also, but I have never found them very successful. You may buy feather jigs with lead noses and eyes painted on them. They are very expensive and a great waste of money, for fish do not really care whether they have eyes painted on them or not. These, again, look very pretty when new, but very sad when they have been in the water for an hour or so. Many sportsmen spend large sums of money on elaborate jigs and metal spoons with patent, and of course infallible, devices to make them run just so, and new and original shapes to make them do this or that. And I myself spent many hours making my lures of bone or rope yarns or American cloth. But, in fact, a piece of cotton waste wrapped round a hook will do.

Our African crew took to this kind of fishing with a gusto and an enthusiasm which themselves became one of our problems. When one of the lines, in the approved Biscay manner, kicked up out of the parallel with its fellows showing that there was a fish on the business end, there was a shout of joy. Everyone, including the engineer, the greaser off duty and the cook, scrambled madly to the rail to pull the line in. Everyone, that is, except the two old Arabs who were saving up to return to their village in the Hadhramuth. One would suppose they were saving their strength as well as their money for this great homecoming, for they were the laziest men in the world. They were two charming old rascals and the ugliest men I have ever seen. They smiled a great deal, one of them showing two sharp black fangs, one on each side of his otherwise toothless mouth. The other was without the two fangs. They expended more energy and thought over the avoidance of work than they would have expended in doing it, and their favourite and most successful gambit was to be constantly praying.

Our bos'n was also an Arab, a neat, compact little man but very reserved. One never quite knew what he was thinking. He had sailed in dhows off the coast of Bombay and had, I found out, done this kind of fishing in them. I suspected that he knew far more about it than I did and must, in that case, have thought my efforts very amateurish and fumbling. But if that were so he kept both his knowledge and his opinions to himself with oriental courtesy or inscrutability, whichever you like.

The rest of the crew, except the engineer, knew nothing about fishing and not very much about anything. When a line kicked up they shouted a strange battle cry of their own invention and made a dive for the side, roaring with laughter, pushing each other and myself out of the way to get there first. But there were times, of course, when they were busy with more important matters, such as eating with their fingers their huge mounds of curry and rice, or sleeping after having eaten them, or praying during the prayer times as laid down in the Koran, at dawn when I was streaming the lines astern, and at sunset when I was pulling them in. Then, mysteriously, there was apt to be no one to attend to the lines at all.

As a result of this disorganization we often lost fish at first and the lines became maddeningly tangled. Steve accordingly stationed men on either side of the deck, one forward and one aft, told them to stay there and watch the lines and haul when they were told. They agreed and put on expressions of earnest alertness. But when an emergency arose, in the form of a fish on the end of a line, they left their posts and charged about shouting and laughing. When there was more than one line with a fish the chaos and confusion were complete, the shouting and the laughter deafening. We often lost fish and gear and time through lack of co-ordination and indiscipline. But they thought it the grandest fun and the dottiest way of catching fish imaginable. Shrieks and peals of mirth accompanied the *Cumulus* on her way up and down and back and forth over the coral shelf of Lathom Island, and later, through the reefs and channels of the coast.

Our engine driver was a Seychellois who had left his native islands for the mainland some years ago and had worked since then in Tanganyika. He was a lively and intelligent young man, superior to other drivers on the coast, and though I should hesitate to say that we had no engine failures while he was in charge, at least we never had any at sea. He had the Seychellois love of fishing and knew exactly how it all should be done. He led the charge to the ship's rail each time a line kicked up, brandishing a gaffing hook, shouting the battle cry which he invented and which the crew took up—'Hard line! Hard line!' He was a cheerful and likeable young man, but he got, as the Americans say, ever so slightly in my hair.

The indiscipline of our crew was matched by the indiscipline of the fish. Unlike the docile germon of the Bay of Biscay, which dies without much struggle, they fought furiously for their lives when hooked on my patent lures. Some, notably the jackfish, charged from side to side on the end of the line in a series of sweeping zig-zags, fouling the lines on either side of them. Others, like the dorado, leapt into the air, flashing like scimitars. In either case they were apt to be hauled on board swathed in a cocoon of their own line and the neighbouring ones. Most of these large and astonishingly virile fish were still wriggling and fighting when we got them alongside. None of us was very expert at gaffing so that at first we lost quite a number of fish through eager but unskilful wielding of the gaffing hook. The Frenchmen used to despatch their germons by running them through the brain between the eyes with a sharp spike. This almost instantly stops their struggles and is a more efficient way than clubbing them with a piece of wood. But even so we found that our tropical fish were so tenacious of life that more than one jab was often needed before the fish was quiet enough to have the hook taken out of its armoured mouth. Fearful entanglements of the lines often took place and sometimes we had to pull them all in on one side of the ship and begin, with patience and perseverance, the long boring business of disentangling them. Fishing lines and hooks, as every amateur fisherman knows, have an eldritch will of their own. Patience, skill and a kind of Teutonic mathematical precision of mind are often needed to deal with them. Imprecations, I found, are of no use at all. No sooner had we disentangled the lines on one side and with relief streamed them astern again than those on the other side became entangled and we had to begin all over again.

The first time we visited Lathom Island the weather was scorching hot and the sea like glass. The round low dome of sand was dim with heat and the only waves breaking on it were tiny idle tongues that licked and died. In the flaming sunrise we lowered the tangons to the required angle and streamed the lines for half an hour before we reached the coral shelf. Almost at once, when we reached the shallow water and saw the piecrust beneath us, the lines began to kick up one after the other and the Africans, now awake, their orisons performed, were ready for the fun. 'Hard line! Hard line!' they shouted, hauling furiously and brandishing the gaffing pole. Big green and royal blue jackfish (*koli-koli*) were hoisted over the side, inexpertly speared. As the sun mounted in the sky the sweat streamed

down from under the broad-brimmed straw hat I always wore
and dimmed my sun-glasses. The hat and the sun-glasses I
found to be absolutely necessary, for without them, even on a
dull day with no sun, a small pain like the pressure of an iron
thumb developed about midday above the nape of my neck.
By three o'clock in the afternoon it was a tight, rhythmically
contracting iron band around the base of my skull and above
my eyes. By sunset it was necessary to take three aspirins and
lie for the rest of the evening in my bunk with my eyes closed.
But if I were suitably armoured against the glare from the sea
and the heat reflected from the deck and ship's structure, I
suffered from no ill effects worse than a tremendous thirst.
When the sun went down at the end of the day's fishing, we
had perhaps a hundred big fish, had lost perhaps a dozen, had
spoilt or lost perhaps twenty or thirty of my lures, and broken a
line or two. We were glad to take the lines in and grease the
hooks and trace wires as I had seen the Frenchmen do at the
end of each day.

We found we could not use more than two or three feet of
thin wire trace at the end of each line because, with bare hands
and arms and bare bodies, we could not handle a greater length
without danger of severe cuts. For none of us wore more than a
pair of shorts, none, that is, except the two old Arabs who were
always covered, as good Mohammedans should be, to below
the elbow and below the knee. But, somehow or other, they
never seemed to have occasion to handle any fish.

On our second visit to Lathom Island a black sea seemed to
climb up at us, bearing white streamers, out of the south-east
and huge dark cumuli swept down upon us trailing veils of rain.
The dome of sand was hidden in foam and spume. The
Cumulus rolled and danced until one felt a kind of sick giddiness,
a drumming in the ears and a spinning in the head. When
we streamed our lines we found that those on the windward
side were blown on top of one another so that the lures fouled
each other and became hooked together. We fastened a short
length of chain, about half a dozen links, on each line to
act as a weight. But each time the ship rolled, the three
lengths of chain swung out and back again like three pendulums,
the range and speed of whose swing were unpredictable. When
they swung inboard anyone staggering along the deck on the

side of the ship that was lifting to the roll was forced to duck
as the innermost chain swooped down and up again close to his
head. We had to take in these lines on the windward side of
the ship and decided at last that in heavy weather we could only
fish on the lee side.

It was around Lathom Island that we broke in this gear and
saw how it worked under conditions very different from those in
the Bay of Biscay. We taught our crew of laughing negroes how
to restrain their ardour and to temper their fervour with a little
method. We taught them how to gaff fish with one quick upward jab of the gaffing pole, instead of making ineffectual
passes with it in the slipstream. We taught them how to stow
the lines neatly and correctly at the end of each day, so that
they could be streamed easily and quickly the following morning. We taught them how to wash and clean the fish after it
had been caught and not to leave it lying in the hot sun. We
taught them not to stream a line again after taking a fish off
the hook without first making sure that the lure and the hook
were in good order and capable of catching another fish. All
these lessons, needless to say, we had to teach ourselves before
we could teach the crew. But I have no doubt at all that every
one of them forgot them all the instant he left the ship, for not
one of them for a moment regarded anything we told him as
having the least practical application so far as he was concerned,
or for a moment thought that it could ever one day be useful in
any life that he might in the future conceivably find himself
leading. It was all just some uproariously funny European
nonsense. '*Shauri ya Mzungu.*' One lesson, however, we never
taught them, in my time at any rate. That was the lesson of
vigilance. We never could teach them the importance of
watching the lines all the time lest they catch a fish unexpectedly, or become foul of one another or catch something like
a large bunch of seaweed and become useless until freed. Perhaps we never taught them this important lesson because to
them it was of total unimportance what was happening to our
lines. When there was a lull in the fishing they curled up and
slept. When we were cruising in waters where it was unlikely
that we should catch a fish, no one watched the lines but ourselves. But this is hardly surprising, for they got nothing extra
even if we caught a thousand fish. When the fishing was dull

they thought of other things, or of nothing at all. When the improbable happened and a line kicked up unexpectedly, we had to rouse the sleepers by shouting 'Hard line! Hard line! Come on there now! Hard line!' And instantly there was cheerful and delighted hubbub.

From our beginnings at Lathom Island we presently extended our range to take in the whole stretch of coastline from Lamu in the north to Mafia and the Rovuma River in the south. We cruised close inshore along the coral reefs and up the eastern exposed coasts of Zanzibar and Pemba Islands, and zigzagged across the strait between them and the mainland. The fish were almost always close in to the reef, so close that Steve was often in doubt about taking the ship in near enough. There were also one or two large shallow shelves where we found fish, such as the large bank to the north of Zanzibar Island. But these were very few and mostly it was a question of creeping cautiously up the coast with look-outs posted at the mast-head watching for unexpected shoals. Some of those scenes and places that remain in my memory had an enchanted beauty, and now in retrospect have the quality of a rare dream. Around Mafia Island was a great stretch of glassy water dotted with many islands. Lines of surf winked on invisible coral reefs under giant cumuli emptying themselves in the distance. They seemed deceptively far away, but were in fact close at hand. Our lines, trailing astern, made eight little V-shaped furrows on the polished surface of the water. The exhaust tonked into the hot air and the deck scorched the soles of the feet. There was no sign of any life, not even a tern fluttering white against the blue. Suddenly the line of foam that had seemed so far away, like giant rollers reduced by distance, their thunder muffled, diminished surprisingly as we approached it and became a line of tiny breakers under the bows, curling coquettishly over invisible shallows. Then we saw the break of foam and momentary flash of silver that showed where fish were busy round the reef, and our lines began to kick up one after the other for the first time for hours.

Chapter Nine

AWAKENING

ZANZIBAR is an old Muslim community where the laws of Islam are still strictly observed and the letter of the Holy Koran is obeyed by a large proportion of the people. The fasts are kept and prayers are said five times daily. Many women still live in purdah and most Arab ladies go heavily veiled in the streets. Indeed it is not long since the purdah was very strict and not very many years ago, at the beginning of the present century, respectable Arab ladies went out only after dark, veiled and escorted by numerous female attendants and men carrying lanterns. Even now they are shielded from worldly tasks and cares and denied worldly joys. They are not allowed to soil their hands with housework or with work of any sort more arduous than light embroidery.

I once went to the house of a young Arab who prided himself on being highly sophisticated and westernized. The house was a modern villa furnished in the western style with the tassels and fringes, the rectangles and electric colours that are so much admired in the East. The time was ten o'clock in the morning and the lady of the house, who was not expecting any visitors, was sitting upstairs in something diaphanous with beads, as for afternoon tea, delicately embroidering on a frame. In the modern kitchen an old African woman was squatting on her haunches cooking a pot of rice over a wood fire in the middle of the tiled floor.

Arab women are not supposed to have any views or to understand anything about anything. In these days, when young men go to Europe and America on scholarships and educational grants of various sorts, this lack of intellectual pretensions on the part of their women folk has an unfortunate result. It often breaks up homes. For when the young men return they find they can no longer communicate with their wives, or with any of their female relations who have remained at home. 'I have divorced my wife,' a young schoolmaster told me. 'She was too stupid.' Fortunately for them, perhaps, it is easier for a Muslim to break the marriage tie than it is for a Christian.

As for amusements there is little for an Arab lady to do even to-day, except gossip. Mixing with the opposite sex in public and, of course, dancing are strictly forbidden. Shortly before I left Zanzibar one of the vernacular newspapers carried a leading article entitled 'Should Women Mix with Men?' This was in response to indignant letters in the correspondence column calling attention to this deplorable and growing practice. The leading article, however, took a broad view of the matter and said that one must move with the times. In this post-war world, the writer thought, it would be found as time went on that women would tend to mix more and more with men. One would just have to try to bear it.

The cinema is permitted as a feminine amusement, if the film is approved by the husband, and in all the movie theatres, except the very newest, there is a special enclosed section divided off from the rest of the seats, having its own entrance. Here the ladies of the purdah may see without being seen and enter and leave unobserved. I often wondered what conclusions they drew, inside their 'bui-bui box', as it was called, concerning the manner and customs of their western sisters as portrayed upon the screen.

In many Muslim countries women may dance provided there is no actual contact with a male partner. In Malaya this had led to a form of dance, known as Joget Modern, in which the boy and girl face one another but do not touch and the effect is often charming. But in Zanzibar any form of dancing is forbidden to women altogether. This, and the general segregation of women which prevails, has, at first sight, a somewhat startling effect on the amusements of the males. I saw this to my astonishment one Saturday evening when I was prevailed upon to pay a visit to the fine social centre which the Government has built for the people of Zanzibar on a site outside the town. In this pleasant and, of course, Neo-saracenic building, there is a big dance or concert hall. A dance is held here every Saturday night and is known as *Rahaleo*, 'the joyous occasion'. I am afraid I failed to see where the joy came in. A band was pumping out lively rum-ti-tum tunes on the stage. The hall was packed with people but I was the only European. About three-quarters of the dance floor was thronged with dancers and there must have been about three hundred people on the floor. But, except for about four girls, they were all men. Yet they danced without the slightest sign of self-consciousness or embarrassment and it was to them obviously a perfectly normal and proper procedure. The remaining quarter of the floor was occupied by rows of seats. Here the women sat, heavily draped in black from the crowns of their heads to the ground. Only their bright eyes showed, following the movements of the dancers. They were like crows upon a bough. They sat for the most part, so far as I could make out, in almost total silence, though now and again two hooded heads would incline towards one another and it seemed that words were being exchanged—words of disapproval and disdain, I have no doubt, concerning the four abandoned creatures only too obviously thoroughly enjoying themselves on the floor. They, one supposed, were the fallen ones and were to be pitied rather than blamed. Heaven would exact its due penalty no doubt, though evidently the time was not yet.

Suddenly near me there was an uproar, angry voices and a scuffle. Two young men were narrowly prevented from coming to blows by others who intervened and led them away to opposite sides of the room, still glaring at one another.

'What are they fighting about?' I asked.

'As usual,' said my friend with a tolerant shrug, 'it is about a woman.'

'But which one?' I said, for the four girls on the floor were dancing round apparently unaware of any disturbance.

'My dear fellow, not one of those!' said my companion in a shocked voice. 'She's over there, the fourth one from the left in the third row. I'm not surprised the boys quarrel over her. She's the most beautiful girl in Zanzibar.'

'Really?' I said. But looking at the rows of seated veiled figures, all apparently exactly alike, I felt I must take my friend's word for it.

Nevertheless all this is changing swiftly. What we are pleased to call 'the Western Way of Life', and especially the more meretricious aspects of it, exerts upon peoples newly awakened to its tricks and toys an extraordinary and powerful attraction. It is felt in Zanzibar as it is felt all over the East. The younger generation of all races is westernizing itself with an eagerness which is a little alarming. For the radio with many knobs, the shiny motor-car, the glittering wrist-watch and CinemaScope are dazzlingly attractive to the young. Do they, one wonders, watching them, in their too-western clothes and hair-do's, crowding into the cinemas, miss the deeper values and standards which are all of our civilization which will endure when its gadgets are out of date or one with Nineveh and Tyre?

The older Arabs still cling to their old ways and fight to preserve the seclusion in which they have dwelt for so long. The fact that there is only one hotel of tourist standard, and that of recent growth, is said to be due to the elders' rooted dislike of tourists in general. I must say one often sees what they mean.

When the mail boats leave Dar-es-Salaam for Zanzibar a tactful little notice appears on the ship's notice board reminding female passengers, in careful language, that Zanzibar is an old Mohammedan community, and that exiguous clothing is frowned upon. 'It is felt', says the notice, 'that ladies will be glad to receive this intimation in advance'—or words to that effect. Yet these exercises in tact do not always dissuade women from going ashore in costumes that Mohammedans consider grossly immodest and, as such, an insult to their faith. One young woman, who went bicycling in the interior of the island with bare midriff and the briefest of briefs, had a hot reception in the villages and had to be protected by the police from a hostile and outraged populace.

When sailors come ashore in the town their carousals in the narrow streets do not increase the respect in which Europeans would like to think they are held. One night a party of sailors from a merchant ship burst into the house of a perfectly respectable citizen because they had seen some women at an upper window, and therefore thought the house was quite a different sort of establishment altogether. The owner of the house called for the help of his neighbours who threw the sailors out after a minor riot in which the sailors drew knives. This caused high feeling in the town. Racial antagonism flared up for a little while. Was one not safe in one's own house? The police acted promptly, however, and the sailors were brought up before the magistrate. They said that they had mistaken the house for a brothel.

'Is it not a fact,' asked one of them in his own defence, 'that this part of the town is notorious for its brothels?'

'Sir,' replied the Indian police inspector, witness for the prosecution, with immense dignity, 'this part of the town is famous for its brothels.' But that was not held to be a valid excuse and the sailors went to gaol.

It is unfortunate that Zanzibar has, as a matter of fact, a peculiar effect on visiting Europeans. They feel a guilty quickening of the pulse and a sense of release from normal restraints, rather similar to the sensation of mild abandon that comes over the most respectable English people on emerging from the Gare du Nord into the streets of Paris. It is due in Zanzibar to the dark alleyways between the overshadowing houses, where you feel that anything might happen even though it never does, to the soft, warm, spice-laden air, to the rattle of palm leaves in the bright moonlight, to hurrying figures with glancing eyes over veils and to the brooding spirit of the past. It is all an illusion really and quite unjustified, but it is a will-o'-the-wisp and leads to a questing impulse and regrettable incidents.

Obviously the seclusion which the Sultanate has for so long enjoyed cannot last much longer, however hard the elders may strive to preserve it. Fast one-class-only floating hotels and the 'Iringa Pioneer' have almost finished it and I was lucky to see it before it vanishes altogether.

I saw it as a happy island. As it has become customary to say in speeches on public occasions, with almost wearisome reiteration, Zanzibar could be held up as an example to other countries ('which I am sure I need not mention'—laughter) of how different races with different creeds and ways of life can live together in a small island in harmony and friendliness. There is no colour bar and no racial distinction anywhere. There are clubs with a racially exclusive membership, but the European club is not the only one. All the races mix perfectly freely in public and visit each other's houses. I went to many parties at which members of all races were present. Yet I

I

suspect that this tolerance is less because the British, the Indians, the Arabs and the Africans have a great affection for one another than because, as yet, no community threatens another. No pressures have developed. They do not tread on each other's toes.

The British are, and always have been, there simply as administrators, doctors, teachers and now, in inevitably increasing numbers, as technical experts of various sorts. They do not own anything. There are no settlers and there is not, and never has been, any question of European exploitation. It is not permitted for a European to own or acquire land in the Sultan's dominions. A few, like my ex-policeman friend, live in retirement in rented houses but they have no stake in the country. There can be no doubt that the British have administered well and have always carefully adhered to the polite outward observances of the Protectorate. The Sultan's anthem is always played and his flag flies everywhere. The administration refers to itself as 'His Highness's Government' and has always preserved the appearance of advising the ruler rather than of ruling itself. This was at one time the true state of affairs when the Sultan was advised by wise and devoted men like Sir John Kirk, Sir Lloyd Matthews and Sir John Hardinge. Of late years this personal rule, involving direct personal contact between the Sultan and his adviser, has tended to give way to rule by a bureaucracy and to not always fortunate interventions by Whitehall. However, there is still personal contact between the British Resident, as the head of the bureaucracy, and the Sultan, and the bureaucracy itself is an intimate and friendly one. All its members are known to one another and to the Sultan himself. Within it there is the hierarchy, the social stratification, largely built up by wives, which is a part of life in any small British community anywhere abroad. One lady told me that on returning from leave she was mildly surprised and gratified to find herself being 'received' by quite a different, and it seemed more exalted, set than that in which she had moved before she went away, while her former friends merely bowed frigidly in the street. This, she discovered, was because her husband had been raised in the hierarchy by an increase in his basic salary. He had, however, forgotten to tell his wife.

It might, I suppose, be said that the British have occupied a

privileged position for too long and are too highly paid as
compared with the natives. But the climate is still a trying one
for Europeans, though it is a healthy enough one now. Their
life remains one of exile and is in many ways circumscribed.
The problem of educating and bringing up children is very
difficult and often involves the break-up of families for months,
or even years. Now, with the rise in the cost of living and the
increasing wealth of other communities, mainly the Indians,
the privileged position of the British is disappearing. Others
are finding that they can do what hitherto has been done by
only one community.

The Indians, who are Muslim Ismaeli Khojas and Bohoras,
originally from Cutch and Gujerat, Hindu Banians and Roman
Catholic Goans, have been the traders in Zanzibar since the
days of Seyyid Said. Now they are powerful by sheer numbers
and many of them are exceedingly wealthy. As everywhere
where the Indians live, their tendency to keep on producing
more and still more Indians is creating a serious problem for
the future. Yet, whatever views one may hold about their
influence, their status as a community or their political outlook,
I always found, from a purely personal point of view, that they
made life in Zanzibar easy and pleasant by means of unvarying
courtesy, instant service and credit so extended as to be embarrassing. Very often the only way to find out what one owed
an Indian shopkeeper was to tell him that one was leaving
the town for ever in a ship sailing in an hour's time. And there
were limits to the number of times one could even do that. I
often heard Indian shopkeepers accused of swindling, over-
charging, profiteering and other secret vices, but I never con-
sciously experienced or appeared to suffer from any of these
activities. 'Beat 'em down, old boy! Beat 'em down! You
can always beat an Indian down but never a Chinese.' In
fact I find that I can never myself beat anyone down. The
thought always comes to me with something of a shock after
I have left the shop that I could have got the article much
cheaper if I had only tried. I really must try to remember next
time.

The Arabs are the owners of the land, the clove and copra
growers. On the whole they are too happy-go-lucky, and also
too lazy, to try by taking thought to make money. Some of

them have become wealthy, by act of God, from their clove estates. Others, during lean times, have allowed their estates to be mortgaged to Indians. They have always resisted any attempt on the part of authority to persuade them to farm scientifically, to conserve their crops or plan ahead. When the crop is good Allah is merciful, and they rejoice and buy an expensive motor-car. When, as a result of ruthless harvesting or for the lack of a few simple measures, the good crop is succeeded by several bad seasons, Allah is punishing them for their many wickednesses and they buy an expensive motor-car, but do it on credit and the Indians win.

But nowadays it is among the Arabs that the new voices are mostly raised for they, apart from the Europeans, provide the intellectual and cultural life of the city. From them come the young doctors, schoolmasters, journalists with the new ideas. They are brash, opinionated and highly intelligent. It is their voices which now cry 'Zanzibar for the Zanzibaris' in the narrow streets. It is they who will shape the future of their ancient island home in the years to come.

The African, the Swahili, forms the background to the picture. His hands build the new Neo-saracenic buildings, the fine white schools, hospitals, social halls that are rising everywhere about the two islands. By his sweat the coconut trees were cleared to make way for the aerodrome. His fingers pluck the cloves which are the wealth of the island. His back bends beneath their weight when they are loaded at the port. A slave for centuries, he still retains unconsciously the memory of slavery which colours his attitude towards his employers and rulers. The European prides himself on being a better employer than the Arab or the Indian and boasts that the African prefers to work for him. But I doubt if this is so, although one is always being lectured by Europeans on How to Treat Africans. The Arab and Indian demand more work and, on the whole, pay lower wages than the European, but they maintain a more intimate and personal relationship with their employees and servants. This itself is something left over from the days of slavery.

I went one evening to an Indian house some way outside the town in order to 'enjoy'. This delightful word, used in the intransitive like this, seems to be peculiar to Zanzibar and may mean any form of enjoyment you like to imagine. In this case, however, it meant playing poker, which I do not enjoy at all, and drinking inordinate quantities of brandy and water, the nastiest drink in the world. We sat on a balcony in a ramshackle bungalow surrounded by coconut trees and mysterious gloomy undergrowth. The houseboy sat cross-legged on the beaten earth outside the balcony on the edge of the circle of light, waiting to be called to bring more drink, to bring food, to bring glasses. From time to time my Indian host would pour him out a generous brandy and say, 'There you are, you old scoundrel!' or something like it. The old servant would take his drink back to his place on the edge of the lighted circle and continue to sit there with it, cross-legged on the ground, watching us, laughing when we laughed and occasionally joining in the conversation from a distance. In a European house such a manner towards the servant would be considered most unusual, and would probably not be understood by the servant and would therefore be unsuccessful. But I was told that in Indian and Arab houses it is quite usual and perfectly understood.

To-day the African is changing too. He is no longer, if he ever was, impressed by the white-suited Bwana Stand-About-and-Shout. He will work willingly, and often well, for those who work alongside him and nowadays prefers to see the European take his coat off. The Swahili is a gentle, good-tempered person and is always anxious to please. It is safe to say that he always does his best. If the best is a poor one it is because he has not been taught any better or does not understand what is wanted. Few Europeans, in the heat of the coast which is bad for the temper, are gentle enough and, shouting at Africans, confuse and frighten them. Those who get the most out of them are those who make them laugh.

I saw Zanzibar, as one now sees all African and Asian peoples, at a moment of destiny. In this little Sultanate, with its beloved but aged monarch, the days are big with impending change. There is a new note in the drums. These changes cannot be stopped but must be guided. I like to think that it is the task of the British to bring to these peoples, now looking forward with hope and a new pride, something better and of more lasting value than radios with many knobs and CinemaScope.

I was transferred to Singapore in June 1952 and left Zanzibar in a big Dutch ship. Parting is half dying and I have suffered many of these small deaths in my time, but few of them tore at my heart quite like this one. My work was unfinished and I had to bequeath it, and what I could in the way of experience, to my young successor fresh out from England. To Zanzibar I could only leave a tear and wishes for the happiness of all her people in the new times that are to come.

When I left our ship my laughing Africans wrung my hands. The two old Arabs placed their palms upon their breasts and bowed. The others stood in a row at the ship's side as the dinghy slowly took me away. They raised their right hands in a kind of salute.

'*Kwa heri, Bwana Mkubwa,*' they said.